# BARBED
# WIRE
# DISEASE

# BARBED WIRE DISEASE

## BRITISH & GERMAN PRISONERS OF WAR, 1914–19

### JOHN YARNALL

*To Grace*

*Cover illustration*: German prisoners in a French prison camp. French Pictorial Service, 1917–1919 (National Archives via pingnews)

First published by Spellmount, an imprint of
The History Press, 2011

The History Press
The Mill, Brimscombe Port
Stroud, Gloucestershire, GL5 2QG
www.thehistorypress.co.uk

British Library Cataloguing in Publication Data.
A catalogue record for this book is available from the British Library.

ISBN 978 0 7524 5690 4

Typesetting and origination by The History Press
Printed in the EU for The History Press.

# CONTENTS

# PREFACE

The number of prisoners taken during the Great War was vast. By 1918, the total number of prisoners held by the belligerents exceeded 6.5 million. The majority of these were held by Germany and Austria-Hungary, 3.4 million, and Russia, 2.25 million. France held 350,000 and Britain 328,000. The remainder were scattered around the other belligerents. Of the 328,000 prisoners held by Britain, about half were located in camps in the United Kingdom and the remainder in British run camps in France and elsewhere. About 185,000 British prisoners were held by Germany.[1]

This study concentrates on British and German prisoners taken on the Western Front, where alleged neglect and ill-treatment became the subject of major propaganda campaigns in both countries. It looks at day-to-day problems as they unfolded and at the more major disputes which were to arise, drawing heavily on published and unpublished official documents, as well as contemporary newspapers and other accounts. This book also identifies many examples of hardship and ill-treatment and some of deliberate physical abuse. But the full story of prisoners in the Great War goes beyond a simple narrative of their experiences and the conditions they faced. That is not to say that these issues are not important, because from the point of view of individual prisoners they are, after all, what really mattered. But such conditions need to be seen against the wider background of the diplomatic, political and military objectives which gave rise to them. This study sets the wider context. Incidents such as the suffering caused to Allied prisoners by the mismanagement of typhus outbreaks in some of the German camps in the early part of the war, or the shooting of unarmed interned civilians during a food riot at a camp in the Isle of Man, stand out as particular examples of unacceptable treatment. By contrast, the treatment by both sides of many prisoners, and of officers especially, reached standards which would be more than acceptable today. The political and diplomatic story is similarly one of both successes and failures. Military considerations overrode diplomatic preferences on numerous occasions, especially in relation to exchanges – perhaps most notably in the case of the British policy to intern rather than exchange enemy civilians at the insistence of the War Office – and also in relation to the decision by both sides to employ prisoners in the war zone. But the predominant diplomatic theme to emerge is the willingness of both sides to invest heavily in the cause of improving the lot of prisoners and ensuring their humane treatment. Their progressive approach achieved much in securing practical improvements in conditions, including agreement on limited prisoner exchanges and internments in neutral countries. Their final achievement in drafting comprehensive agreements to plug the gaps exposed in the workings of the recently agreed Hague and Geneva conventions represented a real step forward. The process of achieving this success forms a major focus of the study. Sadly, much of the work was completed too late to have any great practical impact during the war itself. The lessons learnt were, however, invaluable to those whose task it was to update the conventions at Geneva in 1929, in advance of the Second World War.

# INTRODUCTION

The First World War was the first major war in history to be conducted on the basis of internationally agreed standards for the treatment of prisoners and wounded taken on the battlefield, marking a milestone in the evolution of the treatment of prisoners through the ages. In the earliest times prisoners of war (POWs) had been simply put to death or, if they were more fortunate, enslaved for their labour value. In medieval times, they had been sent to the galleys, not just for the duration but often to stay there beyond the end of the conflict in which they were engaged. Later, it became the practice for prisoners to be exchanged or ransomed by their captors. By the seventeenth century, POWs began to be regarded as prisoners of the state rather than the property of their individual captors. This gave rise to the first international agreements on prisoners. A treaty between Spain and England in 1630 provided for the speedy return of prisoners following the end of hostilities, and a treaty between the USA and Prussia in 1785 sowed the first seeds of regulation on the way in which prisoners should be treated. State involvement also gave rise to the development in the seventeenth and eighteenth centuries of 'cartels', or agreements for the exchange of prisoners based on elaborate tariffs. Such cartels usually included the condition that those exchanged would take no further part in hostilities. These arrangements themselves eventually died out, however, to be replaced by the now more familiar practice of internment for the duration, followed by repatriation.[1]

Despite these improvements, prisoners continued to be treated harshly into the nineteenth century. But during the nineteenth century, as weapons became more destructive and casualties increased, pressure grew to make war more humane. In 1863, the International Committee of the Red Cross was established at Geneva after the Battle of Solferino (1859), where some 40,000 sick and wounded had been left on the battlefield with no mechanism in place for their care. At a diplomatic conference called by the Red Cross in 1864, the First Geneva Convention was adopted by sixteen states.[2] This established the principles that relief should be given to the wounded on the battlefield without any distinction as to nationality, and that medical personnel and their units (to be identified by the Red Cross symbol) were to be treated as neutral and inviolable. The convention was expanded and updated in 1906.[3] The Hague Peace conferences of 1899 and 1907 continued the process of developing international humanitarian law by applying the Geneva Convention to sea warfare[4] and by agreeing conventions (the Hague conventions) governing the conduct of war on land.[5] Amongst other things, the Hague conventions set out detailed rules on the treatment of prisoners. At the time of the First World War, the 1907 Hague Convention and the 1906 Geneva Convention together provided a comprehensive set of rules available to all belligerents. Both Britain and Germany had ratified the conventions and had it as declared policy to comply with their provisions. But even states that had not signed up to the conventions now had before them a set of rules representing contemporary thinking on how POWs and the wounded should be treated.

The underlying theme of the 1907 Hague Convention – and its specific requirement – was that prisoners should be treated humanely. The convention stated specifically that prisoners were in the power of the capturing government and not the individuals who had captured them. Thus governments were responsible and could be held accountable for the fate of those who fell into their hands. Furthermore, the convention made clear that whilst it was permissible to intern prisoners, this was to be done only as an indispensable measure of safety: prisoners were not criminals or convicts and internment was not to be regarded as a punishment. Their belongings and well-being were also to be protected. Personal belongings – as opposed to horses, weapons, etc. – were to remain theirs. Prisoners were to be clothed, fed and accommodated on the same basis as the troops of the capturing government. Officers were to receive the same pay as those of equivalent rank in the country of capture. Participating governments were required to establish bureaux for the exchange of information on prisoners; these bureaux and the prisoners themselves were to be allowed free postage; and facilities were to be provided to enable relief societies to operate. Prisoners were to be repatriated as soon as possible after the onset of peace. These measures established a special and protected status for POWs – a status which recognised their position as legitimate combatants. At the same time, the convention imposed obligations. Prisoners were to be subject to the army laws of the capturing state. Soldiers (but not officers) could be used as labour, but not excessively or in connection with operations of war, and they were to be paid for this. Those who attempted to escape and were unsuccessful could be punished (though successful escapees could not be punished for their escape if they were subsequently captured again). Parole could be requested of prisoners but not demanded; any breaches of parole, however, would result in the removal of their rights and they could then be brought before the courts. Prisoners were obliged to give their name and rank on capture.

For its part, the 1906 Geneva Convention stated that the sick and the wounded were to be treated as POWs, while leaving the door open for belligerents to agree alternative arrangements to internment, such as repatriation or transfer to a neutral country. Medical personnel, army chaplains and others engaged in the collection, transport and treatment of the sick and wounded and in the administration of medical units, were, on the other hand, to be respected and protected, and, if they fell into the hands of the enemy, were not to be treated as POWs. This did not mean that medical personnel were automatically allowed to go free or to move about without let or hindrance. The convention stipulated that, if called upon, medical personnel must continue to carry out their duties under the enemy's directions; medical personnel could be required, for example, to stay with and treat POWs on their own side on their surrender, subsequently being sent back to their own lines only gradually. The convention also imposed other duties. States were required to send to the enemy identification marks or tokens found on the dead and a nominal roll of the sick and the wounded collected by them. They were to keep each other informed of the subsequent movements of the sick and wounded. They were required to collect articles and valuables found on the battlefield or left by the sick and wounded who had died in their hands, so that these could be sent on to those appropriate.

Despite the comprehensive nature of the conventions, the war, when it came, exposed many situations unforeseen by their drafters. Dealing with these was to become a major preoccupation of the British and German

Governments, both internally and in their dealings with each other. The two sides were also closely dependent on and were well served by the neutral governments, especially the United States which acted as protecting power to both Britain and Germany – until the US itself entered the war in 1917.

A major role was played by James W. Gerard, a former associate justice of the New York Supreme Court and US Ambassador to Berlin since 1913. After the US entered the war, Gerard was to gather a reputation for being aggressively anti-German. He gained particular notoriety for a speech he made in New York in November 1917, when he remarked that if the 500,000 German-Americans in the US were to rise up, there were 501,000 lamp posts available to hang them from.[6] His memoirs, *My Four Years in Germany* (1917) and *Face to Face with Kaiserism* (1918), were highly critical of the German regime, including its attitude towards prisoners. But his disenchantment with Germany was gradual rather than immediate and the diplomatic papers show that during his time as ambassador he carried out his duties assiduously. Despite the opinions he subsequently aired, Gerard remained highly regarded at home for the way in which he had carried out his duties in Berlin with impeccable neutrality, enabling him to press his case effectively with both sides.[7] This was especially effective in the case of prisoners, where Gerard demonstrated a particular empathy with prisoners' needs and saw it as his role to maximise their welfare. His work in this area made a major contribution in cooling the temperature between the two sides in the face of often exaggerated reports of ill-treatment, thus avoiding reprisals, as well as paving the way for improving standards generally.

In London, the British Government had the good fortune to have Walter Hines Page as US Ambassador for the whole of the war. Page was renowned for his pro-British leanings, which ultimately led to a rift between him and US President Woodrow Wilson in the face of Wilson's firm policy of neutrality. Page was one of the key influences in finally bringing the US into the war. The diplomatic papers expose a number of instances where the US Embassy in London clearly played down problems over the condition of prisoners held in the UK when reporting to Germany.

Policy responsibility for POW matters within the British Government was effectively split between the Foreign Office and the War Office, with the Home Office having administrative responsibility for civilian internment camps. The lead in looking after the interests of British prisoners held by the enemy was taken for most of the war by the Foreign Office, and in particular by Lord Newton, who was appointed as Assistant

Under-Secretary in March 1916 and head of a newly created POW Department within the Foreign Office later the same year. A former diplomat and Conservative MP until he inherited his title in 1898, Newton was a reforming politician who shared Gerard's empathy with the needs of prisoners and worked diligently on their behalf until the end of the war. Newton had many critics during the war but came to be highly regarded for his success in negotiating prisoner exchanges and internments. Newton himself is said to have commented that this work brought him 'for the first and last time the sweets of popularity'.[8] Continuity on POW matters at the War Office was provided by Lieutenant-General Sir Herbert Belfield, head of the Directorate of Prisoners of War, established in February 1915.

The information available to the British Government about the treatment of prisoners in Germany came from a number of sources, ranging from reports from overseas diplomatic posts, to foreign newspapers and, of course, the reports from US Ambassador Gerard (and subsequently the Netherlands which took over as protecting power when the US entered the war). More direct information about conditions came from escaped or repatriated prisoners themselves, whose reports formed the basis of many of the British Government's initial concerns about treatment and featured heavily in published White Papers. In order to build up a comprehensive picture from such first-hand reports, the government also established at an early stage a special committee ('The Government Committee on the Treatment by the Enemy of British Prisoners of War') to interview all returning prisoners. Such prisoners were in turn forbidden to talk to the press. The Government Committee was chaired by Sir Robert Younger, a Chancery Division judge, and supported for most of its existence by Dame Adelaide Livingstone as its honorary secretary. Dame Livingstone was among the first women to be created DBE for her wartime services in 1918. She was subsequently to secure greater fame as the organiser of the Peace Ballot in 1934–35. The Government Committee published a number of reports during the war based on its interviews. While the committee's publications were without exception critical of the treatment meted out to British prisoners, and clearly formed part of the government's propaganda campaign, the reports of the prisoners themselves form an invaluable primary source for the historian.

Many others outside the government also came to be involved in the care and management of prisoners, most notably the Red Cross and volunteer relief organisations. Such bodies were destined to play a major part in ameliorating the many forms of hardship which prisoners were, by definition, bound to face.

# 1

# CIVILIANS: THE INNOCENT BYSTANDERS

As perhaps the first manifestation of the First World War as total war, enemy civilians were being interned in the UK before any combatant prisoners had been taken by British forces. The large-scale internment of enemy aliens, which came to be undertaken by both sides, was to continue throughout the war. The policy was controversial, invoking public anger in both countries at the perceived injustice of its own citizens being caught up in the conflict as innocent bystanders. At the same time, in Britain especially, there was little public appetite to allow enemy aliens simply to roam free. From a practical point of view, internment imposed costs on both sides in having to feed and house large numbers of internees, as well as diverting scarce administrative resources from more important areas. Throughout the war, attempts were made to reduce or eliminate the difficulties of internment through negotiations on full or partial civilian exchanges. The problems associated with this proved intractable, however, until final success came too late to have any practical effect. While the driving force behind the policy of internment was logical, its application was imperfect and its success questionable. An examination of the official record must bring into question whether, in the end, it proved misguided.

Large-scale internment represented a departure from previous practice. Traditionally, governments had been tolerant towards the presence of enemy aliens. For centuries it had been common to include in treaties provision for civilians to be given time, perhaps six to nine months, in which to settle their affairs before being required to leave the country.[1] Though the Hague Convention did not extend to civilians, discussion during its drafting confirmed the widely held view that it was not acceptable simply to imprison enemy subjects at the outbreak of war. But where civilians were imprisoned, it was also the view under international law that they should be treated in the same way as combatant POWs with all the privileges that such status provided.[2] The view that civilians could not automatically be imprisoned was reiterated in the British Manual of Military Law, issued by the War Office in 1914. But the Manual went on to argue that this did not mean that all enemy aliens could be allowed to go about their business unhindered. First, there was the question of security. It was clearly necessary to be able to regulate those who might be engaged in spying or sabotage. The Manual specifically acknowledged this by referring to the right of every state to take 'such steps as it may deem necessary for the control of persons whose presence or conduct appear dangerous to its safety'.[3] Secondly, the relatively recent spread of conscription gave rise to a newly formed view under international law, that a state could not be compelled to let go unhindered those who would then join the forces of the opposing side. The position of civilians at the outbreak of the war was thus evolving, with no clear and absolute framework setting out how they should be treated.[4]

The scope for a more aggressive policy than had been adopted in the past was particularly attractive in Britain, where sensitivity towards enemy aliens was already high. Fears over spying, sabotage and invasion had been growing in Britain for many years, stoked by writers of fiction such as George Chesney (*The Battle for Dorking*, 1871), Erskine Childers (*The Riddle of the Sands*, 1903) and William Le Queux (*Invasion of 1910*, 1906). Such fear was not confined to the public imagination either. Official concern that German spies were active in Britain, possibly as part of an extensive network, had led directly to the establishment of the British Secret Service (MI5 and MI6) in 1909. Coupled with this, the population of enemy aliens in Britain was large. At the outbreak of war, the enemy population comprised over 50,000 Germans and 10,000 Austrians. Some of these were simply on holiday or were the passengers or crews of visiting merchant ships. Others were diplomats, professionals or itinerant workers such as waiters. Many were long-term residents, such as the husbands or wives of native citizens. In contrast to the position in Britain, there were fewer than 10,000 British citizens in Germany. This disparity in numbers was to influence directly the attitude of the two sides throughout the war.

Unlike the British Government, it is clear that Germany had no predetermined policy towards enemy civilians. Events in Germany in the first few days of the war appear to have been spontaneous and unco-ordinated. There were reports of Russians and French being seized by the crowds and in some instances shot, and even Americans being subjected to the suspicion generated by foreigners. US Ambassador Gerard records:

A curious rumour spread all over Germany to the effect that automobiles loaded with French gold were being rushed across the country to Russia. Peasants and gamekeepers and others turned out on the roads with guns, and travelling by automobile became extremely dangerous. A German Countess was shot, an officer wounded and the Duchess of Ratibor was shot in the arm. It was some time before this excitement was allayed, and many notices were published in the newspapers before this mania was driven from the popular brain.

There were rumours also that the Russians had poisoned the Muggelsee, the lake from whence Berlin draws part of its water supply. There were constant rumours of the arrest of Russian spies disguised as women throughout Germany.[5]

In Berlin, the official German reaction on 5 August was to round up all British subjects. Gerard notes that:

During the day British subjects, without distinction of age or sex, were seized, wherever found, and sent to the fortress at Spandau. I remonstrated with von Jagow [the German Minister of Foreign Affairs] and told him that that was a measure taken only in the Middle Ages, and I believe that he remonstrated with the authorities and arranged for a cessation of the arbitrary arrests of women.[6]

Following this initial reaction, the German Government quickly became more relaxed. Instead of being automatically interned, British subjects were soon allowed considerable liberty, being required only to report to the local police station during the day, and being forbidden to remain out at night. While not officially allowed to leave, many were in fact able to escape, making their way to Britain across the neutral frontiers. Such people clearly saw their future as intolerable within Germany, though some at least were far from happy at having to leave, as a letter from C.B. Maxse, the British Consul-General in Amsterdam, to Sir Edward Grey, Foreign Secretary, records:

Since the stream of British refugees set in through Holland I have had occasion to remark that many British subjects, who have resided for some time in Germany, have apparently lost all patriotic instinct. I have reported on this subject in previous despatches dealing with the reception of British refugees in this country. I have even had a British born woman of the educated classes in my room at this office, who told me that she sincerely hoped that Germany would win and the British be beaten. This class of person absolutely refuses to believe any statements regarding German atrocities in Belgium, the way the war was initiated by that country's double dealing, or even to read any British newspapers or official publications that may be handed to them. I am happy to say that their number has not been great, but they have been exceedingly virulent. I have made it a rule to ask them in reply why, holding such views, they did not wish to remain in Germany and become naturalized there, especially as in some cases they had previously told me that they had lost touch with their families in England.[7]

For its part, the British Government made clear its policy from the outset. On the day after the outbreak, McKenna, the Home Secretary, introduced a bill to enable restrictions to be placed on aliens by means of Orders in Council. McKenna justified the move in the following terms:

Information in the possession of the Government proves that cases of espionage have been frequent in recent years and that many spies have been caught and dealt with by the police. Within the last 24 hours no fewer than 21 spies, or suspected spies, have been arrested in various places all over the country, chiefly in important military or naval centres, some of them known to the authorities to be spies.[8]

The bill secured an immediate passage through parliament and Orders in Council started to be made the following day. Aliens were required to register with local officials and prohibited from entering designated areas, such as those within the vicinity of ports, dockyards and military installations. They were prohibited from travelling without a permit and from possessing firearms, communications equipment and other items. They were also prohibited from reading German language newspapers and from working in the banking business.

Alongside these measures the War Office issued a separate order providing for the immediate internment of all German and Austrian males between the ages of 17 and 42, excepting those who could clearly demonstrate that they were exempt from military service. At an urgently convened meeting of government departments, however, it became clear straightaway that this policy could not be fully implemented because of a lack of suitable accommodation to house the large number of prospective internees involved. It was therefore decided that internment would be restricted initially to those Germans whom the police regarded as dangerous, viz. spies and saboteurs. Later in August, following concern by the commissioner of police about the large number of Germans now unemployed, it was further agreed that those who might become dangerous through unemployment or destitution should also be interned, and on 7 September it was decided to intern all reservists, with unmarried or destitute men being taken first. After between 8,000 and 9,000 had been arrested under these arrangements, internment was again suspended through lack of accommodation. A further purge instituted on 20 October brought the number interned to 12,400, out of a total German population in the UK of 55,686 men, women and children.[9] The pattern of prioritising the internment of enemy aliens according to availability of accommodation and in reaction to events was then to continue for much of the war. In December 1914, for example, McKenna reported to the Cabinet that the policy of internment was causing hardship and many aliens were now being released – 1,100 had been released in November on report from the police that they represented no danger. He went on to say that the War Office was now considering a general release of all those interned since 20 October, subject to police vetting of the individuals. But in a further reversal provoked by public outrage following the sinking of the *Lusitania*, Asquith announced in May 1915 the internment (subject to individual exceptions) of all non-naturalised men of military age.[10] By December 1915, the total number of enemy alien civilians interned in the UK had reached 32,272.[11]

The British policy on internment was strongly resented by the German Government, which took the position that it was wrong in principle to detain anyone not in the armed forces. German public opinion was also outraged. In October 1914, the German Imperial Foreign Office issued an ultimatum threatening the arrest of all male British subjects in Germany between the ages of 17 and 55 unless the British Government confirmed by 5 November that all Germans not especially suspicious had been released. Having failed to receive such confirmation, the German Government duly carried out its threat, leading Gerard to try to de-escalate the situation in a note handed to Grey on 13 November:

Although it may already be too late to be of much practical effect, I feel it my duty, in the interest of humanity, to urge you to obtain some formal declaration on the part of the British Government as to its purpose in ordering the wholesale concentration of Germans in Great Britain and Ireland, as is understood here to be the case. It is known here that many of the Germans interned belong to the labouring classes, and that their position is actually improved by their internment, and it is recognised that the British Government has the right to arrest persons when any well-founded ground for suspecting them to be spies exists. Great popular resentment has been created by the reports of the arrests of other Germans, however, and the German authorities cannot explain or understand why German travellers who have been taken from ocean steamers should not be permitted to remain at liberty, of course under police control, even if they are compelled to stay in England. The order for the general concentration of British males between the ages of 17 and 55, which went into effect on the 6th instant, was occasioned by the pressure of public opinion, which has been still further excited by the newspaper reports of a considerable number of deaths in the concentration camps. Up to the 6th considerable liberty of movement has been allowed to British subjects in Germany, and, as you were informed in my telegram of the 5th, many petitions were received from them setting forth the favourable conditions under which they were permitted to live and carry on their business, and urging the similar treatment of German subjects in England. I cannot but feel that to a great extent the English action and the German retaliation has been caused by a misunderstanding which we should do our best to remove. It seems to me that we should do all in our power to prevent an increase in the bitterness which seems to have arisen between the German and English peoples, and to make it possible for the two countries to become friends on the close of the war.[12]

As has already been noted, the fundamental difference between the policies adopted in Britain and Germany arose mainly because of the huge disparity in the number of enemy aliens held by either side. Grey had already sought US assistance in making clear to the German Government the 'reasonableness' of the British policy in the light of this.[13] Grey argued that the large number of enemy aliens in the UK caused legitimate concern to the military authorities responsible for the national defence. For the government not to have acted in the way it had, with the consequent risk to the public safety, would have represented a dereliction of its duty. This had been the sole driving force behind the government's actions and there had never once been any intention 'to indulge in a domestic act of hostility towards German subjects as such, or in any way to inflict hardship for hardship's sake on innocent civilians'. He then went on to state that every effort was being made to mitigate the inconvenience to those detained and to provide the best possible treatment under the circumstances. He hoped that in the future the necessarily austere conditions in the civilian internment camps would be improved further, and that the defects in procedures and conditions which had inevitably arisen from the need to act quickly would be rectified. By contrast:

> The German Government, on the other hand, have not the same excuse for proceeding to a wholesale arrest of British subjects in Germany, since, owing to the small number of them, the scattered condition in which they live, and the different character of the classes to which they belong, they cannot, under any circumstances, be regarded as constituting the same danger to Germany that the masses of German subjects in Great Britain constitute to this country.

The possibility of securing the repatriation of British subjects was first considered by the British Government just a few days into the war, in the face of mounting concern about the conditions they were facing in Germany. Almost simultaneously, the German Government offered to allow all remaining British subjects to leave, provided the British Government would release all the German citizens held in the UK.[14] While the British Foreign Office would have been more than happy to go along with this proposal, the War Office found it unacceptable on the basis that an 'all for all' exchange would result in Germany gaining a clear manpower advantage. During inter-departmental discussions, the War Office pressed this point and went on to secure a HMG 'established principle' that in all present and future exchanges no side should gain militarily at the expense of the other.[15] In the light of this principle, the British Government then set about negotiating, with some success, a more limited exchange which would exclude all male civilians of military age and those already in custody for crimes or under suspicion of espionage. The German Government agreed to release all women and children and arranged special trains to the Dutch frontier for the purpose (Britain had been allowing women and children to leave since the outbreak but Germany had not) and agreement was also reached on the exchange of physicians and clergymen of military age. By the end of October 1914, the German Government announced that all British civilians, except those between ages 17 and 55, were now free to leave the country.[16] But apart from piecemeal agreements providing for the exchange of invalid civilians or civilians incapacitated from military service and other minor categories, a more comprehensive agreement relating to those of military age remained elusive.

Concern over the fate of British civilians held in Germany had exposed a fundamental policy rift between the Foreign Office and the War Office that was to persist for most of the war. The Foreign Office, supported by a substantial body of public opinion, took as its prime objective the need to alleviate the hardship faced by British citizens held in Germany. The War Office, on the other hand, remained firm that nothing should be done to increase the military manpower available to the enemy even if, in the process, this exacerbated the hardship faced by British citizens. War Office intransigence on this point extended so far as to resist even the exchange of older civilians at present unfit to serve, causing Lord Robert Cecil at the Foreign Office to write at one stage to Harold Tennant, Under-Secretary of State for War:

> I cannot help thinking that our military authorities are unnecessarily rigid as regards the standard of invalidity applied to German civilians in this country who may claim to be repatriated as unfit for military service. While I have no doubt that the German authorities are sending into the trenches numbers of men who are not fit to go, this does not really strengthen their fighting force, does it? It is merely a counsel of despair adopted to enable them to keep up the appearance of formidable numbers when the reality has in fact begun to disappear. There seems, therefore, no reason why sickly Germans of forty five years of age and upwards should not be sent back, and to refrain from doing so affords the Germans some ground for refusing to send back British subjects who are really useless for military purposes.[17]

At the end of 1915, the Foreign Office renewed its attempts before the Cabinet to soften the War Office's stance on exchanges.[18] It argued that the conditions facing all British POWs in Germany, combatant and civilians alike, would become intolerable as the blockade strengthened its grip. And while British POWs in Germany were supported by food parcels – a practice likely to increase – German POWs in Great Britain were mainly fed and clothed at the expense of the British taxpayer. As far as civilians were concerned, the papers noted that 'a number of the older civilians are suffering a good deal – especially from the mental effects of long imprisonment under conditions which, though relatively improved, are still severe for men of education'. Even though the Cabinet accepted a sub-committee's recommendation of February 1916 – that the Home Office, in consultation with the War Office and the Admiralty, should draw up rules for the repatriation of those over 50, and those over 45 who were unfit for service at the front (except in both cases if the intelligence services disagreed) – the War Office and Admiralty quickly made sure that it would come to nothing. A note by Lord Newton, circulated to the Cabinet in May, recorded that so many conditions had been attached to the resulting scheme at the insistence of the War Office and Admiralty that it was doubtful that its adoption would have much effect.[19]

Newton then returned to the general case for action to relieve the suffering of British civilians in Germany. Newton pointed out to the Cabinet that by now most had been confined for nearly two years and that great hardship would result if they had to spend another winter there. He returned to the question of their mental state, commenting that: 'Confinement is especially trying to the middle-aged and well educated, to which categories most of the interned belong, and it is stated on authority of persons recently released that a considerable number of prisoners are beginning to show signs of insanity.' Newton went on to argue that following the introduction of conscription by the British, objections to a wider exchange of civilians were no longer applicable, since the Admiralty and War Office would now have a claim on repatriated civilians in the same way as the Germans. There were also considerable savings to be had from getting rid of as many of the interned Germans as possible as they were costing the taxpayer £50,000 to £60,000 a month. Newton concluded by meeting head on the War Office argument that any substantial exchange would automatically assist the enemy militarily:

Amongst the Germans interned are boys of under 18 and men above the military age; others who are detained because they are considered to possess certain qualifications which may be of assistance to the enemy, such as a knowledge of chemistry or engineering; men of indifferent health and physique, who have never performed any military service, and men who have married English wives and have sons serving in the British Army. There are also amongst the interned a considerable number of undesirables, who are suffering from venereal diseases of a more or less malignant type; well known agitators, and bad characters with the worst possible police records. In such cases the individual military value to the State must be infinitesimal, and common sense suggests that to get rid of them permanently would not only be of great benefit to this country, but to the detriment of the enemy.

It should also be borne in mind that many of the interned, although previously well disposed, will emerge from their confinement, upon the conclusion of the war, impoverished and animated with the bitterest hostility against this country. In addition to constituting a dangerous element in the population, they will increase the social and economic difficulties which must inevitably follow the release of hundreds and thousands of men liberated from naval and military service.

It is obvious that the requirements of the Admiralty and War Office must be paramount in this matter, but it seems open to question whether any potential military or naval gain to the enemy would not be amply compensated by the advantages which we should obtain by a much wider exchange of civilian prisoners, quite apart from humanitarian considerations.

Newton's arguments were augmented by Grey himself in a further paper setting out the arguments for and against an exchange of civilians, circulated to the Cabinet in August.[20] In this Grey listed a number of factors in favour of an exchange. He argued that an exchange would solve 'the problem' of the disposal of between 20,000 and 30,000 Germans on the conclusion of peace; it would result in the civilian camps becoming available for large numbers of combatant POWs; and it would add to Germany's food-shortage problems, while saving Great Britain some trouble and expense. Grey also believed that the German Government would agree not to employ repatriated civilians in military or naval operations, while acknowledging that should they not honour such an undertaking, a substantial number of men of military value would be placed at their disposal.

Some wearing down of the opposition by the War Office and Admiralty to exchanges did appear to have occurred when negotiations were opened up with the German Government between August and October 1916 on a British proposal for an exchange of all civilians aged over 45. In a note to Laughlin, the US Chargé d'Affaires, Grey explained that HMG were 'most anxious to arrange for the immediate release of civilians over 45, owing to the deplorable accounts which are reaching them as to the mental condition of many of the older men both in the British and German internment camps'.[21] But despite German acceptance and a counter proposal for the full release of all civilians and repatriation for those who wanted it – coupled with an undertaking by the German Government that any prisoners so released would not enter the army or navy – the British War Office were finally to renege, yet again, on the original proposal. They now insisted on adding to the exchange of all over-45s the rider that each party should have the right to detain for military reasons twenty persons who would otherwise be released. The German Government were finally to acquiesce in October 1916, regretting in passing the British rejection of a general exchange, 'as the only excuse for their detention is removed by non-employment in the army'.[22] Agreement on the exchange of over-45s, which formally came into effect on 2 January 1917, represented in principle a significant milestone, but in practical terms its success was short-lived, due primarily to lack of transport. In addition, the intensification of the submarine campaign, the breaking off of diplomatic relations between the United States and Germany on 3 February, and the declaration of a blockade zone by Germany, all conspired to inhibit any real chance of progress. The exchanges were in fact suspended in February, by which time only 370 Germans and seventy British had been released. Of the seventy British, forty-five were at that time still in Holland waiting for transport, and only twenty-five had actually reached home.[23] The breakdown of the agreement was greeted with dismay in Britain, where support continued to be strong for a total exchange.

The irritation felt within the Foreign Office at the continuing hard line being taken by the War Office, and their rejection of a formula which appeared to offer a full and final solution to the problem of enemy alien civilians, brought to a head the rift that had been growing since the outbreak. At the end of September 1916, Grey formally recommended to the Cabinet that responsibility for prisoners should be removed from the Foreign Office and given to the War Office and Admiralty, in order to bring the principle into line with the reality, and to make clear to the British public where the blame for the continuing retention of British civilians in Germany should lie.[24] As a result, primary responsibility for POW affairs was transferred to the War Office. The Foreign Office retained responsibility only for matters concerning US representation of British interests. A new POW Department, under Lord Newton, was established to look after the interests of British POWs.

Further substantive progress on civilian exchanges had to await agreements that were to be reached at The Hague in 1917 and 1918 (see

Chapter 11). The 1917 agreement made some progress in providing for the resumption of repatriation under previous agreements and for some 1,600 German and 400 British incapacitated civilians to be interned in the Netherlands. But the major breakthrough came in the 1918 agreement, which finally provided for the voluntary repatriation of all civilians (including those interned in the Netherlands under the 1917 agreement) subject to the right of the British authorities to retain up to seventy prisoners and the German authorities up to forty. The disparity in numbers held by either side was to be compensated for by the release of an additional number of British combatant POWs. The agreement went on to provide that no civilian repatriated under its provisions would be employed by either side in any naval or military service, including the mercantile marine, nor would he be called upon to undertake compulsory national service. Despite these agreements, wrangling over their implementation, coupled with an interruption in repatriation sailings in June 1918, again limited their practical effectiveness, much to the renewed anger and dismay of both the British public and parliament. Such was the extent of the wrangling that by the Armistice only 6,840 internees had been repatriated to their own countries or transferred to camps in Holland since the beginning of the war.[25]

Much has been written about the role of attrition in the First World War and the unnecessary suffering that it caused. The extent to which attrition formed a fundamental part of British military thinking is clearly demonstrated by the policy of the War Office towards enemy alien civilians held in the UK. As has already been made clear, the War Office made no secret of the fact that the military regarded depriving the enemy of manpower as a top priority. It made no apology for the fact that the imbalance in numbers ruled out, for them, the prospect of any substantial or 'all for all' exchange. The following extract from a War Office Committee Report in March 1917 makes the War Office's case:

> Any increase of the resources of manpower of the Central Powers must tend to prolong the war, and as the war is to a great extent one of attrition, the best and really most humane course to follow is to place and keep out of action as many of the enemy as possible.
>
> Taking all the circumstances into consideration; and more especially in view of the disparity of the numbers involved, the proposal of a general exchange of civilians should not, in the interests of the State, be entertained.[26]

In the context of total war, there is something to be said for the argument that abandoning 5,000 British citizens in Germany was a price worth paying for the greater good. Yet even supposing (quite unrealistically) that all the German citizens held in the UK would, if released, have found their way into the German armed forces, the effect would hardly have been great – 50,000 represented, for example, a mere 1.1 per cent of the 4.5 million Germans mobilised at the outbreak of war.[27] There were also other arguments, advanced repeatedly by the Foreign Office, that rather than being for the greater good, this policy actually harmed the British war effort by imposing the financial costs of holding over 50,000 Germans in the UK, and the manpower costs of having to divert resources to hold them or otherwise look after them. To these must be added the very real contribution that the release of British citizens would have made to the war effort by improving public morale. The possibility of negotiating a solution which enabled an exchange without adding to the enemy's available manpower – as finally negotiated under the 1918 Hague Agreement – was available to pursue from the outset. But while the War Office paid lip-service to attempts in this direction, in practice it obstructed progress towards agreement – or the implementation of such agreements as were actually reached. The War Office position thus prevailed, with no evidence that it either improved security within the UK or that it shortened the war. The British internees held in Germany, many of whom were there for four years, paid a heavy price for this essentially blinkered approach.

# 2

# APPLYING THE
# CONVENTIONS

For many years before the war, both sides had devoted much time and effort to developing theories for conducting warfare and had held elaborate exercises and manoeuvres for testing them out. But neither side had prepared any detailed contingency plans for handling large numbers of prisoners, partly because such an issue was 'not susceptible to manoeuvres', and partly because of the general feeling that any conflict would be short, so that prisoners would need to be held for a short time only before repatriation.[1] In the event, the rapid influx of prisoners from the outset put the organisational capabilities of the belligerents under severe pressure. By 1 February 1915, the German authorities held 18,000 British combatant prisoners, 39,000 Belgian, 245,000 French and 350,000 Russian; the British held 15,000 and the French some 50,000.[2] The accommodation and other arrangements for handling these prisoners had to be put together on an ad hoc basis, often with unsatisfactory results. But for the longer term both sides quickly started to develop formal standards and policies for the treatment of prisoners in accordance with the Hague and Geneva conventions.

The need for both sides to be able to exchange information on prisoners was recognised by the Hague Convention, which stipulated that belligerents should establish information bureaux for this purpose. Within one week of the outbreak, the British Government had established a Prisoners of War

Information Bureau under the directorship of Sir Paul Harvey, a serving senior civil servant. The bureau opened for business on 17 August.[3] Its staff, also drawn from the Civil Service, initially totalled fifty (almost all women), recruited for their knowledge of German. The work of the bureau extended beyond the basic requirements of the conventions, being organised into five main divisions: establishing individual records of all POWs held throughout the British Empire for use at the end of the war and for periodic transmission to the enemy, with copies going to the Red Cross; receiving from British hospitals information about sick and wounded prisoners and preparing reports for transmission to the enemy; forwarding to the enemy lists of enemy dead found within the British lines; receiving and taking charge of all personal effects found on the battlefield or of those who had died as prisoners; and answering all enquiries from whatever source about POWs or enemy dead, furnishing inquirers with the addresses of POWs and, if asked for, their state of health, and redirecting mail sent to prisoners 'care of' the bureau.[4] At the peak of its activities the bureau was dealing with some 400 enquiries a day from Germany alone, with a staff in excess of 300. The bureau took particular pride in being able to deal efficiently with personal callers at its offices at 49 Wellington Street, The Strand, who were asked to set out their queries on a standard form, an answer being brought back to them within a few minutes. By September 1914, the German Government had also set up a bureau,[5] and on the 21st of that month the first list of prisoners from the British bureau was transmitted to Germany via the US Embassy. Despite some initial wrangling about the quality of information provided by the respective bureaux, and subsequent suspicions by the US that the German authorities occasionally obfuscated and delayed over providing lists and concealed the existence of prisoners,[6] there is no evidence of any fundamental rift between the two sides over the work and objectives of the bureaux.

Action was also quickly taken to provide free post for prisoners and to facilitate the free dispatch of parcels, again as required by the Hague Convention. Other matters took longer to resolve. The convention stipulated that, in the absence of any specific agreement between the belligerents, captors should provide food, quarters and clothing to prisoners on the same basis as to their own troops. This provision became the subject of detailed regulations. Both sides developed statements of their policies and exchanged these over the first few months. Their approach was remarkably similar. Both attempted to lay down standards that provided comfort for the prisoners within the inevitable restrictions of confinement. Such

standards would provide a blueprint to be followed by camp commandants and others in authority at the same time as satisfying the enemy that
their captured personnel were being treated in a humane way. The German
Government forwarded their first such statement in November 1914.[7] This
gave prominence to the position of officers and the need to protect their
status. As a starting point it stated that officers and men were not generally
interned in the same place together. Officers and officials of corresponding
rank were accommodated in fortresses rather than camps. Generals were
provided with a living room and a bedroom; staff officers with a single
room; and other officers either a small individual room or a large room
accommodating several together. Captured officers were permitted to have
orderlies of their own nationality for their personal service and, within the
limits of what was available to prisoners, could have whatever food they
desired on special payment. NCOs and men were usually kept on drill
grounds, artillery target grounds or on special grounds in the vicinity of
unfortified towns. Accommodation, space allocation, heating and lighting,
etc. were provided to the same standards as hut camps and garrison quarters
generally, and food provided on the same basis as that applicable to German
NCOs and men. The German statement made the specific point that effort
was made to provide specially for NCOs, particularly older ones. Medical
services corresponded to those provided in German hut camps in peacetime and captured medical personnel were utilised for this purpose. Lastly,
prison camps were clearly separated from other camps, and were under the
supervision of commanders who directed the assignment, feeding, guarding
and services of the prisoners.

In subsequent statements, the German Government elaborated on the
detailed arrangements. The standards for officers required that accommodation should be light and airy, with heat, light and shower baths provided for
free. The accommodation had to be hygienic with at least 15 cubic metres
of breathing space per man. In addition, each officer was to be provided
with: 'Bedstead, with mattress, bolster, bed linen, and two blankets; chair or
stool; an appliance for hanging up the clothing, and a place for storing the
eatables (where possible, closets, cabinets, or chests of drawers); wash bowl,
water glass, towel, table (a place at the table for each), pail.'

Orderlies were to be quartered in the same camp as the officers, and were
to be provided in the ratio of one man to five to ten officers. They were to
be responsible for the cleaning of clothes, living rooms, courtyards and halls,
and for heating and table services, etc. Since officers paid for their own food

and clothing, the daily menu had to be nutritious, varied and moderately priced, to enable them to be able to meet the costs of other items such as laundry. Beer and light table wines were permitted; canteens were available for the purchase of plain foodstuffs, except cigar tobacco and chocolate, though these items may be sent to them in parcels. Books and periodicals were permitted under censorship. For NCOs and men, a standard of 5 cubic metres breathing space was applied. Sleeping provision comprised cloth sacks (palliasses) filled with straw or wood shavings. Each prisoner was allocated two woollen blankets, a towel and eating utensils. Accommodation was shared by a number of men, with each quarter being provided with the necessary tables, seating places, linen, drinking cups, clothing hangers and shelves, etc. A bathing installation and a wash house for laundry were provided in each camp. Sufficient lighting was to be provided, by electricity if possible. As far as clothing was concerned, the German standards stipulated that NCOs and men would remain in the uniform that they has brought with them on capture until this wore out, at which time proper articles of replacement clothing would be provided to them 'from the booty of war'. When this was used up, new clothing would be specially purchased. The standard clothing supply consisted of suit, necktie and cap, shirts, socks, warm underwear, shoes, overcoats and woollen blankets to protect against cold. Prisoners were permitted to write two letters of four pages (six for officers) each month, which could be supplemented by weekly postcards. The rules could be waived in exceptional circumstances.[8]

While expressed differently, the rules adopted by the British Government aimed for similarly high standards. As in Germany, officers were to be housed separately from soldiers, in country houses or in officers' quarters in barracks. Their accommodation would be comfortably furnished without luxury and servants would be found from among the prisoners. Accommodation for prisoners generally was provided on board ships, in barracks, in large buildings taken over for the purpose and in specially constructed huts, all warm and well lit. The aim of the British authorities was to do everything possible to make the day-to-day life of prisoners tolerable. To this end, 'captains' were elected by the prisoners themselves, to whom commandants looked for general control of the camps, and through whom representations were received. Prisoners did their own cooking and generally looked after the cleanliness and good order of the camps. Arrangements were made for prisoners to wash their own clothes and hot shower baths were provided in most cases for prisoners' use (with the hope that this facility would soon be extended everywhere). In each camp a committee was formed from among the prisoners to organise amusements and to frame suggestions for occupation, 'either intellectual or athletic'. Prisoners were sometimes employed in making roads, building huts for themselves, and clearing ground, in which case they were paid at the same rates as British soldiers for similar work. Books were supplied in each camp, and philanthropic individuals or bodies often helped with the provision of occupation or amusement. An ample supply of 'first-class' clothing, soap and towels, etc. was held for the prisoners at each camp and was supplied to those who needed it free of charge. Prisoners were allowed to retain small sums of money ($£1$) for their own use within the camp, with the camp commandant retaining larger amounts on the prisoners' behalf – receipts always being given. Similarly, gifts for prisoners were permitted, subject to inspection by the camp authorities. Prisoners were permitted to write two letters a week, each consisting of two pages of ordinary writing paper, lined. More could be written in exceptional circumstances. Letters were censored. There was no limit on the number of letters a prisoner could receive. After some initial censorship, new rules were also quickly introduced allowing prisoners to see English newspapers at the discretion of the commandant. Specifically excluded were newspapers of a 'sensational, socialistic, or inflammatory stamp, as well as those which are gratuitously offensive to our enemies' – and should any demonstration occur in connection with the information contained in the newspapers, the concession could be withdrawn. Sanitary arrangements at each of the camps were under the control of the medical officer in charge, who in turn was in frequent touch with the local medical officer of health. In addition, two officers, experts in sanitation, frequently visited the camps, 'with a view to making the conditions, as nearly perfect as possible'. As evidence of the success of these arrangements, the British Government noted that the total number of deaths from natural causes at all places of internment (civilian and military) up to the beginning of December 1914 totalled only five – one from valvular heart disease, two from aneurism of the aorta, one from dropsy and one from typhoid (contracted before arrival in the camp). Each camp had its own resident medical officer and small hospital for treating minor cases of sickness. More serious cases were moved to local hospitals or to the German hospital in London. Soldier and sailor prisoners were removed to military hospitals and treated in exactly the same way as British servicemen, including the separate treatment of officers in officers' wards.[9]

The quality, quantity and style of food provided in the camps were to become major areas of contention throughout the war. But while in practice the quality of the diet varied greatly from camp to camp and from time to time, both sides conscientiously set out to develop standards intended to provide a satisfactory level of subsistence. At the outset, the British Government laid down the following daily rations for each prisoner:

Bread, 1lb 8oz or biscuits, 1lb
Meat, fresh or frozen, 8oz or pressed, 4oz
Tea, 1/2oz or coffee, 1oz
Salt, 1/2oz
Sugar, 2oz
Condensed milk, 1/20 tin (1lb)
Fresh vegetables, 8oz
Pepper, 1/72oz
2oz cheese to be allowed as an alternative for 1oz butter or margarine
2oz of pear, beans, lentils or rice[10]

According to one source, while the diet in British camps varied, it provided working POWs with 4,600 calories a day at its most generous; and even when it had declined later in the war to 3,000 calories a day, it was hardly unsatisfactory.[11] In addition to these free rations, canteens were provided to enable POWs to purchase tobacco, fruit and other minor luxuries, at the same price as applied to British soldiers.[12]

For its part, the German Government laid down a 'performance standard', requiring camps to provide plain food of sufficient quality and variety, adapted to match the work carried out by the prisoners. Prisoners were to receive the same quantity of bread as German troops lodged in civilian quarters. They were to receive three meals a day:

In the morning: Coffee, tea, or soup.
At noon: A plentiful fare consisting of meat and vegetables. The meat may be replaced by a correspondingly larger portion of fish.
At night: A substantial and plentiful meal.

Commandants were made specifically responsible for applying these standards, for increasing rations to meet particular needs where necessary, for ensuring that diets did not become monotonous and for adapting diets where possible to 'the habits of living of the various nations'. The principles laid down that continuous and careful supervision of the food under co-operation of medical officers was absolutely necessary. As in the British camps, canteens were also provided for the purchase of food and other personal items at 'fixed low prices'.[13]

Particular problems arose in Germany during the first few months of the war over the quantity and quality of food provided by private contractors in some of the camps. New regulations copied to the British Government via Gerard in April 1915[14] gave camp commandants detailed instructions on how to deal with this. The regulations made clear that the self-management of catering was preferable to the use of contractors, since nearly all complaints about food had come from camps using contractors. Where it had not been possible to terminate contracts (and efforts should continue to be made to do this) a strict control on contractors should be maintained. The authorities were clearly as concerned about profiteering as they were about the welfare of the prisoners, stipulating that those failing to satisfy proper standards following a warning should have their contracts terminated; and any excuse that recent price rises were the cause should be met 'by pointing to the enormous gains previously made by the contractors, which have already been remarked upon in the Reichstag, and that therefore they can afford to supply at a loss now'. The regulations continued:

> All requests to make an allowance on any contracts that are terminated or to take over remaining stocks at a higher price than their present value are to be refused. On the contrary, it can be claimed that on account of his former profits, if a contractor is released from his agreement, he should pay a bonus to the military authorities. It is also just and possible to exact compensation from a contractor on account of deficiencies in the quantities supplied, and of improper profits in the past.

Looking more generally at the management of catering, the regulations emphasised the need for camps to have sufficient trained staff. All those involved – from officers fitted to control catering arrangements, officials managing financial and commissariat branches, NCOs who might supervise kitchens, to private soldiers who might be employed as cooks – were required to undergo a week's training at other camps capable of serving as a model of what was required. Day-to-day responsibility for catering in each camp was to be given to a kitchen committee, appointed by the commandant, to include the camp surgeon, the paymaster or official in charge of the financial and stores departments, and any other persons deemed suitable. The committee was to be responsible for all purchases, with particular regard to nutritive values – 'If there is a suspicion of under weight or adulteration, samples are to be sent to the nearest food laboratory for examination'. And:

> In this connection, anything that might be open to criticism, or might cast reflection upon the integrity of the supervising staff of the camp, even in the smallest degree, must be strictly obviated - for example, such as supplying the guards with food from the prisoners' kitchens, or accepting favours from contractors and purveyors.

The regulations dealt specifically with the role of prisoners, stressing the importance of their co-operation. Particularly 'cleanly and capable' prisoners were to be employed for the preparation of food, and NCO or civilian prisoners were to be permanently attached to the kitchen to supervise the staff and communicate to them the wishes of the prisoners. As to diet, the tastes of the prisoners were to be met as far as possible, with 'home dishes' being provided and religious customs being considered as far as possible. The normal daily average dietary provision was then set down as 85g of albumen, 40g of fat and 475g of hydrate of carbon, or a total of 2,700 calorific units, for prisoners of medium weight doing light work, with 10 per cent less going to people doing absolutely nothing (e.g., those in hospital) and 10 per cent more going to those doing heavy work. Examples of daily menus were given, with the requirement that diets for each month were to be sent by each camp to the Accommodation Department of the Ministry of War, and:

> It is the duty of the medical officer to bring to the notice of the commandant in writing, and to insist on their being made good, any deficiencies in the feeding arrangements which may come to his knowledge. Otherwise he will be held responsible for any harm ensuing to the prisoners from inferior or insufficient food.

The exchanges of correspondence over accommodation, maintenance and food standards did not result in any agreement on what the correct standards should be, nor was that required by the Hague Convention. The published documents did however indicate that in these areas both sides fully sub-scribed to the objectives of the convention. In other areas the position was more difficult. One of these was officers' pay. The Hague Convention required belligerents to pay captured officers (but not men) the same pay as the equivalent rank in the country of capture, with the sides reimbursing each other after the conflict. This left open questions such as what consti-tuted equivalent rank and whether pay should be at active or inactive service rates. Grey put forward detailed proposals for agreement on 24 September 1914.[15] These suggested that all captured officers, whether belonging to the land or sea service, should be treated alike, and that whatever their length of service their pay should be at the minimum of the equivalent rank in the British infantry. Ad hoc arrangements should be made for officers of a very high rank. All in receipt of such pay would be required to pay for their own food and clothing. Grey went on to suggest that mutual arrangements should also be made to enable officer prisoners to remit part of their pay to their families and dependents, since these would otherwise either remain unprovided for, or the respective governments would have to make addi-tional provision themselves. Pending a response to the proposals, the British Government proceeded to pay captured officers half the pay of equivalent infantry ranks and to provide them with free messing and medical provision. Captured officers were allowed to purchase such liquors as they wished, with their only expense being clothing, which they were expected to pay for themselves. In March 1915, the British Government found out from the German branch of the Geneva Red Cross that the German authorities were paying substantially below the rates for equivalent ranks and deduct-ing two-thirds for messing (at Crefeld the deduction was reported as being 100 per cent).[16] In response, the government stated that the convention was clearly no longer a regulating factor and proceeded to pay captured offic-ers above the rank of captain as captains, and those at captain or below at the same ratio to minimum British rates as the German Government were paying in relation to German rates. From such pay, captured officers would be required to defray the costs of their rations and messing.[17] While the British Government left the door open for further discussion and agree-ment, this never seems to have happened.

Application of the detailed provisions of the Geneva Convention also caused difficulty. The convention provided for those engaged exclusively in looking after the wounded or sick to be protected at all times and if captured not to be treated as POWs. At the same time the convention laid down that a belligerent who was compelled to abandon wounded and sick must, where practicable, leave behind a portion of medical staff to take care of them; and medical staff falling into enemy hands could be retained to look after those included in a surrender for so long as their services were necessary for this purpose. They were then to be returned as military circumstances permitted. Thus, although medical personnel were not to be treated as POWs, this did not mean that they were free to act or move about without let or hindrance. The potential for flexible or controversial interpretation of these provisions was to be a cause of concern to both sides during the course of the war, as well as offering the opportunity to hold on to medical staff for longer than strictly necessary, which both sides exploited. There was concern quite early on about the imprisonment of captured British medical personnel at the German prison camps at Crefeld and Torgau, leading the British Government to propose on 21 December 1914 a mutual exchange of such prisoners.[18] For their part, the German Government objected to the release by the British of a number of German doctors via Spain. Not only was it alleged that they were held for too long, but the route of their release made it extremely difficult in practice for them to actually return home. This particular problem prompted the German Government to put forward detailed proposals for a reciprocal agreement on the treatment of medical personnel in January 1915.[19] The proposals comprised three strands. First, it was noted that the sense of the Geneva Convention was that medical personnel could be retained to provide support until the medical staff of the capturing army were in a position to take over. Thus, if the capturing army did not have sufficient staff immediately available there was nothing wrong in requiring detained medical staff to accompany the sick and wounded to reserve hospitals and prison camps and to continue their work there until proper permanent arrangements could be made. Secondly, the proposals noted that under the Hague Convention responsibility for the care of prisoners was placed specifically on capturing states, so 'the doctors of the enemy State cannot be compelled to devote their services to the sick and wounded prisoners beyond the first emergency'. The proposals defined 'the first emergency' as including the sudden outbreak of an epidemic among the prisoners. Thirdly, the routes chosen for the return of medical staff should enable those returned to reach their destination as quickly as possible, whilst at the same time ensuring that they were not able to gain useful military intelligence about enemy operations in the war zone. This argued generally against direct routes of return, and the

German Government proposed instead that exchanges between Germany and France should be executed via Switzerland, those between Germany and Great Britain via the Netherlands, and those between Germany and Russia via Sweden.

These proposals were effectively rejected by the British Government in March 1915, resulting in the issue remaining unresolved for the duration of the war. The British Government argued that captured medical personnel should only be required to continue working for as long as the sick and wounded remained in the unit for which they were responsible. They should not be responsible for any sick and wounded transferred to hospital or prison camp or for the care of prisoners from any unit other than their own. In a direct response to the German reference to epidemics, the British considered that captured personnel should not be required to undertake any 'fresh' work, as this seemed to imply that should medical personnel be required to continue work already commenced, this should not extend beyond the immediate necessities. In short, the capturing state was only entitled to use captured medical personnel to tide over an immediate emergency, and should themselves take over care with the minimum of delay. When this had been done, the captured medical personnel should be sent home as soon as possible. The British Government concluded that if Germany accepted this interpretation they would be prepared to engage in the mutual release of captured medical personnel immediately. Again, there is no evidence that the German Government replied to this, leaving both sides to continue in their own way throughout the war.

The steps taken during the first six months of the war to set out, if not to agree, the ground rules for the treatment of prisoners exposed both strengths and weaknesses in the Hague and Geneva conventions. The differences between the two sides over the treatment of captured medical personnel stemmed from lack of precision in the wording of the Geneva Convention itself. A remedy to this had to wait for the redrafting of the convention in 1929. While the 1929 convention continued to require medical personal to be returned as soon as possible, it also specifically required that while awaiting return they should continue to carry out their duties under the direction of the enemy, making it only 'preferable' that they should be engaged in the care of the sick and wounded from their own side.[20] While there was also some lack of precision in the Hague Convention with regard to the pay of captured officers, failure to comply with the convention seems to have been a conscious decision on the part of the German Government. The official

reason for this, if any was given, now seems lost, but the most likely explanation is the disproportionate cost that the German Government would
have had to face because of the substantially greater number of prisoners
that they held as compared to their enemies. If indeed this was the case,
the decision turned out to be particularly shrewd as the Treaty of Versailles
ultimately provided for the parties to waive all reciprocal repayment of sums
due for the maintenance of POWs in their respective territories.[21]

Despite these weaknesses, the overall framework provided by the conventions for the welfare and maintenance of prisoners can only be regarded
as a success. By early 1915, mechanisms existed on both sides to provide
information about prisoners in a timely and systematic way, and for prisoners to communicate and to receive relief post-free. The accommodation
standards published by both sides appeared adequate or better, as did the
approach which they adopted towards providing an adequate diet. But the
real test was whether the declared objectives and standards were always met
in practice. Throughout the war, and in the early days especially, there was
concern on both sides that they were not and that in reality many prisoners
were being treated badly.

# 3

# GERMANY: PROBLEMS & INSPECTIONS

When Gerard visited the POW camp at Döberitz, a few miles west of Berlin, on 20 August 1914, he found the conditions entirely satisfactory. The camp contained only a small number of prisoners and it had been possible to house them in existing purpose-built barracks. Gerard noted, 'There were only a few British among the prisoners, with a number of Russian and French. I was allowed to converse freely with the prisoners and found that they had no complaints.'[1] But by the time of Gerard's next visit at the end of September, the course of the war had resulted in a significant increase in the number of prisoners and a marked deterioration in conditions. Many prisoners were now housed in horse tents surrounded by barbed wire. Not only were the conditions poor but there was also a shortage of basic necessities. The men complained about the insufficiency of the food: 'One loaf of good black bread is given to three men; each man has a cup of coffee in the morning, some soup in the middle of the day, and a cup of coffee at night, and this constitutes their sole rations.'[2] They asked for tobacco and money to buy supplies at the camp canteen. The prisoners also had only one blanket each, no change of underwear and no overcoats, since they had been compelled to abandon their overcoats and equipment on being captured. On his own initiative, and utilising his own resources, Gerard took immediate steps to provide relief. He obtained supplies of underclothing and blankets from the large department stores of Berlin and their wholesalers and sent these to the camp. He also sent sticks, crutches and wheelchairs for the wounded, as well as extra food and 'nourishing delicacies', such as 'chocolate, eggs, and port wine'.[3]

Events at Döberitz were becoming typical of camps throughout Germany. The growth in the number of prisoners was rapidly outstripping the resources needed to clothe, feed and house them. Gerard was quick to alert the British Government to this, prompting a major relief operation for British prisoners in Germany over the winter of 1914/15. In early December, uniforms and clothing for captured British officers were sent directly from England, and towards the end of the month Grey reported that £20,000 was being made available for the ad hoc relief of British POWs pending the establishment of more formal machinery. On 14 January 1915, Grey stated that the government was placing at the disposal of the US Embassy £1 per man per quarter, or £20,000 per quarter, for the benefit of all British POWs (including civilians) held in Germany.[4] The effort involved in managing the ensuing relief effort was substantial. As a matter of course prisoners arrived at the German camps ill-clothed and ill-equipped. Gerard initially established a warehouse in Berlin to hold central stocks and recruited packers to organise their distribution, an arrangement subsequently changed in favour of direct delivery to the camps.[5] By March 1915, American Express had been given a contract to undertake such deliveries.[6] In the same month, Gerard reported that, to date, some 9,648 items of clothing (including boots, caps, mufflers and gloves) had been supplied to British prisoners in Germany[7] – a significant figure when set aside an estimated British combatant POW population in Germany of 18,000 at 1 February 1915.[8]

The joint British-American relief operation undoubtedly ameliorated many of the hardships facing prisoners on capture – hardships made significantly worse by the onset of winter. But the need for relief, particularly its urgency and scale, had an immediate impact on the British Government, which saw in this evidence of deliberate callousness towards British POWs by the German authorities, in turn giving rise to a propaganda campaign which was to last for most of the war about the alleged ill-treatment of British prisoners. The evidence for deliberate and widespread ill-treatment is nevertheless uncertain. In the case of Döberitz, for example – effectively the catalyst for the start of the campaign – conditions following Gerard's visit at the end of September 1914 seem quickly to have improved. The counsellor of the American Embassy in Berlin visited the camp on 17 October and produced what might be regarded as a very favourable report on conditions there.[9] He found the men to be cheerful with few complaints, and none about the food. There were some objections about the thickness of the blankets and some requests for caps, soap, towels and books (the embassy would be sending out more books, though the report noted that there was already a large circulating library of English books within the camp). The men did their own cooking and ample arrangements were to be made for them to do washing throughout the winter. A large amount of space had also been set aside for exercise. While the report acknowledged that prisoners were still accommodated in tents, it noted that a large number of wooden huts had been built, each lit by electricity and properly heated. Every hut would house 100 men in a large room, with a small room set aside for the British NCOs in charge of the building. Huts would be grouped in 'colonies' of ten, with each 'colony' allocated a kitchen, two lavatories and a store house.

By November, the huts had been brought fully into use, and by the spring of 1915 their numbers had been increased further. The next formal inspection by Gerard and his colleagues took place on 30 March 1915, at which time he was able to report a further general improvement in conditions.[10] By then the British population of the camp amounted to some 3,600 NCOs and men, out of a total population of some 8,000. The prisoners were healthy and in good spirits, with such complaints as there were relating almost entirely to the food – the German material prepared by Russian cooks did not suit British tastes. The author of the report (Jackson) observed, however, that these complaints 'were the exact counterpart of complaints made to me by German prisoners in England'. The British prisoners were required only to do their share of camp fatigue work and they had no objections to that. Again, the camp was described as being in a healthy location, and the new barracks – which were intended for use by German soldiers at some time in the future – were at least as good as those used by Germans in the same neighbourhood. All in all, 'The impression of the whole was excellent, and one received the idea that everything that could reasonably be expected was done for the men by the authorities in charge'.

The early problems of Döberitz therefore seem to have been quickly overcome. Indeed, such was the atmosphere in the camp that in January 1915, Motor Scout Cecil A. Tooke, a prisoner and prominent artist 'whose Christmas and Easter cards are well known all over the world', was asked by the British prisoners to design an illuminated address for Colonel Alberti, the camp commandant, on the occasion of the latter's seventieth birthday.[11] And in March 1915 the commandant himself allocated a marquee to the prisoners for chapel on Sunday and for use as a theatre during the week. The civilian British chaplain at Berlin, who visited the camp each fortnight, procured various instruments with the help of English ladies resident in Berlin and established a small orchestra from amongst the prisoners which then gave concerts (in the 'Döberitz Empire') every two or three weeks. Further evidence of the general mood of the prisoners at around that time is given in the US inspectors' report of their visit to the camp on 30 March 1915, when they recorded that several prisoners had asked if they might volunteer for work on German farms without being considered as giving 'aid to the enemy' and incurring the risk of forfeiture of pay. (Grey's ultimate response to this question, viz. 'that His Majesty's Government do not wish them to work in the manner referred to',[12] was in fact to cause a great deal of confusion, being taken by the prisoners to mean that they should not work at all – contrary to the requirements of the Hague Convention – as opposed to Grey's intention that they should not put themselves forward and volunteer.)

Despite these generally encouraging and comforting reports, the British Government was reluctant to let go of its earlier concerns about conditions at Döberitz. In March 1915, it published an article written by 'a US citizen' – sent to Grey by HM Ambassador in Washington – following a visit to the camp in the very early days.[13] The conditions described in the article were no doubt those which had given rise to Gerard's alarm the previous October. The author was careful not to attribute blame, acknowledging that conditions in the camp no doubt arose out of military necessity, and accepting that everything that could realistically be done for the prisoners was probably being done. If anything, the author was attempting to draw attention to the plight of POWs generally rather than the unacceptable conditions at Döberitz. Nevertheless, the picture presented was of '9,000 very miserable men', lacking warm clothing, vermin-ridden, with no way of keeping themselves clean, sleeping two in a bed in horse tents – some of which were patched and very old – each housing between 200 and 500 prisoners. While the men were given enough food, the stew-based diet (referred to by one prisoner as 'skilly', which even his pig would not eat) was particularly unacceptable to the British and French, though liked by the Russians. According to the article, despite all this, the main hardship suffered by the prisoners was that they had nothing to do.

For their part, the German authorities felt well able to rebut all these criticisms when the article was put to them for comment. Their reply (not published) included:

it is to be noticed that the visit which must be the one in question was under-taken at the most unfavourable time conceivable, seeing that at that period the prisoners were still living in tents many of which were blown down or damaged by the Autumnal storms. On account of this circumstance and the wetness of the season, the camp apparently gave the visitor the impression of being particularly unliveable-in. Even if the report does not contain an actually untruthful description of what he saw, he at any rate judges everything with-out making the slightest intelligent allowance for the particular conditions of war. It will suffice, in this respect, simply to point to the obviously far worse conditions which prevailed during the Autumn of that year in the internment camps for German civilian prisoners at Newburg [sic] in England.[14]

As to the more specific comments and complaints, the German Government refuted the charge that Döberitz contained 9,000 miserable and sickly men, stating that they were in fact all strong and healthy. Nor did it see anything wrong with 'stable-tents', since these were better and warmer than others. It went on to point out that many German prisoners in other countries were held in tents in winter, while those countries did not have to deal with the same number of prisoners as Germany. And although it accepted that 'the English' found life monotonous, it contended that they had only themselves to blame, because at Döberitz, as elsewhere, they tried to escape from even the lightest tasks. On the question of hygiene, the German Government stated that all POWs had the opportunity to wash their whole bodies each day, and as far as food was concerned and the reference to 'skilly':

> It may happen that the English do not find new dishes so palatable as the extrav-agant fare which England provides for her mercenaries. Groats, which English soldiers are reported to have spoken of as too bad to give to pigs, are readily eaten by many Germans: and they are even a favourite dish in certain parts of England.

Another camp which gave the British Government early cause for concern was the prison fortress at Torgau, in Saxony, a camp for officers. Torgau had attracted the attention of the Foreign Office following the arrest of two doctors employed by the Red Cross near Namur, in contravention of the Geneva Convention.[15] These were sent to Torgau where there were already twenty-eight officers and five privates of the RAMC. (The Red Cross asked the Foreign Office to intervene, but while the German authorities offered to release the doctors subject to a guarantee of reciprocity, the Foreign Office declined.) Julius G. Lay, the US Consul-General in Berlin, visited Torgau on 15 and 16 October 1914 and interviewed both the commanding general and the prisoners. He identified a number of 'objectionable features', most of which he believed could be dealt with if the commanding general could be satisfied about the conditions under which German officers were being held in England. To this end, he asked his counterpart, the US Consul-General in London, to visit one of the camps in England and to report his observations. The 'objectionable features' themselves, while clearly impacting on the daily life and comfort of the prisoners, fell a long way short of ill-treatment. The officers had recently been forbidden beer; since the water and the mineral waters provided were 'unfit to drink' Lay considered that limited wine and beer could not possibly do any harm. An extension of 'lights out' from 9 p.m. to 10 p.m. was urgently requested. Water closets and latrines were currently being used by all ranks and all nationalities, including German soldiers and civilian workers; Lay asked for a water closet and latrines to be set apart for English officers and the same for French officers. White bread had recently been forbidden for the officer prisoners, despite evidence that ample flour was available in the town. Enlargement of the kitchens and the provision of new boilers had been necessary and the officer POWs had been asked to pay for this, when the matter was clearly not their responsibility. The prisoners were allowed no newspapers, and letters had been delayed through holdups in the censorship processes. Lay concluded: 'When the officers at Torgau can procure palatable and wholesome mineral waters to drink, have additional and separate latrines installed, buy white bread, as rye bread makes them sick, and be allowed special medicines, the conditions under which they live can be regarded as satisfactory.'[16] A report by Jackson of the US Embassy following a further visit to Torgau in May 1915 found no continuing problems.[17]

In his report on Torgau, Lay had referred to rumours there of ill-treatment of British NCOs and men at other camps: 'Rumours of their exposure to the elements, their starvation and their treatment, are rampant all along the line.' The US Embassy considered that there were no grounds for such rumours, but many nevertheless appeared to have been based on good authority. A report written by Major Vandeleur of the 1st Cameronians, who had escaped from Crefeld in December 1914 (see Chapter 6), provides an example. Most of Major Vandeleur's report[18] deals with his journey between capture and arrival at Crefeld. He himself acknowledges that at Crefeld there was not so much to complain about. There was some overcrowding, with Major Vandeleur and his four fellow officers being put in a room intended to accommodate six people, but which already housed ten. Food was regular, but of poor quality. There was provision for exercise and order-lies were provided (one for every fifteen officers) for the purpose of keeping the rooms clean. However, 'Officers had to make their own beds and brush their boots in nearly all cases. The beds we slept on were as provided for German soldiers, and were very hard and uncomfortable'. Although reli-gious services were permitted, the Lutheran parson provided made so many unpleasant remarks about the late king and the British that the captured officers decided to hold their own services. In concluding his report, how-ever, Major Vandeleur turned to information supplied by the orderlies at Crefeld, and by English and French medical officers who had been at other camps, about the 'barbarous way in which British soldiers are being treated in the various laagers by the Germans'. According to this information, many of the other camps were composed of tents; the men had in many cases had their greatcoats, clothing and money taken from them; they had to sleep on sodden and rotten straw which had not been changed for months; and feed-ing arrangements were bad. According to Major Vandeleur, 'All the men who came as orderlies were crawling in vermin and half of them were suffering from the itch. The medical officer had to isolate these men before they could be employed as servants'. Moreover, the British were being singled out to undertake all the menial tasks in the camps, so as (according to the French orderlies) to create ill-feeling between French and British soldiers. In Major Vandeleur's opinion, 'something should be urgently done to try to ameliorate the lot of the British soldier who is a prisoner in Germany'.

The German authorities were just as dismissive of these complaints as they had been about Döberitz.[19] As far as Major Vandeleur's own position was concerned, they stated that the rooms at Crefeld were large enough to prevent any overcrowding, and as to the beds, 'German soldiers' beds must be good enough for POWs'. The number of orderlies had increased from one for every fifteen officers to one for every five officers during Major Vandeleur's stay. Officers had never had to make their own beds or clean their own boots. As to the food, 'Major Vandeleur seems to hold that any dishes not known in England or not prepared in the English way are bad'. And as far as the rejection of the Lutheran parson was concerned, 'The reason given by the English officers for not desiring any more visits from the Evangelical minister of religion was, "not his disagreeable remarks about the late King, but his indistinct pronunciation"'. The German authorities also refuted the claims about the treatment of prisoners generally. They rejected the claim that British prisoners had had their overcoats and tunics taken away from them – 'Many have sold them or lost them at play with more pecunious French or Belgians'. And as to the orderlies being covered in vermin, 'It is, with a few exceptions, untrue that English orderlies were afflicted with lice ... The truth is, however, that the English, like the Russians, but in distinction from the French and Belgians, always arrive in the internment camps filthy and lousy'.

Reports of ill-treatment, especially ill-treatment directed specifically against the British, continued to take hold and came from a variety of sources. In a note to Page, US Ambassador in London, dated 26 December 1914, Grey referred (second hand) to a French priest who had returned from Minden to Rome, and who was reported to have given an account of the cruelties practised upon the British prisoners by their guards. While the French prisoners were well treated and the Russians not so badly, the British were, allegedly, singled out for ill-treatment:

> According to the French priest, the German soldiers kick the British prisoners in the stomach, and break their guns over their backs; they force them to sleep out in marshy places, so that many are now consumptive. The British are almost starved, and such have been their tortures that thirty of them asked to be shot.[20]

A further example is contained in a note from the British Ambassador in Petrograd, written on 9 December 1914, which recorded a visit from 'a Russian Medical Officer' who had reported that two British officers held on the Baltic island of Dänholm bei Stralsund were being less well treated than their Russian counterparts.[21] The British officers had allegedly been placed alongside less well-educated Russians who spoke no English. The Russians could buy books, the British could not. The German lieutenant in charge was openly insulting to the British. The food was bad, both in quantity and quality. It comprised three pieces of bread a day made with potato meal: lunch was mostly potatoes; the evening meal consisted of bread and a small slice of sausage. On 30 December 1914, HM Ambassador, Petrograd, reported a visit by another Russian medical officer who 'confirmed' the unfavourable treatment of British prisoners at Dänholm bei Stralsund.[22] The medical officer stated ('on the authority of a Belgian sergeant') that men there, including the British, were subjected to a regime of extreme harshness. They were quartered in earthen huts which were undrained, unheated and unlit. The food was less in quantity and worse in quality than the officers' food. The POWs had to work on draining marshy country around the camp. Many suffered from rheumatism and their general condition was deplorable. Again the German authorities denied the substance of the complaints, identifying the Russian medical officers as two disaffected ex-prisoners at Dänholm who had been moved on from there because they had refused to serve as doctors to the Russian prisoners. Their conduct had been provocative and they had complained about being housed in accommodation normally occupied by German soldiers. Complaints about the quality of the food at the camp were simply untrue and there was no ill-treatment. If the British were being less well-treated than other prisoners, this was 'intelligible considering that in the early days the English officers behaved in a very haughty and insubordinate fashion'.[23]

Reports such as these, together with the irrefutable need for the massive relief programme for British prisoners being implemented by Gerard, had already caused the British Government to protest formally at the end of 1914 about the failure of the German Government to comply with the Hague Convention, noting particularly 'the inhuman treatment to which it is unfortunately evident that many British prisoners of war in Germany are being subjected' and 'the manner in which British prisoners of war in Germany have been singled out for ill-treatment'.[24] In some cases allegations of ill-treatment were indeed found to be valid by the US inspectors themselves. At Altdamm, near Stettin, while the camp authorities were praised for their efforts in difficult circumstances, specific complaints by the prisoners about the rough treatment of the guards, together with complaints about insufficient food, clothing and blankets, were not denied.[25] And at the end of March 1915, an inspection of the officers' camp at Burg bei Magdeburg found that the seventy-five British prisoners there were scattered about the camp and housed with officers of other nationalities in large rooms used for all purposes. There were no separate mess and recreation rooms and while the health of the prisoners was good the ventilation and sanitation 'left something to be desired'.[26]

As the British Government continued to pass on complaints, Gerard for his part tried to calm the situation, noting that up to 4 May 1915, twenty-nine inspection reports had been provided by the US Embassy in Berlin and these had established that most rumours of poor conditions or ill-treatment were without foundation or exaggerated. In those camps which he had visited personally he had heard practically no complaints, except about the insufficient quantity of food; the prisoners nevertheless looked in good health. He cited the case of Göttingen as an example:

> I received a telegram from the British Government ... stating that the prisoners in Göttingen were in great need, and received the telegram only a few days after having visited Göttingen, and had found there a model camp, hearing absolutely no complaints from the British there, except as to the kind and the amount of food. The men, however, were all cheerful and of most healthy appearance. In this camp the latrines, kitchens, &c., are in fine condition; bath arrangements are good, and there is an excellent steam laundry. It was also quite refreshing to find that professors of the University and Lutheran pastors and other people in Göttingen have, since the opening of the camp, taken great interest in the prisoners, helped the camp commandant in every way, and aided in founding a camp library. Great praise is due to Professor Strange, of Göttingen University, for taking the lead in this work. The packages from England are promptly received in all the camps, and the arrangements which we made with the American Express Company seems [sic] to be working very satisfactorily in this respect.[27]

After the US had entered the war, Gerard added as an aside that not everyone in Göttingen had shared Professor Strange's enthusiasm for helping prisoners, as the professor had woken up one morning to find that his house had been painted red, white and blue by some of the local population.[28] Gerard concluded his comments by stating that no British soldier now needed clothes in Germany, and that any British soldier who did require them need only notify his camp commandant.

The evidence about conditions in Germany during the early stages of the war is therefore conflicting. There can be no doubt that the rapid movement of armies during the first few months produced prisoners in such numbers and in such condition as to overwhelm many of the original camps in Germany. The relief effort organised by Gerard on behalf of the British Government over the winter of 1914/15 clearly played a major role in ensuring that British prisoners quickly received the clothing and other basic necessities needed to make their existence tolerable. Within the camps, accommodation and food obviously varied, but the official German attitude that allowance needed to be made for the harsh conditions of war must be at least partly credible. Despite this, however – and the fact that overall conditions were destined to improve rapidly – there is still a question mark over direct German culpability for the poor conditions found in a number of camps, most notably in relation to outbreaks of typhus which were to occur at Wittenberg, Gardelegen and elsewhere, and which are dealt with more fully in Chapter 5. Gerard's attempts to calm down the situation are nevertheless understandable. He needed the continuing co-operation not only of the German Government but also of individual camp commandants and other army officers to be able to carry out inspections. In most cases where poor treatment was identified, this appeared to arise out of unpreparedness or incompetence rather than deliberate intent. When ill-treatment was exposed, for whatever reason, intemperance in writing the resulting reports was not likely to be of help with regard to the future. This was even more so against the background of British policy to play up allegations of ill-treatment whenever these were rumoured or found. US personnel inspecting camps in the UK faced similar considerations and also erred on the side of temperance in presenting their reports. That the US inspectors played down some of their worst findings and deliberately leaned towards conciliation rather than confrontation is borne out by Gerard's own admission in his memoirs that there were indeed many instances in the early stages of the war where prisoners were harshly treated by the Germans.[29]

The complaints that did emerge during the early stages quickly began to focus on three main themes: the singling out of British prisoners for unduly harsh treatment; the unacceptable nature of the diet; and the housing together of all nationalities. The 'singling out' of the British was to become an enduring theme throughout the war, with the British Government holding publicly that this was a deliberate German policy. The German Government consistently denied this, blaming the 'English' for bringing problems on themselves, for example by being too haughty, reluctant to work or too critical of a foreign diet. The US inspectors seem to have been split on the issue. Gerard claimed not to have found any difference whatsoever in the treatment of prisoners of different nationalities, nor indeed to have received any complaints on this score,[30] while McCarthy, one of his inspectors, had no doubt that German policy was influenced directly by an intensity of feeling directed specifically towards the British.[31] Another inspector, following a visit to Burg bei Magdeburg in March 1915, appeared to be offering an alternative explanation when he commented:

> The discipline is German and some of the rules appear unnecessary and objectionable to British officers. Moreover, young British officers have more

animal spirits than their Continental comrades, and some of the things which are done thoughtlessly are misunderstood and taken amiss, and are followed by disciplinary measures.

So far as I have been able to ascertain, there is no discrimination against British officers or soldiers, but it is certain that some camp regulations appear more onerous to them than they do to members of Continental armies.[32]

It seems likely that cultural differences and different attitudes to discipline were indeed at the root of many of the complaints by the British of ill-treatment, though the extent of this is obviously difficult to judge from this distance in time. There is, nevertheless, little tangible evidence to support the view that the British were routinely singled out.

As has already been noted, British complaints about camp food effectively mirrored those of German prisoners in British camps. For many British prisoners black bread was regarded as inedible per se, being widely believed to cause serious stomach upsets. The stew-based diet which accompanied it, while normal to the average German citizen, was equated by many of the British prisoners to a poor diet, even though its calorific value might have been sufficient. The monotony of the diet also sapped morale, with Gerard himself later remarking, 'Think of living as the prisoners of war in Germany have for years, without ever having anything (except black bread) which cannot be eaten with a spoon.'[33] Even within its own terms, the quality of the German diet varied from camp to camp (depending on the purchasing skills of the camp commandant), as did its quantity. When asked by Grey to investigate reports that British prisoners at Süder-Zollhaus, near Janneby, were starving, Gerard reported back that, though not starving, the prisoners were undernourished and suffering illness through insufficiency of food in a working camp, and that a new commandant had now been appointed.[34] Centrally, the German authorities took seriously the need to feed prisoners adequately and were throughout the war to review and amend diet regulations. They also took early steps to minimise problems by giving prisoners as much control as possible over the content and production of their own diets. For British prisoners especially, the impact of the camp diet was to be substantially reduced through the receipt of parcels from the UK which, as early as autumn 1914, provided sufficient food to meet their daily requirements.

Of the main complaints advanced by the British Government in the early days, the German practice of housing all nationalities together was, in clear distinction to the others, both deliberate and pernicious. The detailed reasoning behind the Prussian War Ministry's decision to adopt this policy is not clear. It may be, as the German Government said in response to complaints, that the policy was designed to demonstrate to the prisoners, and by implication to their respective governments, that they were not natural allies. McCarthy believed that the practice was simply an extension of the policy of singling out the British for especially harsh treatment. He cites the comment of one British prisoner that 'you do not have to be civilised to be an ally'.[35] Or it may have been simply that the Prussian War Ministry took the view that segregation was a nicety it could not afford to spend time pursuing amidst all the other more pressing matters of war. Whatever the reason, the effect of the policy was deleterious. National differences led to irritation and were often subversive to discipline and good order – even, for example, in relation to such matters as whether to open or close windows at night (with the Russians preferring a 'fug' and the British fresh air). But much more seriously, by bringing the nationalities together at close quarters the German authorities enabled the spread of typhus from the Russians, where the disease was endemic, to prisoners of other nationalities, where the disease was effectively unknown, to devastating effect. It was perhaps largely because of this, together with the obvious point that prisoners were more likely to be well behaved and amenable when housed with their own kind, that the Prussian War Ministry gradually rescinded its policy of non-segregation around the end of 1915.[36] It is worth noting that under the 1929 Geneva Convention belligerents were specifically enjoined not to house different nationalities or races together in the same camp if this could be avoided.[37]

Gerard's contribution to improving the lot of British prisoners in Germany and cooling the temperature between the two sides during the early part of the war was clearly substantial. It is especially to his credit that he personally took the initiative in organising relief and visiting the camps, and that he was then prepared to devote considerable embassy resources to continuing the work. But his initiative was also to assume a longer-term significance when he successfully persuaded Bethman-Hollweg, the German Chancellor, to allow him to pursue the development of a more formal inspection regime with the German authorities and the British Government.[38] Following detailed negotiations with both sides, Gerard finally secured agreement to a scheme under which each government agreed to provide the other with a full statement of its policy on the treatment of prisoners and complete details of the conditions under which they were to be held. These were to be supplemented by copies of any instructions issued from time to time to camp commandants. Accredited representatives of the US embassies in the UK and Germany would then have the right to inspect camps in the respective countries at twenty-four hours' notice. During their visits, the US inspectors would have the right to interview prisoners within sight but out of earshot of the guards or other camp officials. The subject matter of such interviews was to be restricted to the wishes and complaints of prisoners. For their part, the inspectors would in the first instance attempt to resolve any problems with the camp authorities before referring them to higher authority. In this respect, the German Government insisted that problems could only be referred higher if the camp commandant had specifically stated that he could not or would not comply with the inspector's findings.[39]

The formal scheme finally came into operation during March and April 1915, and by the middle of the year parallel diplomatic effort had resulted in similar schemes being brought into force right across Europe. The workload imposed on the US was substantial. During the two years leading to the US' own entry into the war, the inspectors carried out many hundreds of visits and produced many hundreds of reports. In Germany alone they made over 200 inspections in 1916, against a target to re-inspect each camp every four months, or after only one month in the case of a bad report. In France, inspections were scheduled for every nine months, there being insufficient inspectors available to meet the original target of one visit every six months.[40] All reports of visits were copied by the respective embassies to each other and to the governments of both sides and until 1916 the British Government published the reports in the form of Parliamentary White Papers as a matter of course. After the US entered the war, the task of carrying out inspections passed to the Netherlands and other neutral governments.

The US was rightly proud to have effectively developed an entirely new arm of international protection and relief work. As McCarthy himself noted: 'To develop and establish a principle of inspection … is a definite achievement … It will indeed relieve much suffering. I have no doubt that this matter will be established as a principle of international law, and be embodied in conventions such as those established at The Hague.'[41] As he predicted, the principle was duly embodied in the Geneva Convention of 1929.[1]

# 4

# THE BRITISH EXPERIENCE

The primary focus of concern in Britain during the first few months of the war was, naturally, the fate of British prisoners in Germany. Nevertheless, there was also much concern and debate about the treatment of enemy prisoners in Britain. While the British authorities had far fewer combatant POWs to deal with than Germany, the decision to intern large numbers of enemy alien civilians (see Chapter 1) put severe pressure on the accommodation and other resources needed to house large numbers. As the war progressed, camps in Britain were typically located in the west and north-west of the country, away from the south and east coast ports, and even in Ireland. But initially, accommodation had to be seized wherever it was available. The first combatant POWs went straight to Dorchester in August 1914, while some of the first civilian internees were held for a time at London's Olympia. Old workhouses, skating rinks, disused industrial premises and existing army barracks were all commandeered. For a time, prison ships were also brought into use. The fact that such accommodation often had to be used before it was properly adapted, and was in many cases intrinsically unsuited for its purpose, caused inevitable hardship, just as the same factors were creating hardship for British prisoners in Germany. Like the British press for its part, the German press categorised such hardship as ill-treatment and campaigned accordingly. Within Britain, concern about hardship being suffered by German prisoners, especially civilian internees, was to some extent shared by the public and politicians, both on humanitarian grounds and out of concern that poor conditions would give rise to reprisals against British prisoners in Germany. At the same time there were perhaps just as many who, far from being concerned about hardship, were critical that German prisoners, especially officers, were being made too comfortable. From both sides of the argument an acceptance grew, as it had in Germany, that a formal regime of independent inspections and reports offered the best way forward.

Unlike Germany, reports of hardship in camps in Britain related predominantly to civilian internees. This was partly a reflection of sheer numbers. At the end of 1914, the POW population in Britain totalled 17,433 civilians, as opposed to only 6,388 naval and military.[1] It was also no doubt partly a reflection of the fact that civilian internees were more difficult to handle. While combatant POWs were used to discipline and more readily accepted the rigours of camp life, civilians brought with them a high degree of resentment at having been separated from their families, deprived of their liberty, and subjected to discipline. Internees also came from all parts of the social spectrum and in many cases difficulties were caused by internees being housed together with people not of their own kind. To make matters worse, unlike Germany, where British civilian internees were generally held separately – eventually in one camp at Ruhleben – German internees in Britain were in many cases housed in the same camp as combatants. It was the practice in such cases to try to segregate both categories within the camp, but the overall ethos of the camp administration nevertheless tended to favour the combatants, with civilian internees often being treated with suspicion as potential spies, complainers or troublemakers.

Problems became highlighted as early as November 1914, when civilian internees at Queensferry Camp, Flints, petitioned the Foreign Office against their conditions.[2] The camp had been set up in a disused factory which had been unattended for five years. At the time of the petition the camp housed about 1,100 prisoners who, the petitioners claimed, were aged from 14 to 72. The men complained that the building was unclean, unsanitary and had rain pouring through the roof. The inmates had mostly to sleep on palliasses placed on a floor of concrete, iron, soil and a small portion of wood. On arrival they just received one, then a second blanket. There was no ventilation, and there were only two urinals and four buckets placed in two outhouses for the use of all the men. Cooking facilities were inadequate and there was insufficient food. There were only eight 200-gallon kettles to be used for all purposes to feed the inmates. On arrival the men were not inspected by a physician, the hospital was located too near to the main building, with the sick being obliged to sleep on the floor and pay for their medicines, and the camp exercise area was too small. Similar themes emerged at Newbury. The former Liberian Ambassador to the UK, who had subsequently moved to Germany, visited the camp at the beginning of November 1914 and identified a series of problems which the camp commandant told him had been raised with the War Office on a number of occasions to no effect.[3] These included that the conditions were 'too rough' for some of the 'better classes' – for example, six reservists taken from a Brazilian ship were being held in one stall of a stable when they should have been treated as officers – and that most men were under canvas, with some not being fit enough to be housed in this way. A far gloomier picture of conditions at Newbury towards the end of November 1914 was contained in a report circulated by Churchill to the Cabinet.[4] While this report had been compiled by a German firm in Hamburg following visits to a number of camps in the UK and elsewhere, and was therefore unlikely to have been absolutely impartial, the basic criticisms it contained seem to have been accepted as valid by Churchill, who confined his covering remarks to saying, 'although the report contains some inaccuracies, the compilers have done their best'. The report included:

> The camp at Newbury is the worst. Prisoners are stabled together, with 8 to 10 being housed in a stall for a single horse, which could not properly hold more than 3 or 4 human beings. The accommodation is unheated and the prisoners have had to sleep on straw which remains unrenewed for two months at a time. Each prisoner has only one or two blankets which cannot be dried in the sun. The food is bad and insufficient, boots and clothing are scarce, and medical aid and medicines almost non-existent.

Other camps covered by the report included Dorchester, which was criticised for its poor food and lack of cleanliness, and the fact that there were only three baths and twelve basins for 1,200 men to wash each morning. There was also only one camp interpreter, who was described as 'an unpleasant man'. A ship's doctor held at Frithill-by-Frimley, with self-evident exaggeration, compared the enclosed open-air camp there to the Boer concentration camps, forecasting that, 'unless amendment is introduced, hundreds and thousands are simply bound to perish miserably as a consequence of irresistible diseases, the result of both insufficient food and inhuman treatment'.

Not only did the British Government accept such criticisms as valid, but it also regarded them with serious concern. One Foreign Office official described the situation at Queensferry as 'a gross scandal', and, widening his comments to include other camps, went on:

> I understand that there is much friction between the officials of the Home Office, the War Office, and the Police, and that, what [sic] between them, there is a degree of callousness in dealing with the unfortunate prisoners which appears to me not worthy of this country, quite apart from the way it reacts on the treatment of British subjects abroad. After all most of these prisoners whom we feel compelled for general reasons of policy and public safety to intern, are perfectly innocent. Many of them are totally unaccustomed to a life of hardship and to unclean and unsanitary surroundings.[5]

Grey himself took the view that while the treatment of combatant POWs had been uniformly good, the treatment of interned alien civilians had indeed been a failure. But while the War Office too acknowledged that there had been problems, it restricted itself to putting these down to simple practicalities rather than any overt or unintended callousness. For example, the War Office's view on Queensferry was that the conditions there were simply 'the inevitable result of sending a large number of persons without any notice to be shut up in a disused factory which had in no way been prepared for them', and that everything possible was being done to remedy the situation.[6] The War Office's own internal report of conditions at Frimley and Newbury in October 1914 found everything at Frimley to be in perfect order, with no cause for complaint, except that 'in the civilian camp all classes were herded together, and that Germans of the lowest and probably criminal classes were mixed with people of higher and better stamp'. At Newbury, conditions had been found by the War Office to be even better, with different classes of civilian being as far as possible segregated. The War Office report concluded:

> It is naturally unpleasant for men, who have lived in luxury and have never roughed it, to be put into bell tents in the Autumn, but I absolutely repudiate the assertions, that have been made in Germany and elsewhere, that there has been any want of consideration severity or hardship in the case of the prisoners or interned in Frimley or Newbury Camps.[7]

Despite the more relaxed attitude of the War Office and its obvious attempts to defuse the situation, the evidence is that the overall picture was far worse than it claimed. Chandler Anderson of the US Embassy visited Newbury at the end of November and found conditions to be so bad there that he decided to make no detailed report of his visit. He found within the camp civilians over military age, who should not have been detained; a lack of accommodation for dealing with wounded men; and wounded military POWs who should have been in hospital. He found the washing accommodation to be 'disgusting'. Given the adverse reports that had already appeared in the German press about the conditions at Newbury (see Chapter 3), Anderson decided simply to make a report of a short and vague nature, saying that the camp did not compare unfavourably with the camps in Germany holding British prisoners. Any report better than this would be open to contradiction by anyone who had been there, and any worse report would be 'misunderstood' in Germany.[8]

Of the many reports of poor treatment and conditions, one incident, which occurred at the camp for civilian internees at Douglas, Isle of Man, in November 1914, stands out from the others. Douglas was one of the first camps to be established at the start of the war and was based on an existing tented holiday camp. When it opened as a prison camp in September 1914, the accommodation was adequate, with an approved capacity of 2,400. But as the seasons changed, conditions worsened. Numbers at the camp also grew rapidly giving rise to overcrowding. Within a month, the population of the camp had grown to over 3,000. By November, general discontent about conditions had become focused on the quality of the food, culminating in a riot on 19 November during which the guards opened fire, killing five prisoners and wounding nineteen others. The British Government reacted quickly, inviting the US to send in an inspector to report on the incident. Chandler Hale of the US Embassy in London accordingly visited the camp on 25 November, six days after the shootings. On the advice of Grant Duff, HM Ambassador in Berne,[9] Hale's report was subsequently published on 29 December.

Hale presented a glowing picture of the camp.[10] Compared to any of the other camps he had visited in the UK or Germany, he found conditions to be good. While acknowledging that it was 'somewhat crowded', he noted that 1,000 men would be transferred to a new camp on the other side of the island at Peel (Knockaloe) as soon as accommodation was ready for them, 'probably in a few weeks'. Meanwhile, of the 3,300 inmates, 2,800 were housed in tents with wooden flooring, while the remaining 500 were housed 'in two large comfortable buildings'. The latrines and washing facilities were very good and were kept clean, and there was hot and cold running water. All of the camp would eventually be housed in huts when a building programme, currently underway, was completed. The diet was excellent and meals were taken in 'a large glass-roofed, steam-heated, and electric lighted building, where 1,600 can eat at a time'. As to the riot, Hale pinned the blame squarely on a number of troublemakers among the prisoners:

> The riot started, it is alleged, as the result of bad potatoes. The authorities admit that one shipment proved wormeaten, and they were rejected after a few days. On the 18th November the men declared a hunger strike at dinner. The following day they ate their dinner without any complaint, and immediately after the withdrawal of the guards from the rooms, the prisoners suddenly, and evidently by pre-arrangement, started to break up the tables, chairs, crockery, and everything they could lay their hands on. Upon the appearance of the guards, the rioters charged them armed with table legs and chairs. The guards fired one volley in the air, but it had no effect. Finally, and in self-protection, they fired a second round which resulted in the death of four Germans and one Austrian, and the wounding of nineteen others.[11]
> I talked freely with the wounded and also with many others, and gathered that the prisoners were in the wrong and had only themselves to blame. One of the most intelligent men I talked with, a German, said that a considerable percentage of the men were a bad lot gathered in from the East of London, with several agitators amongst them who preached discontent and insubordination which was really the direct cause of the trouble. I am satisfied this was so, as I saw the whole camp and every detail connected with it, and have nothing but commendation for the entire organisation and the kindly treatment accorded the prisoners by the Commandant and his subordinates.

Hale's report of the shootings and his assessment of conditions at Douglas were understandably used by the British Government to rebut accusations that German citizens were being ill-treated in British camps. Further vindication was provided by the formal coroner's inquest into the shootings held on 20 and 27 November. In giving evidence to the inquest the guards were uniformly consistent in arguing that they had no alternative but to open fire in the dining hall. They could not get near enough to the rioters to contain them by use of bayonets because of obstacles in their way. Had they negotiated the obstacles they would have left themselves open to being overpowered and having their rifles taken. No one had actually given the order to fire, but the rioters ignored requests to put up their hands, leaving the guards with no alternative but to shoot. The jury accepted the guards' testimony, taking only ten minutes to find that the five deaths 'were caused by justifiable measures forced on the military authorities by the riotous behaviour of a large section of the prisoners'.[12]

Despite this exoneration, Hale's report nevertheless seems to have presented a sanitised version of the actual conditions at the camp. A report by the Destitute Aliens Committee (a joint committee of the Home Office, War Office and Local Government Board),[13] received in the Home Office on 4 December, was much more critical. A file minute records, 'This report contains very frank criticism (not for publication) of various shortcomings largely due to great pressure and inexperience in the management of the [Isle of Man] camps. It is to be compared with the laudatory account given by the American Embassy.'[14] While the committee supported the verdict of the inquest, it had no doubt that the large numbers assembled in the dining hall (2,400) had contributed to the incident and called for the vast overcrowding in the camp to be reduced. It also noted that an officer should always be present in the dining hall in the future to prevent the situation getting out of hand again. To avoid lack of interest and recreation breeding discontent and insubordination, the committee recommended the encouragement of all forms of employment, drilling and other exercise. It also noted that food for the internees was presently provided for them by the camp owner, who received 10s a head for each prisoner. The committee considered that the internees themselves, many of whom were chefs, cooks and waiters, should be directly involved in the camp catering.

Recent research supports the view that Hale's report was either superficial or deliberately played down genuine problems which the prisoners had faced.[15] This indicates that the background to the riot had a number of unsatisfactory features going wider than simply a bad batch of potatoes. The camp commandant, who was also the island's chief constable, appears to have overseen a regime based on harsh discipline more appropriate to a prison than a place of internment – a consequence, it is suggested, of his previous experience with concentration camps during the Boer Wars. The prison guards also appear to have been inexperienced or incompetent, with the commandant complaining specifically about the excessive drinking of one of his officers. And while it is true that the inadequacies of tented accommodation were acknowledged by Hale, the resulting hardships seem to have been understated. In a number of instances the tents had actually collapsed, with their occupants having to dig trenches to allow water to run out of the camp. There were also suspicions that in providing food the camp owner was profiteering at the internees' expense. Alongside these problems, there were also reports of criminal offences being committed by the prisoners, refusal by some of them to work, and insulting and threatening language. These perhaps serve to underline the overall atmosphere of the camp as a place of discipline rather than simply as a holding place for enemy aliens. Conditions at Douglas ultimately improved, but the events surrounding the riot clearly highlighted severe weaknesses in the early management of the camp. There can be little doubt that, had British citizens been subjected to similar events in Germany, there would have been a justifiable outcry from the British Government, parliament and press.

Alongside concern about the events at Douglas, the British Government also attracted criticism for its use of prison ships. Nine ships were used to hold both civilian internees and military and naval POWs, with the first being commissioned for use on 28 October 1914. On 28 December, the War Office recorded a total of 8,321 prisoners held on the ships, comprising 5,340 civilians and 2,981 military and naval POWs.[16] The ships were moored in groups of three, with the *Andania, Tunisia* and *Canada* moored off Ryde, Isle of Wight; the *Ascania, Scotian* and *Lake Manitoba* (subsequently replaced by the *Uranium*) moored at Portsmouth Harbour; and the *Saxonia, Ivernia* and *Royal Edward* moored at Leigh Channel, Southend. All the ships were modern and offered a degree of shelter and comfort denied to those forced to occupy tents at the onset of winter. In practice, however, the ships presented their own problems. Being confined on board heightened the sense of 'imprisonment' felt by many and increased the resentment felt by those who strongly objected to being interned at all. Close confinement also exacerbated the problem of the social classes being mixed together. Overall, tensions were hardly eased in this respect by the decision of the prisoners in some instances to allocate the available accommodation on the basis of ability to pay. On the *Royal Edward*, for example, the system comprised a first-class mess, charging 2s admission; a first-class club, for those of 'higher standing', which included first-class cabins, and which only the wealthy could afford; and steerage, with bunks stacked in threes. While this satisfied some, it further alienated many. Different problems existed on the *Saxonia*, which accommodated a 'rougher element' and accordingly comprised only one class. Here trouble arose from attempted escapes, unjustified complaints about the food and 'undesirable females' attempting to board ship. On a general inspection of the ships, Jackson of the US Embassy in Berlin found the conditions on the *Tunisia* to be generally 'depressing', with navy prisoners sick from the tropical diseases they had brought with them following their capture in Africa; mail had been temporarily suspended because of an unspecified breach of regulations and no newspapers were being delivered to the ship.[17] Lowry of the US Embassy in London found problems on the *Uranium*, housing 743 prisoners, including 300 merchant sailors from Cameroon, who justifiably complained of lack of space for exercise and overcrowded sleeping accommodation on the lower decks.[18]

Though one writer has suggested that the use of prison ships represented something of a propaganda coup for Germany, and that their use was discontinued as a result,[19] the reality is that they were only ever intended as a stopgap measure. The greatest pressure for them to be withdrawn came from within the UK itself, and in particular from within the House of Commons. One MP expressed concern at the security implications of mooring ships in Portsmouth Harbour, enabling prisoners to gather and pass on naval intelligence to the enemy – a problem acknowledged by the government.[20] There were also concerns about the amount of valuable shipping being tied up for non-productive use (102,205 tonnes in total) and the costs of the arrangement, with the charter price of the ships reaching some £86,000 per month. As one MP put it during a debate on the navy estimates on 15 February 1915: 'For the purpose of economy it would have been cheaper to take the whole of Grosvenor Square, and furnish it handsomely, and keep them [the prisoners] all there rather than to use these valuable steamers, of such importance to the country, for that purpose.'[21] Two of the prison ships were given up at the end of February 1915. The remainder were all returned to traditional use by the summer of 1915.

Accusations of profligacy were also directed at the government in relation to the camp for captured German officers at Donnington Hall, Leicestershire, this time coupled with allegations of excessive luxury. Concern was first expressed by the local community which observed the taking over of the hall followed by extensive works to refurbish and add to the accommodation. When it opened on 10 February 1915 the camp had capacity for 174 prisoners.[22] This was then added to by the construction of additional barracks. By the end of February there was sufficient accommodation for 320 officers and eighty POW servants. Quarters were built outside the barbed wire for a guard of three officers and 100 men, plus administrative staff. The final cost of the work, according to the government's own figures, was £17,000,[23] which even before it was completed attracted strong criticism. Many objected in principle to the use of 'large country mansions', such as Donnington Hall, at a time of reports of poor treatment of British prisoners in Germany. Others objected to such features as the provision of electric lighting at Donnington at a time when British soldiers at Knightsbridge Barracks had to make do with gas.

The government was finally compelled to answer these mounting criticisms. It took as its starting point the fact that Donnington Hall had been acquired simply because there was nothing else available. In a detailed statement on 8 March, the War Office attempted to rebut accusations of inappropriate luxury by describing the accommodation in detail. A few baths had been installed in one room, at the rate of one bath per fifty officers – 'not an extravagant allowance'. Officers were allocated less floor space in the bedrooms than was allowed per man in a barrack room in peacetime, and the large bedrooms were 'distinctly crowded in appearance'. It was proposed to put as many as twelve officers in each of the additional wooden huts that had been built, 'without any partitions'. Each officer had 'a strip of cheap carpet by his bed' and 'a plain washstand and half a cheap chest of drawers', so that 'the style of furnishing the bedrooms corresponds to that in servants' bedrooms and cannot be described as luxurious'. Furthermore, 'no billiard tables are provided'.[24] Despite this attempt at reassurance, controversy over Donnington Hall continued, with its alleged high cost again being raised in the Commons Easter Adjournment Debate on 15 March 1915.[25] The prisoners benefited particularly from the fact that the full capacity of the camp was not utilised until very late. By August 1915, for example, the number held totalled only 161, of whom forty were enlisted men acting as servants for the remainder. This enabled each officer to be allocated about 60 square feet of floor space. The other living conditions were also good. Acquisition and preparation of food was overseen by a committee of German officers. Each officer paid 2s a day for messing and a typical daily menu at this time was:

- Breakfast: Porridge, cod steaks, butter.
- Lunch: Cold meats, fried potatoes, beetroot salad, butter.
- Dinner: Vienna steaks, onions, beans, mashed potatoes, pancakes.

Other food items were available for purchase. One author has noted that the prisoners at Donnington Hall could eat as well as anyone else in Britain at the time, and most would have regarded it as 'an idyllic country club'.[26] It is not surprising that the prisoners themselves felt they had no grounds for complaint. Friedrich von Bülow, the brother of the former German Chancellor Prince Bernhard von Bülow, who was himself a prisoner at the camp, expressed 'complete satisfaction with his treatment'.[27] A sentiment which in turn caused one Foreign Office official to comment somewhat acidly: 'Herr F von Bülow seems to be quite enjoying himself. It must be somewhat tantalizing to have to gaze at the "splendid park" fallow deer etc grazing at large thro' the barbed wire.'[28] Complaints about the opulence of Donnington Hall continued well into the war.

Public, press and parliamentary interest in POWs continued unabated. The topics were wide-ranging. There was concern that recent outbreaks of foot and mouth disease might have been caused by German prisoners bringing the disease into the country on their clothing, prompting an assurance by the War Office that prisoners would be kept away from farm stock.[29] There were suggestions that prisoners at Shotton, Queensferry, were being provided with butter and vegetables, while the soldiers guarding them were not,[30] and that officers at Donnington Hall ('to save the trouble of walking a mile') were being ferried by motorcar, while the National Reservists guarding them had to walk.[31] The Home Secretary was questioned about the German convalescent hospital in Hitchin, where the chairman of the local magistrates had suggested that the entire staff consisted of enemy aliens, and that security was being endangered by the hospital's location overlooking the town and its railway station. On the same day the Home Secretary also had to deal with criticisms that prisoners at Knockaloe had been allowed to drill with dummy rifles with their own instructors.[32]

Within the House of Commons, the focus shifted more and more to the quality of management in the camps and the need for independent inspections. The War Office was subjected to criticism on both counts, much to the annoyance of MPs who were concerned at the damage that reports of poor conditions could do to Britain's reputation abroad and the implications for British prisoners held in Germany. During a debate in February 1915, one MP referred to a camp containing 2,000 prisoners which lacked adequate drainage and where 'great loads of repulsive rubbish and refuse have to be carried away and buried every day'. The MP had pointed this out two months previously and nothing had been done. Another said:

I think it should be known that the War Office today is so full of officialism, or is so frightened of a little investigation, that Members of this House are refused permission to see what is going on in the various camps. The practice is so stupid and dangerous that it gives rise to unfounded rumours and criticisms: a committee should be formed to manage camps, or MPs given the status of visiting justices.[33]

The case for some form of independent inspection of the camps was not being made solely in the House of Commons. In a letter to the War Office in January 1915, Sir Arthur Conan Doyle wrote:

Might I venture respectfully to make a suggestion [for the reciprocal inspection of prison camps].

Either the Germans would refuse, which would in itself confute their allegations, or they would accept, which would put an end once for all to their assertions of barbarity by which they seek to justify their own ill-doings.[34]

In truth, the reluctance of the War Office to allow inspections seems to have been based more on irritation at the distraction of having to show endless numbers of visitors around the camps than on what such visitors might find, as the following note from the War Office to Sir Edward Grey on 15 December 1914 indicates:

The [Army] Council feel sure that Sir Edward Grey will concur in the Council's opinion that it is undesirable that constant visits to the various places where Prisoners of War are interned should be made and they consider that such visits should not be more frequent than is really necessary. They are accordingly prepared to make arrangements for an officer to accompany small parties of properly accredited individuals to such places of internment as may be found necessary.

It would be desirable that the number of individuals composing such parties should be limited to four or five, and the Council venture to suggest that preference should be given to American subjects over those of other nations.[35]

But pressure from the Foreign Office to allow friendly journalists and others to visit the camps undoubtedly bore fruit in calming down concern – especially foreign concern – about the treatment of prisoners in the UK. Colonel Dietrich Schindler, a Swiss, was allowed to visit camps in

England on the recommendation of Grant Duff in Berne in order to counteract malicious reports in the Swiss press. Schindler's visits to Handforth and Queensferry served this purpose particularly well when he was able to report in the Swiss newspapers that the internees at these camps were generally content and the conditions were as good as could reasonably be expected.[36]

The overall picture emerging in the early days of the war was thus in many ways similar to that in Germany. While there is no evidence of the barbarity and deliberate ill-treatment that each side accused the other of perpetrating, many prisoners undoubtedly suffered hardship. Much of this can be accounted for by lack of preparedness on the part of the authorities for the major task suddenly confronting them. A degree of incompetence within the Home Office and an unsympathetic (if to some extent understandable) attitude within the War Office, inevitably added to the problem. Also as in Germany, significant variations in treatment arose as a result of the autonomy which both sides gave their camp commandants. Nevertheless, despite much criticism in the UK that prisoners were being treated too lavishly, rather than too harshly, there was a general recognition in the country that the way to ensure that British prisoners were treated properly in Germany was to ensure German prisoners were properly treated in the UK. The Foreign Office stood firm on this and pressed throughout for standards consistent with the Hague Convention to be maintained. The arrangements for independent inspections agreed with the German and US Governments, which came into force in March and April 1915, ensured that this would be seen to be the case.

# 5

# WITTENBERG, GARDELEGEN & TYPHUS

The causes of most of the hardships faced by British prisoners in Germany during the first few months of the war – lack of food, clothing and bedding, inadequate accommodation and poor hygiene provision – all came to a head at Wittenberg at the end of 1914. In addition, the prisoners there suffered directly from the consequences of the Prussian War Ministry's policy not to segregate prisoners by nationality. Rigid enforcement of this policy resulted in the spread of epidemic typhus, a disease endemic among Russian troops (many of whom had themselves developed a resistance to the disease) throughout the camp. How the authorities reacted to the events at Wittenberg and at other camps suffering from typhus epidemics in 1914 and 1915 became the subject of special focus by the British Government during the war, being held up as particular examples of the general ill-treatment of British prisoners by the German authorities. Such was the strength of feeling that when in 1916 the International Committee of the Red Cross asked belligerent governments to abandon the practice of reprisals, the British Government rejected the request, citing the handling of the typhus epidemics at Wittenberg and Gardelegen (along with the sinking of the *Lusitania* and the executions of Nurse Cavell and Captain Fryatt), as particular reasons why the option to exact reprisals was still needed (see Chapter 7).[1] The publication of two separate reports on the events at Wittenberg and Gardelegen[2] inevitably engendered much bitterness and debate among the British public at the time. These documents, though by definition one-sided, provide a full narrative of events to draw upon.

The camp at Wittenberg was one of the first to be established at the beginning of the war. It lay some 2 miles outside the city itself at a place called Klein Wittenberg and was located on a flat, sandy plain, devoid of trees and shrubs – according to Gerard, 'in a very unattractive spot next to the railway'.[3] The camp covered some 10.5 acres and consisted of eight compounds, each containing an average of six wooden bungalows. Each bungalow was split into two barracks, each in turn intended for some 120 men. Thus the design capacity of the camp was in the region of 11,500 men. But the massive influx of prisoners in the first few months of the war meant that by the end of 1914 there were some 17,000 to 19,000 men in the camp (180 to 200 prisoners in each barrack), resulting in severe overcrowding. Of the total, only 700 to 800 POWs were British. There was a much larger contingent of French and Belgians, but the vast majority were Russians captured at the Battle of Tannenberg in August 1914. The deprivations resulting from overcrowding were made much worse by the exceptionally severe winter of 1914/15. In the camp's first experience of winter, the heating was found to be inadequate. There were only two stoves to each bungalow which, even had this number been enough, were often short of fuel. Nor did the men have sufficient clothing or adequate sanitary facilities. Their overcoats had often been removed on capture and had not been replaced. Their remaining clothing was often in rags and blankets had to be used as a substitute. Many prisoners had neither boots nor socks, nor changes of underclothing. There was no laundry and for personal ablutions there was only one trough or tap per compound (2,200 to 2,400 men), which was frequently frozen. No hot water was available, except that which came from the cook house. None of these deprivations was made any better by the incompetence of the camp commandant and his unsympathetic attitude towards the prisoners in his care.

As the war progressed, formal disinfection and quarantine arrangements were introduced for all prisoners arriving at camps in Germany to combat typhus and other infectious diseases.[4] But these were not yet in place at Wittenberg in December 1914, where the only means of disinfection was provided by a single cup of soap issued to each barracks at intervals of several weeks. The potential for the spread of disease was made significantly worse by the fact that the camp possessed only one mattress for every three prisoners, with the commandant insisting that every British prisoner should share his mattress with one French prisoner and one Russian. While the camp authorities were clearly culpable in allowing typhus to flourish, if not for actually encouraging it, it was their reaction to the ensuing epidemic which singled them out for the most serious criticism of inhumane treatment contrary to the Hague Convention. Rather than devoting proper resources to containing the epidemic and treating the sick, the authorities chose instead to protect their own health by evacuating the camp, handing over responsibility for its management to the prisoners themselves and responsibility for medical treatment to six captured British doctors sent there for the purpose. From December 1914 to August 1915, with one or two minor exceptions, the entire German staff and guard remained outside the camp, shouting directions to the prisoners from beyond the barbed wire entanglements. Supplies for the men were pushed into the camp over chutes; food and medical supplies were passed in on a trolley over about 20 yards of rail, worked by winches at either end so as to avoid all direct physical contact between the prisoners and the outside world.

The six British doctors at Wittenberg had been sent there from nearby Halle, where they had been held with seven others since November 1914. On 10 February 1915, the thirteen had been told that they were to be distributed around the camps. The six assigned to Wittenberg were Major Fry, Major Priestley, Captain Sutcliffe, Captain Vidal, Captain Field and Captain (then lieutenant) Lauder. Of these, two at least had already suffered on the way to Halle. On the journey from Cambrai, Major Priestley had become caught up in the general hysteria of the early months of the war and had been accused of using dum dum bullets. He had been removed from the train at Valenciennes and subjected to intimidation from the local population before proving his innocence under questioning. Captain Vidal had been forced to subsist on only one loaf of bread and one meal of soup for a whole week during his journey from Cambrai to Torgau, which took place between 15 and 20 September 1914.[5]

The published report on Wittenberg paints a vivid picture. According to the report, on their arrival the six doctors were met with appalling scenes of men wandering up and down aimlessly in unlit rooms or lying on the floor, gaunt and verminous, and generally in such a deplorable condition as to cause Major Fry to break down. Because there were no mattresses in the hospital, many of the prisoners did not want to go there, with the result that there were many sick scattered around the camp. And in the absence of stretchers, all the typhus cases had to be carried to the hospital on the tables from which the men ate their food, with there being no possibility of washing the tables afterwards because there was practically no soap in the camp. The diet was bad and insufficient: the bread allowance was a 1kg loaf for ten men; breakfast was black (acorn) coffee and bread; the midday meal comprised soup, broad beans, potato flour, grease and the minimum of meat; the evening meal consisted of thin soup containing margarine. At the outbreak of the epidemic, the canteen selling bread and other articles had closed. Within the camp hospital conditions were even worse. During the first month of the epidemic the food ration for each patient had been half a *petit pain* and half a cup of milk per day. The only soup to be got came from the main camp kitchen and, according to one of the prisoners, was transported in a wooden tub without a cover, resulting in the soup itself arriving full of dust and dirt. There were no bedpans or toilet paper available and there was a lack of soap and medical supplies. Not only were the patients infested with lice, but there were many cases of post-typhus gangrene due to the men having no socks to keep their feet warm.

Despite having to deal with as many as 100 typhus cases at a time, the report describes how the doctors were able gradually to improve these conditions, through hard work, organisation, and tirelessly seeking and obtaining supplies. Captain Vidal especially is credited with obtaining soap from England. By the end of July 1915, the epidemic had effectively been beaten, at a cost of 185 deaths from 1,975 cases of typhus recorded between 15 January and 23 July 1915. Of the original six British doctors, only three – Major Priestley, Captain Vidal and Captain Lauder – survived, the others having contracted the disease and died. The contribution of the German medical authorities had been negligible. The camp physician, Dr Aschenbach, entered the camp only once during the whole course of the epidemic. This took place about four weeks after Major Priestley's arrival, when some sort of order had evolved. Dr Aschenbach arrived in a complete suit of protective clothing, including mask and rubber gloves. His inspection was brief; it is alleged in the official report that he simply took some bacteriological specimens for his research work at Magdeburg and left.

The handling by the German authorities of the typhus outbreak at Gardelegen was very similar. Gardelegen, a camp near Stendal on the main railway line between Berlin and Hanover, was established in November 1914. Like Wittenberg, the authorities at Gardelegen were ill-prepared for the severe winter of 1914/15 and their attitude towards the prisoners was hostile. The camp was severely overcrowded, resulting in palliasses being spread across the entire floor. The official report notes that one hut:

contained in the breadth four rows of straw or shaving palliasses so arranged that laterally they were touching and terminally only left the narrowest passage-way between. Here men of all nationalities were crowded together. In these huts, devoid of tables and stools, the men lived, slept, and fed. They sat on their bags of shavings to eat their meals; they walked over each other in passing in and out; they lay there sick, and later on, in many cases, died there cheek by jowl with their fellow prisoners. The atmosphere by day, and still more by night, was indescribably foetid, and this was their sole alternative to going outside in their meagre garments for fresh air.

There was widespread malnutrition: food parcels had not yet begun to arrive (the Russians did not have them anyway) and the camp diet was not sufficient for a normal adult. Sanitation was inadequate, with only one standpipe leading to a trough for 1,200 men to do their cleaning. Some men went for several months without a shower or bath. As elsewhere, the men were not segregated by nationality and at Gardelegen it had been officially ordered that they were to be mixed in each barrack room in strict proportion to the overall number by nationality in the camp. At the time of the typhus outbreak in February 1915 there were about 11,000 prisoners in total in the camp; 4,000 Russians, 6,000 French, 700 Belgians and about 230 British. Two days after the outbreak, a German medical commission arrived to inspect the camp, by which time, according to the published report, all the men in the camp were infected with lice, as were their clothing and blankets. Within two hours of the commission's subsequent departure, the Germans had evacuated the camp. From outside, the commandant summoned to the fence a number of British medical officers who had been transferred from Magdeburg shortly before, together with a number of French and Russian doctors already in the camp. He told them that the camp was now in quarantine, that nobody was allowed to enter or leave, and that supplies would be sent over the fence daily. In a close echo of Wittenberg, the Allied doctors, under a senior French physician, then reorganised the camp and began combating the epidemic, utilising additional food and medical supplies obtained from the German authorities. Eventually, a German doctor (who had been expelled from Egypt by the British) also entered the compound to work alongside the others. In all, the epidemic at Gardelegen lasted for four months, during which time 2,000 prisoners contracted the disease and 300 died.

Similar stories to these were told about many other camps, and although Wittenberg and Gardelegen were singled out for the publication of special reports by the British Government, they were by no means the camps most seriously affected by typhus. Of 18,000 prisoners at Cassel, for example, there were 7,000 cases of typhus, with a mortality rate of 11 per cent, and at Cottbus there were 1,765 cases, resulting in 200 deaths.[6]

While individual camp commandants clearly had responsibility for what went on in their camps and must be held accountable for unnecessary hardship experienced by the prisoners in their care, the practice of evacuation by the camp authorities in the face of typhus epidemics bears all the hallmarks of a centrally imposed policy. Evidence to support this is to be found in the report of an interview by one of the US camp inspectors with the German Inspector General of the POW Camps of the IVth Army Corps in March 1916.[7] Discussing Wittenberg, the Inspector General argued that typhus had practically been unknown in Germany before its introduction by the Russian prisoners, that the symptoms were unrecognised and that the German doctors had not at first known how to treat the cases which appeared. He continued that:

> the isolation of the camp, and the order forbidding the German guards to enter it, had been absolutely necessary to prevent the spread of the disease to the city of Wittenberg, where most of the guards had their homes, and that, as a result of these precautions, there had not been a single case among the civilian population.

This at least gives some explanation for the actions of the German authorities. But while it is an explanation, it hardly seems a justification, as intended by the Inspector General. Typhus may indeed have been unknown to the local military medical services in Germany, but it was by no means unknown to the civilian authorities or generally in war, where traditionally more people had been killed by diseases such as typhus and cholera than by enemy action. Wider medical consultation could quickly have established its nature and its causes. And whatever dangers there might have been of spreading the disease to the civilian population, the authorities had both a specific obligation under the Hague Convention to look after the prisoners in their care and a humanitarian duty to alleviate suffering. Sending in captured doctors hardly fulfilled this – the more so if they really did not know the nature of the problem they were dealing with. The culpability of the German authorities in insisting that all nationalities should be mixed should not be overlooked. Even when, during the height of the epidemic at

Wittenberg, Major Priestley and Captain Vidal asked for the British prisoners to be housed separately to prevent the spread of the disease from the Russians, the camp authorities refused on the usual ground that the British should get to know their allies better. The British doctors estimated that the direct consequence of this refusal was the death of fifty British military POWs and nine civilians.

After the epidemic, the physical conditions at Wittenberg substantially improved. By October 1915, Major Priestley and Captain Vidal, who were by then under the charge of a German medical officer, reported that the camp hospital was now excellent in all respects, as was the general health of the camp, with only a few minor illnesses occupying but a small amount of their time. The quantity of food provided was now sufficient, and its quality had improved – though this could still be better. Cleaning and sanitation were also satisfactory. Perhaps most significantly the British prisoners were now being housed together. But underlying the improvements in physical conditions there still persisted an unpleasantness in the camp brought about by the harsh regime imposed by the commandant. At the one extreme this involved physical violence and intimidation, with reports being received of prisoners in the bath house being punched by the guards, including one prisoner with a crippled arm who was slow to get dressed and the striking of a British medical officer by one of the German NCOs. Underpinning the regime of violence was the use of guard dogs brought into the camp at night. Short of violence, there were also gratuitous acts or omissions clearly designed to make the life of the men unpleasant. For example, despite adequate relief funds being available, the commandant refused to ensure that the British prisoners had sufficient overcoats. Neither did the men receive full pay for the work they carried out. There were delays in the distribution of parcels and canteen prices were unnecessarily higher than outside the camp. Even at the most basic level no provision was made for the men to enjoy satisfactory recreation such as football and other games, with walking offering the only opportunity for exercise.

By sheer perseverance, and by raising the matter directly with von Jagow, Gerard was able to secure some change in attitude. The dogs were removed from the camp and some thirty-seven British civilian prisoners at Wittenberg were transferred to the more congenial surroundings of Ruhleben. Gerard also even secured the punishment of the German NCO who had struck the British medical officer, resolving the issue to the satisfaction of the officer himself. Nevertheless, Gerard's lasting view was that

Wittenberg was undoubtedly the worst camp he had visited,[8] a view shared by one of his inspectors, who noted:

> My whole impression of the camp authorities at Wittenberg was utterly unlike that which I have received in every other camp I have visited in Germany. Instead of regarding their charges as honourable prisoners of war, it appeared to me the men were regarded as criminals, for whom a regime of fear alone would suffice to keep in obedience. All evidence of kindly and humane feeling between the authorities and the prisoners was lacking, and in no other camp have I found signs of fear on the part of the prisoners that what they might say to me would result in suffering for them afterwards.[9]

It was not until early 1916 that the problems of Wittenberg were finally resolved by the replacement of the camp commandant. A report by the US inspectors of a visit in March 1916 noted that the new commandant, who had been in post for some six weeks, was already being spoken highly of by the prisoners. He had already made a number of improvements – for example: the clothing situation was now satisfactory; the men were being paid fully and promptly; the distribution of parcels had now been speeded up by the employment of British prisoners in the parcels room; and the canteen now stocked sufficient provisions at satisfactory prices.[10] There were no further officially published adverse reports on Wittenberg for the rest of the war. For its part, following the epidemic, Gardelegen ceased to be used as a camp for holding British prisoners.

Throughout the debate about conditions at Wittenberg the German authorities had steadfastly refused to accept that they had acted in any way improperly. Press coverage in Britain and the United States in the wake of the publication of the British report and Gerard's subsequent visits provoked strong diplomatic reaction. Nevertheless, the German authorities were clearly stung by international accusations of inhumane treatment. On 31 March 1919 a special commission established by the new German Government to look into alleged violations of international law against prisoners, examined in detail the British Government's published report on Wittenberg. The commission, which sat in Berlin, comprised: Professor Schücking, Professor of International Law at Marburg (chairman); six politicians drawn from across the parties; Privy Councillor Eckhardt, Foreign Office; Captain Vanselow, Admiralty (Armistice Commission, Spa); and Colonel von Fransecky, Chief of the POW Department at the War Ministry.

Lieutenant Breen of the British Military Intelligence attended the proceedings in plain clothes as a member of the public, sitting alongside Ridder van Rappard, the Netherlands Minister Resident. Lieutenant Breen's report of the proceedings was subsequently endorsed by van Rappard as an accurate account.[11]

The commission examined documentary evidence and heard from German witnesses only, though Lt Breen considered that it nevertheless appeared to be trying to be impartial. In addition to expert testimony, there were two witnesses for the defence – Dr Aschenbach, the Wittenberg Camp physician, and Dr Schiel, a camp officer. Both put forward evidence either excusing events at the camp or denying specific allegations. They accepted that there had been an initial delay in dealing with the typhus epidemic, arguing that for twenty years prior to Wittenberg no outbreak of this kind had occurred and that it had taken a month to diagnose correctly the disease as 'Fleck Typhus'. The camp was overcrowded and during this time Russian, French and British prisoners had continued to be housed together in accordance with the instructions of the Prussian War Ministry. No advantage would have been gained from segregating the prisoners later as by then the infection had already become general. As to the detailed points set out in the British report, Dr Aschenbach first dealt with charge that only one mattress had been provided for every three prisoners. He defended this on the basis that the mattresses provided for use in the lazaret had been unsuitable and appeared to be intended for bunks on board ships. Four mattresses had therefore been sewn together in such a way that three men could be comfortably accommodated on each of these larger mattresses. While not commenting directly on the number of blankets provided, he denied that prisoners had suffered from frozen feet and stated that where amputations had taken place these were the result of gangrene, 'a concomitant of this special form of typhus' (an analysis which was supported by medical experts appearing before the commission). The defence also strenuously denied that there had been a shortage of bandages and syringes. As to the withdrawal of German personnel from the camp, and the provision of supplies over a mechanical chute, these measures had been undertaken in order to prevent the spread of the disease outside the camp. In defending himself against the allegation that he had absented himself from the treatment of the prisoners, Dr Aschenbach argued that as the Allied doctors were in charge of their own countrymen, there was no need for him (or his assistant) to interfere. He had confined himself to general supervision of the sanitary condition of the camp and the discipline of the hospital staff. He also insisted that medical comforts, wine, cognac and milk had all been supplied to the camp in sufficient quantity. To substantiate this he produced vouchers for the purchase of these items in the town (though Lt Breen notes that no statements of the amounts of such supplies were presented, nor any evidence that they had actually reached the prisoners themselves). All in all, Dr Aschenbach argued that the evidence given by the three British doctors who had returned to England was 'deliberately false'.

Having listened to the defence, and to the evidence of medical experts who noted that the percentage mortality at Wittenberg had been lower than in other camps where the British Government had not protested, the commission found that no violation of international law had taken place at Wittenberg in 1915. It subscribed to the view that the evidence of the British doctors could not be relied upon, considering it too objective and noting that 'The doctors were no doubt irritated at being retained in Germany for a lengthy period, and recounted in many instances things heard but not seen by them'. In presenting its detailed findings, the commission agreed that greater precautions might have been taken and greater preparations made in advance to meet the outbreak of contagious disease in the camps. The different nationalities had not, however, been concentrated together for the purpose of spreading the infection. It found that food supply in the camp was sufficient and that the employment of doctors who were POWs to give medical treatment to prisoners of their own nationality was in accordance with international law. Lastly, it found that the allegation of cowardice contained in the published British report was unjustified; on the contrary, Dr Aschenbach and his assistant deserved praise for their activity.

It is obviously not possible on the basis of Lt Breen's inevitably brief account to glean all the nuances of the commission's thinking or its detailed conclusions. The absence of direct evidence from the Allied doctors or from any prisoners must, however, clearly detract from the credibility of its findings. The allegations that the regime at the camp was unduly harsh, contrary to the Hague Convention, appear to have been ignored. By concentrating on individual points in the British report and excusing or denying them, the commission seems to have studiously avoided the bigger picture of events at Wittenberg, which were not only reported by the British doctors but also supported by Gerard and others. It has already been noted that the British and German Governments failed to agree on the circumstances in which captured medical personnel could be used to provide care for prisoners (see Chapter 2), but by putting the complete care of the camp in the hands of captured doctors at Wittenberg and elsewhere, the German authorities seem to have stretched even their own relaxed interpretation of what was permitted by the Geneva Convention, as well as abrogating their general duty of care under the Hague Convention.

# 6

# FROM CAPTURE TO THE CAMPS

Studies of the treatment of POWs inevitably concentrate on life within the camps. For many prisoners in the First World War, however, the hardships experienced from the point of capture to their arrival at the permanent camps were as great, if not greater than, any they would encounter subsequently. While ill-treatment at the point of capture did not feature as a major concern in the published correspondence between the respective governments, atrocities nevertheless occurred on both sides. In the first few months of the war, officer prisoners at Crefeld reported that they had collected evidence (without giving details) that British officers and men had been killed after capture.[1] In May 1915, Consul-General Maxse at Rotterdam wrote to Sir Edward Grey passing on an unsubstantiated allegation by a German deserter that on the capture of 84 British and 300 French troops on 26 December 1914, the British were ordered to be killed 'with bayonet and butt'.[2] And in one of the few cases to be brought to trial after the war, in this instance at the instigation of the French Government, a lieutenant-general and a major in the German army were formally charged with issuing orders to kill prisoners and wounded, and with obeying such orders and passing them on to subordinates to be carried out (see Chapter 13). But most such acts would be spontaneous, carried out without or contrary to orders in the heat of battle or its immediate aftermath. Snipers or machine-gunners who had imposed substantial casualties on attacking troops, for example, might not expect to receive the highest standards of humane treatment on capture, or even be allowed to survive attempted surrender. One German author records the case of British troops being killed while attempting to surrender during battle simply because there was no facility for taking them back behind the lines: 'They could easily have put up a fight, for we made up just a handful of little fellows, but they instead stood on the upper step and hastened to raise their hands. We could not escort them back, and so we made short work of them with hand grenades.'[3] In 1918, one escaped British prisoner reported:

> We were defending a trench and held out to the last, when we were surrounded and had to surrender. The Germans beckoned us to come towards them, and as the first of three of us – privates – showed ourselves to obey they were deliberately shot; the rest of us were taken prisoners.

Another escapee said:

> At the time of my capture a German officer was standing near the trench, and close by him there was a private with his bayonet fixed. One of the men of my battalion was scrambling out of the trench, intending of course to surrender. The private ran at my comrade to bayonet him. The officer ordered the private to halt, but no attention was paid to the command, and the officer without hesitation shot the private in the head with his revolver, killing him on the spot. The British soldier had not been touched. This happened close to where I was standing.[4]

Despite such events, tragic though they obviously were, the evidence is that for the most part they were relatively isolated, with both sides trying as far as possible to treat captives humanely. More common, perhaps, was the practice of looting. One German author writing after the war argued that looting was an exclusively Allied practice, since 'no such looting by the Germans was reported by the Entente'. He identified the French as particular culprits, with '*La bourse or la vie*' being a familiar cry, and with the removal of articles during searches on capture and then not being returned being a routine procedure. The following event, alleged to have taken place at St Hilaire on 27 September 1918, is cited as an example:

> Shortly after being captured, while going through the communications trench, my watch was torn from my arm at the point of a revolver. All articles

which had been taken from us, such as handkerchiefs and the like, we were allowed to buy back at extravagant figures. For instance, at Vitry le Francois, a cheap cotton handkerchief was sold for three francs fifty, or perhaps twenty times its real value. The merchant in this case was the sergeant-major of the camp. That was the experience of all the thousands who came to the camp at Vitry le Francois, with negligible exceptions ... The story of pillage goes like a thread through all the reports I have.[5]

While the French may have been singled out for the harshest criticism, the British and other nationalities were not spared, though the claim here was that while the French carried out their thefts in the spirit of 'brutal anger' and with 'heartless cruelty', British troops usually displayed 'a certain good-natured geniality, a businesslike solemness or looked upon the matter as a sporting proposition':

> A group of several hundred Englishmen formed about us. All of them looked friendly and benevolent ... Every prisoner, every wounded man and every corpse had been relieved of his watch and other noticeable valuables, for the collection of watches etc seemed the main object of the war to many Tommies, some of whom had as many as a hundred in old sandbags.

One of the prisoners said, 'I would never have thought that the English were such rogues. I always thought they were as decent as ourselves.' Another regretted that the German soldiers had not known of this British custom at the time of the Spring Offensive and that they had let the prisoners keep all their belongings, only occasionally demanding a cigarette.[6] And: 'The English displayed a childish eagerness for souvenirs.' 'When the Englishman had satisfied his thirst for souvenirs, he usually treated his prisoners well.'[7] Another observer was less charitable, but also perhaps less reliable, in claiming:

> Thoroughly trustworthy men have assured me that men were killed for refusing to hand over their watches. I myself had never a chance to witness such cases, but I do not regard them as impossible at all. For we must bear in mind that the British attacking troops were totally intoxicated. [L. Reuss, student of political science, Markt 5, Ohrdruf, Thuringia][8]

Despite the author's claim that looting was an exclusively Allied practice, it was clearly carried out by both sides. While acquiring personal property from prisoners was specifically forbidden by German regulations, looting by German troops was far from uncommon.[9] One observer (an American Red Cross deputy commissioner) has stated, for example, that it was not unusual for American prisoners to be robbed of all their money and other personal effects before reaching their permanent camp. He cited the case of prisoners who complained to him during a routine camp inspection that 'when made prisoners, German soldiers, even officers, took from them watches, rings, shoes, and other private property'.[10] Yet another German memoir attempts to shift some of the blame for looting to the prisoners themselves, citing the case of a group of British prisoners who, in an attempt to ensure they survived, offered money and valuables to their captors, only to be told that what was really wanted was cigarettes: 'It was not long before we all had fags sprouting from our lips.'[11] It is perhaps inevitable that looting should sometimes have taken place at the local level without the sanction of higher command. This seems especially so in the case of the desire for 'souvenirs', which may well have been extracted without any serious menace – though this distinction would not, of course, have been particularly meaningful to the prisoners concerned.

Following capture, prisoners (especially officers) would often be interrogated. They would then be transported to established camps, either directly or via temporary 'cages' constructed in the battle zone to hold prisoners while detailed forward transport arrangements were being made. It was German policy to transport other ranks in box cars with straw-covered floors, with those severely wounded or in need of medical care being conveyed in ambulance trains.[12] Officer POWs would, where possible, be conveyed in passenger coaches (third or sometimes second class). Prisoners would go to camps assigned to the German Army Corps which had captured them, though sometimes this might involve journeying via other camps – sometimes as many as five or more – along the way.[13] After problems in the early days of the war caused by the spread of typhus, prisoners arriving at an established camp would, as a matter of course, be placed in quarantine for up to three weeks, where they would be fumigated and their clothing disinfected. They would then be assigned permanent quarters within the camp. An alternative to this, when the facilities existed and the numbers were not great, was for quarantine to take place while the prisoners were still in the battle zone.

Despite the carefully laid down procedures, journeys to the camps could be not only uncomfortable but also stressful. Prisoners on both sides complained of humiliation and intimidation, often involving the enemy civilian population. The British Government Committee on the treatment of prisoners alleged in particular that POWs transported to Germany during the first four months of the war were subjected to 'incessant moral brutality', with the prisoners being exposed to jeering, insults, spitting and hostile crowds. The behaviour of the German Red Cross was regarded as, 'the most revolting':

> At every station there would be found an elaborate installation of food and drink and materials for medical aid, presided over by women wearing the Red Cross. Consistently they refused anything whatever to the English, however desperate their needs. When asked by a wounded officer for a glass of water, one of these ladies burst out laughing and said: 'Nothing for you English'. They would show food to the starving prisoners and then remove it, calling the attention of the crowd and observing that it was, 'not for the swine'. They would bring water and soup in cans and pour it out on the platform in front of the Englishmen.[14]

Many other examples are given of deliberate humiliation of captives. Private W. Arnold of the Dorset Regiment reported that 'The Scots were pulled out and called "Fräulein", and their kilts were lifted up'.[15] And at a time when the British press was full of stories of atrocities committed by German troops in Belgium, so too were wild stories circulating in Germany about uncivilised practices being undertaken by the British. One of the more bizarre of these involved the standard British-issue clasp-knife. Captain Middleton, RAMC, reported:

> One rather interesting incident occurred when the English-speaking orderly produced one of our men's regulation clasp-knives and asked what the spike in it was used for. I told them a variety of its uses, and finally added that in the mounted branches it was used for picking out stones from horses' feet. I did not believe the significance of their enquiries until later, when I found that the universal German opinion was that these clasp-knives were weapons of offence, and that the spike was used for picking out the eyes of the wounded. It was a long time before we were allowed to forget it, and it is needless to say that this general belief did not lessen the warmth of hatred with which we were received. [Journey from Halle to Hanover, 28–30 August 1914][16]

Other RAMC officers also described hostile incidents over clasp-knives during their journey from Mons to Torgau between 1 and 4 September 1914:

Here [Aachen] a mob of drunken Uhlans and railway employees were incited by a German officer – a colonel – to take us to our carriage. He said it was scandalous that we, who had gouged out the eyes of German wounded with the marlinspikes of our clasp-knives, should travel in a second-class carriage, while German wounded were in trucks. Several of the mob had these English clasp-knives and were threatening to practice upon us, some tried to hit us through the window, and some were making efforts to get into the corridor when a young officer came up and quelled them. [Captain Beaman][17]

And:

At Aachen there was a very hostile demonstration. There was a troop train standing at the same platform. The men swarmed out to look at the prisoners and abuse them. The train guard produced a field service pocket knife and showed the soldiers the marlinspike which he said the prisoners had used to gouge out the eyes of wounded Germans. (NB – The same form of pocket knife used in the German army.) [Major Furness][18]

The German press had also mounted a fierce campaign about the alleged use by British troops of dum-dum bullets, outlawed by the Hague Convention. Such was the success of this campaign that the British Government was forced categorically to deny their use in the House of Commons.[19] Meanwhile, POWs on their way to the permanent camps in Germany suffered from the spin-off, with the civilian population shouting 'dum-dums' at them as they passed by. As mentioned in the previous chapter, Captain (subsequently major) Priestley of the RAMC was removed from his train at Valenciennes, on his way from Cambrai to Halle in September 1914, for questioning having been accused himself of using dum-dum bullets.

There seems little doubt that the harassment of prisoners on their way to the camps was fairly common, and that if anything such action was condoned, if not actively encouraged, by the German authorities. Gerard recalls that, against the background of many reports of such incidents, he was pleased one day to read in the *North German Gazette* that a number of individuals had been fined or imprisoned for 'improper conduct towards prisoners of war'. According to the article, their names had been printed, 'in order that they may be held up to the contempt of all future generations of Germans'. Gerard's pleasure at the apparently humanitarian motives of the German authorities soon turned into disappointment when he learned that the civilians had in fact been punished for helping the prisoners rather than annoying them. The whole story had stemmed from an incident in a north German town predominantly occupied by Danes, who had helped passing prisoners suffering from hunger and thirst by providing them with food and drink.[20]

Alongside harassment and threatening behaviour, there were also stories about ill-treatment of the wounded on their way to the camps, as exemplified by the case of Captain Thomas of the Munster Fusiliers:

One night in the train the tube in my throat became nearly stopped up, and I could not breathe, so the *Unter-Offizier* in charge called a doctor who was on the train, and he came and poked at it with a piece of stick that he had cut out of the hedge on the line, and so freed my respiration a little … I who was much worse was sent to the camp at Torgau, where I arrived late in the evening of the 1st of October, having been travelling for five days and four nights continuously in a cattle truck with only a hard board to lie on. On arriving at the station at Torgau, I was made to march in fours with some French soldiers, just arrived as orderlies, to the camp, a matter of about a mile. Although I was gasping for breath and so weak I could hardly stand up, I was prodded along by German soldiers with bayonets. [St Quentin–Torgau, c. 28 September to 1 October 1914][21]

But while reports such as this present an appalling picture, the Government Committee was able to acknowledge that a slow improvement in the transport of wounded prisoners did take place with the first use of hospital trains at the end of 1914.[22]

Of all the accounts of the hardships faced by POWs on capture in the early days, that given by Major Vandeleur of the 1st Cameronians (already referred to in Chapter 3) is particularly informative. Major Vandeleur had been taken prisoner at La Basée on 13 October 1914, and had escaped from Crefeld in December. Having learned to speak fluent German at Heidelberg University before the war, he had been able to secure his escape by travelling by train towards the Channel. During the journey he wore German officer's uniform and shared a box of choice cigars with German officers; he is alleged to have walked into his London club still wearing German uniform.[23] On his return he was able to give a full account of his experiences.[24] Major Vandeleur was taken prisoner by the Prussian Guard Cavalry; he was personally well treated, being given food and shelter, unlike the other officers and men captured with him who were confined in a church overnight without food. Major Vandeleur attributed his own good treatment to the fact that he was perceived as a likely source of useful information, being bombarded with numerous questions, especially with regard to the alleged use by the British of dum-dum bullets and the state of the British army. On the following morning he was marched with four other British officers and 200 men to Lens. At Lens, he told his captors that he could march no further because of a leg wound and was then driven by motor to Douai, with the remainder of the party following on foot – a considerable distance. At Douai, he was at first detained on the square in front of the Hôtel de Ville, guarded by a sentry who subjected him to 'continual abuse and revilement'. When the rest of the party finally arrived, they were all held in a shed overnight. The only food they received was a little given by the French Red Cross. No straw was provided and since the men's greatcoats had been taken from them they were forced to walk round all night to keep warm.

According to Major Vandeleur's account, in the face of opposition from the guard further food was given to the prisoners by the French Red Cross on the morning of 17 October, following which, at about 2 p.m., they were marched to the railway station, again being 'reviled at and cursed all the way by German officers as well as German soldiers'. One of the British officers was spat on by a German officer. For their onward journey to Cologne, the prisoners were loaded into closed-in wagons from which horses had just been removed. In the wagon occupied by Major Vandeleur there were also four other officers and fifty-two men. Of the men, fifteen were British soldiers and thirty-two were French civilians 'of all grades of society'. Since the wagons had an accepted capacity of six horses or forty men (with the doors open to enable some ventilation) this resulted in severe overcrowding and room for only some of the men to sit on the floor – an unpleasant enough experience in itself since the floor was 'covered fully 3 inches deep in fresh manure', with the stench of horse urine 'almost asphyxiating'. According to Major Vandeleur, the whole journey took place with practically no ventilation, no food and no opportunity of attending to the purposes of nature. While French prisoners in the wagon were given some potato soup at the German-Belgian frontier, the British prisoners were deliberately kept until last and given only the small amount of bread and soup that remained after the French prisoners had taken what was wanted. And all along the way the prisoners were cursed by officers and soldiers alike at the various stations:

at Mons Bergen I was pulled out in front of the wagon by the order of the officer in charge of the station, and, after cursing me in filthy language for some 10 minutes, he ordered one of his soldiers to kick me back into the wagon, which he did, sending me sprawling into the filthy mess at the bottom of the wagon. I should like to mention here that I am thoroughly conversant with German, and understood everything that was said. Only at one station on the road was any attempt made on the part of the German officers to interfere, and stop their men from cursing us. This officer appeared to be sorry for the sad plight in [sic] which we were in. I should also like to mention that two men of the German Guard also appeared to be sympathetic and sorry for us; but they were able to do little or nothing to protect us.

Up to this time I had managed to retain my overcoat, but it was now forcibly taken from me by an officer at a few stations further on.

Major Vandeleur's report contains some inconsistencies, possibly attributable to poor transcription or simply carelessness in narration. He states in one part of his account that his confinement in the railway wagon lasted for three days and three nights, and in another that this leg of his journey lasted for thirty hours; neither of these statements is consistent with the actual dates of travel given in his report, which implies a railway journey overnight. Also, he refers in one part of his report to being accompanied in the wagon by fifteen British soldiers and in another to being accompanied by twenty-five. Nevertheless, his report overall is compatible with other accounts of the conditions and hardships faced by prisoners being transported to the main camps. His concluding argument that British officers and men were systematically singled out for harsher treatment than other prisoners on the basis of orders by higher authority is also consistent with the allegation being pursued at the time by the British Government, and simultaneously being denied by the German authorities.

Major Vandeleur's report was put directly to the German Government, which referred it on to the German military authorities. The overall tone of their detailed reply received in July 1915[25] (not published) was one of disdain. It commenced with the statement that since so much time had elapsed since the events reported were alleged to have taken place, it was not possible to examine them one by one but 'This much, however, is certain, that the statements are pretty untrue and partly immeasurably exaggerated. Major Vandeleur appears to take not the slightest account of the peculiar conditions imposed by war.' The reply acknowledged that there may well have been particular hostility towards the British POWs since 'There certainly did exist a strong and justifiable feeling of bitterness against the English, as wounded German soldiers returning from the front brought back large numbers of English bullets with a "dum-dum" action, and brutal weapons (two-edged dirks, "Doppeldoche")'. And more generally:

> If the English pretend that they were attended to during the journey only after the French, the reason is to be found in the quite comprehensible bitterness of feeling among the German troops, who respected the French on the whole as honourable and decent opponents, whereas the English mercenaries had, in their eyes, adopted a cunning method of warfare from the beginning, and, when taken prisoners, bore themselves with an insolent and provocative mien. That any such distinction in treatment was ordered by superior officers is an untruth.

As to Major Vandeleur's detailed comments, the reply noted that the poor conditions of confinement referred to at Douai were due simply to the lack of suitable accommodation, the conditions being no worse than those facing the captor's own troops. It was 'out of the question' that POWs received no attention or that the French Red Cross were obstructed in issuing food and drink, though ladies of the French Red Cross had been found to be offering alcohol to POWs, which was prohibited. It was also 'beyond the bound of possibility' that a German officer had spat at Major Vandeleur (though it should be noted that Major Vandeleur had in fact claimed that it was another officer that had been spat at rather than him) or that his greatcoat could have been taken by force, 'having regard to the mentality, up-bringing, and social status of the whole class of German officers'. And while accepting that there may have been some overcrowding because of shortage of wagons, it was again 'out of the question' that the cattle truck in which Major Vandeleur had been transported could have been in the state he described, 'in view of the cleanliness which prevails without exception in German railway carriages'; the problem must therefore have been caused by the prisoners themselves immediately defiling the carriage by relieving themselves. Finally, in justifying the transportation of an officer in a cattle truck, the German authorities resorted to a personal attack on Major Vandeleur himself:

> At Douai in those days, an English officer – perhaps wrongly set down as Colonel – said, 'he would speak with no German officer – at most he would

spit at one'. He remarked to another German officer ... that he would respect no German officers except those in the Horse Guards. This ill-bred behaviour was rightly requited by making the offender travel in a cattle truck. There is much to be said for the belief that the officer in question was Major Vandeleur.

The only concession made by the authorities to Major Vandeleur's report was to note that while there was no record of German soldiers swearing at prisoners, orders had now been given to keep POWs separate, 'in order to obviate such an occurrence'.

The German military authorities therefore made little attempt to rebut Major Vandeleur's individual complaints. It is clear that their overall view – shared by the Imperial Foreign Office which passed on their reply without comment – was that nothing so serious had happened beyond the undoubted hardships which had to be expected by troops and captives alike in the middle of a war. For the Government Committee, the key point was not so much the detailed complaints made by Major Vandeleur and others, but that the reports coming out of Germany seemed to add up to a deliberate strategy of singling out the British for unduly harsh treatment and that, far from hardship simply being a factor of war, it represented 'a remarkable record of organised cruelty'.[26] That the British Government was sincere in this belief is evidenced by the marginal comments made by key personnel within the Foreign Office on the German response. One Foreign Office official described it as an attempt to refute the irrefutable, while another, Sir Horace Rumbold, described it as, 'approved German journalese at its worst', commenting that 'it would be easy to pick the whole effusion to pieces'. His minister, Lord Cecil, asked for the report to be sent to the War Office, noting that the ill-treatment of prisoners during transport depended on a great body of evidence besides Major Vandeleur's.

Whether there was any substance in the British claim of deliberately targeted ill-treatment is at this stage impossible to assess. A direct comparison of the British and German transport arrangements in the first few months is difficult. For one thing, the number of prisoners taken by the Germans far exceeded the numbers taken by the British. Secondly, until 1916, prisoners taken by the British were generally taken to the United Kingdom, providing a different set of logistics. There is, nonetheless, a close similarity between the accounts given by British prisoners of their treatment by the Germans and recorded tales by German prisoners of their treatment

by the British and French. The same German author cited above quotes
Lieutenant Heinricks of Potsdam:

> In the middle of December 1914 I was transported to Brittany with about
> a dozen wounded Germans in a cattle car; it took two days, and we were
> without straw or any attention, without food or medical care. I was seriously
> wounded, but every request for coffee or food, such as was given the French
> wounded, was refused with the remark: 'The Boches don't need anything'.
> At a railroad station outside of Paris a sub-lieutenant entered the car and
> asked if there were any officers there. Naturally I replied in the affirmative, for
> I hoped to be able to interpret for the men, but the only result of my answer-
> ing was that the fellow stepped on my wounded leg.
> In the hospital at Vitré (Brittany) the doctor cut about in my wound, which
> was already infested with maggots. As this was intensely painful, I whistled
> through my teeth, whereupon with true French politeness, he shouted: '*Vous
> n'etes pas dans une ecurie, ici!*' – 'You're not in a stable here!'[27]

The author gives other examples of transports taking days without food
or water and of insults by the civil population. Inaccurately, and in direct
contradiction of British accounts, however, he concludes: 'And the German
civilian population – as the enemy freely acknowledge – never indulged in
violence towards helpless or wounded prisoners, or even as much as abused
or derided them.'[28]

These German reports were published in 1922 for the purpose of dem-
onstrating that Germany had been treated unjustly regarding allegations of
ill-treatment and war crimes; wrongdoings had taken place on both sides
and Germany had not been treated even-handedly. The timing and the
purpose of the publication, together with the remarkably close similarity
between the German reports and those already published by the British,
must give rise to a question about whether they were fabricated deliberately to rebut the British criticisms. On the other hand, it is possible that the
accounts justly demonstrated that similar practical difficulties confronted
both sides in dealing with an immediate and unfamiliar problem, and that
the human nature of both captors and captives differed little between the
two sides.

After the first few months of the war, the capture and transportation of
prisoners assumed a more regular pattern as systems became more organised. Sudden defeats and victories in battle could nevertheless still put a

severe strain on those systems. For example, the German Spring Offensive of 1918 resulted in an exceptionally large number of prisoners being taken by the Germans in a very short space of time. The British Central Prisoners of War Committee reported that between 21 March, the date of the offensive, and July 1918, the names of some 3,000 British officers and 41,000 NCOs and men had been notified as captured, bringing the total number on their books to 90,230[29] – effectively a doubling. These numbers, together with the inevitable chaos and disorganisation brought about by the fast-moving battle, resulted in the same sort of treatment and conditions as had been reported in 1914. One British prisoner, captured at 9 a.m. on 21 March at Lagnicourt, was marched with a band of prisoners, including a number of wounded, to Villers, arriving there at 3 p.m. Thence they were taken across country to a cage which they reached at 9 p.m. They spent the night in the open without food or drink, other than water from a small stream. The next morning at 10 a.m., still without food, the men were marched to Marchiennes, arriving at 6 p.m. They had only coffee on the journey and at Marchiennes were given coffee and a small piece of bread only.[30] Other cases involved marches of three days with little water, no food and sleeping in the open air; some included wounded prisoners, with no food, even though the escorts had provisions themselves.

As the war progressed it became common practice to detain prisoners in the battle zone to carry out work on such things as roads and railways before (or sometimes instead of) sending them on to permanent camps. The legality of this was debateable. The Hague Convention did not specifically forbid the employment of prisoners in the battle zone, but exposing them to danger clearly ran counter to its spirit. And while the convention did not rule out work near the front, it did expressly forbid the employment of prisoners on work connected with 'the operations of war'. The term 'operations of war' was not, however, defined, and for the duration both sides studiously avoided agreeing or adopting a definition. The British Manual of Military Law stipulated that POWs should, if possible, be removed from the frontier districts[31] and the British military authorities had at first disliked the idea of using prisoners behind the lines as a potential nuisance and distraction. They were won over by experience, however, and, in order not to contravene the Hague Convention, issued regulations that prisoners in France were not to be employed within range of the enemy's artillery nor on any work in connection with defence or handling munitions of war.[32] Out of concern for the conditions being faced by German POWs in

France and the dangers resulting from the ever-increasing range of artillery, in 1917 the German Government successfully pressured the British and French Governments to agree to withdrawing all prisoners to a distance of at least 30km behind the firing line (see Chapter 7).

Those engaged in work behind the front suffered some of the harshest and most dangerous conditions faced by prisoners on either side. Though some of the dangers were temporarily ameliorated by the decision to withdraw to 30km, the German military were subsequently to renege on this agreement during the final few months of the war. Returning British prisoners during this time related many stories of danger, hardship and employment on munitions, clearly contrary to the Hague Convention. For example, following the 1918 German Spring Offensive, British POWs near Arras were employed on road-making, building light railways and carrying ammunition from one dump to another. The work was arduous, starting with reveille at 3 a.m., with coffee but no food. Following a march, work on site started at 8 a.m., with a break from 12 noon to 1 p.m., and further work until 5 p.m. The prisoners worked a seven-day week with no food being provided before tea at 7 p.m. 'Tea' comprised soup (made of dried fish or lentils), one loaf to three men and no coffee. No clothes or food parcels were given to the men and sanitation was poor. At Villers, about 12km behind the line, a British POW reported having to carry shells to different German batteries. There, an ammunition dump covered by a Red Cross flag was spotted by the Allies who shelled it, killing several men. There was also a dysentery epidemic due to the poor food. No blankets, beds or straw were provided and the sanitary conditions were very poor. A POW at Ecoust, 9km from Villers, also reported being under shell-fire from the Allied guns, despite the military equipment there being stored in a marquee flying Red Cross flags. He described the condition of the prisoners there as 'pitiable', through want of sleep, starvation, ill-treatment and being forced to work, whether sick or well, with no chance to wash or change clothes. At Sailly, men were required to load shells and protested, only to be told that German POWs were being required to do the same at Arras. Cameron Highlanders taken at Arras on 28 March 1918 were required, as soon as they were taken prisoner, to serve a German held gun with ammunition for two hours and to dig out a position for it under British fire. There are many other similar stories.[33]

The whole process from capture to arrival at a permanent camp held the focus of the British Government and the British public, especially during the early days of the war. An indignity clearly not foreseen by the drafters of

the Hague Convention was the exposure of prisoners to insults and humiliation by the civilian populations. Both sides subsequently agreed to prevent
this. The practice was finally outlawed under the Geneva Convention
1929.[34] As to the other hardships faced by newly captured prisoners, it is
perhaps easier from this distance than it was at the time to accept the argument that many were simply the inevitable consequences of war, especially
when set against the even greater hardships being experienced by many
who had not been captured. They were hardships, nonetheless, and it is clear
that having survived the traumas of capture, transportation and possibly
work near the front, for most (though by no means all) prisoners, arrival at
a permanent camp would generally represent the start of a more settled and
less unpleasant existence.

# 7

# REPRISALS

It is surprising that taking reprisals against prisoners was not prohibited by the Hague Convention. Both sides took advantage of this omission. The British Government professed early on to be against reprisals, on grounds of both practicality and principle. Neil Primrose, Under Secretary of State for Foreign Affairs, told the House of Commons on 10 March 1915, that reprisals against Germany would fail because the German authorities would always be more ruthless than the British in carrying them out. He added – perhaps making a virtue out of a necessity – that, 'We have entered this war in a generous spirit, and I think in a spirit worthy of the best traditions of our history, and to those traditions we must remain faithful'. This assessment of German ruthlessness turned out to be accurate and tempered British policy throughout the war. But despite this, and its claim to be against them, the British Government repeatedly looked to reprisals – just as the German Government did – as a possible means to redress injustices and grievances. By the end of the war, the British Government had revised its public position away from being against reprisals in principle, to justifying them as an expedient recognised by all civilised countries.

The first serious use of reprisals took place in early 1915 following the launch of the German campaign of unrestricted submarine warfare. This campaign gave rise to widespread public outrage in Britain; outrage shared by Winston Churchill, as First Lord of the Admiralty. In retaliation, Churchill decreed that in future all captured German submarine crews would be placed in naval detention barracks as 'criminals', rather than in camps as 'honourable prisoners of war'. For Churchill, the sinking of naval and merchant shipping alike, without warning, represented acts of atrocity 'against the laws of nations and contrary to common humanity';[2] he argued that those who committed such acts, even though acting under orders, automatically forfeited their rights as POWs under the Hague Convention. Churchill's move was at first widely popular, despite misgivings in *The Times* and elsewhere about the morality of his policy,[3] misgivings privately surpassed in the Foreign Office, and by Grey in particular, by fears about its implications for the fate of British prisoners held in Germany.[4] But events were moving in Churchill's favour. On 28 March 1915, the cargo-passenger ship *Falaba* was torpedoed en route from Liverpool to West Africa, and on 31 March, the submarine campaign reached its peak, with twenty-nine ships being sunk in a single day. This enabled the Admiralty to carry the day in maintaining a firm stance in reply to a German threat to imprison one British officer for every member of a German submarine crew held in detention.[5] The Foreign Office removed from their reply to the German Government a proposed counter-threat by Churchill; not to rescue German submarine crews from the sea if they went ahead with the imprisonment of British officers ('the result will be reprisals. It is difficult to see where such reprisals would stop')[6] and a threat to investigate the German submarine action after the war in order to bring home responsibility (in an unspecified way) to those concerned. The reply held the line that submarine prisoners would continue to be segregated, however. At the same time, in an attempt to defuse the situation, it stressed that, though segregated, these prisoners would be 'treated with humanity, given opportunities for exercise, provided with German books, subjected to no forced labour, and ... better fed and clothed than officers of equal rank now in Germany'. The reply was shown to the king and, at Churchill's request, the correspondence with Germany was published in the press.

The Times supported this position, arguing that it was already well established that simply 'obeying orders' was not a valid defence for those committing atrocities.[7] The House of Commons showed no interest at all. *The Times* even stood firm when, on 14 April, it reported 'rejoicing' in the Berlin press that the German authorities had carried out their threat and placed thirty-nine British officers in prison[8] to correspond with the ten German officers and twenty-nine submarine crew currently in detention in Britain.[9] And in a leading article on 26 April, headed 'Driving Home the

Moral', *The Times* equated the German imprisonment of the thirty-nine with their use of poison gas at Ypres, both being examples of Germany's willingness to violate the established conventions of warfare. From the list of names of the thirty-nine which had now been published, *The Times* deduced that the German authorities had deliberately gone out of their way to select for punishment members of the most prominent British families and regiments (an assessment subsequently confirmed by Gerard),[10] concluding that, 'The whole proceeding will strike Englishmen as unjust, petty, and spiteful. It is, of course, a mere attempt at blackmail, and to no attempt of that kind can we dream of yielding.'[11] But within government the fate of the thirty-nine British officers, and the actual conditions under which they were being kept, was moving to the forefront of Foreign Office concern. Reluctantly – and only after insisting that the request should come from Grey himself – Churchill agreed to a Foreign Office proposal to allow the US Embassy to visit the German submarine prisoners in detention barracks as a means to secure reciprocal visiting rights in respect of the British officers held hostage in Germany.[12] When the matter came before the Cabinet on 26 April, the 'general opinion' was that 'differential treatment' of German submarine prisoners should continue, subject to the apparently undermining caveat that care needed to be taken to observe the provisions of the Hague Convention, 'which do not allow prisoners of war to be confined'.[13] On 27 April, Churchill was obliged to make a statement to the House of Commons.[14]

In his statement, Churchill was both robust and conciliatory. His introduction, clearly directed towards the German Government, took care to distinguish between submarine prisoners per se, who were entitled to be treated as ordinary POWs, and those who had been 'engaged in wantonly killing non-combatants, neutrals, and women on the high seas'. Those engaged in such acts could not be recognised as on the same footing as 'honourable soldiers'. Churchill acknowledged that the situation was 'not free from difficulty', because the crimes committed had not been foreseen in international law; it was not possible, therefore, to tell what punishments might be available after the war to deal with the crews involved or what reparations might be levied against the German state. In the circumstances, all submarine prisoners captured after 18 February would be kept separate from ordinary POWs. In the concluding part of the statement, Churchill stressed that despite segregation, the prisoners were being kept in 'humane' conditions, though he declined to give details of those conditions pending a 'neutral' inspection. As for the thirty-nine British hostages held in Germany,

Churchill was clearly prepared to sacrifice them as martyrs: 'Whatever material ill-usage is inflicted on the gallant gentlemen upon whom it is in the power of the Germans to revenge themselves, they will have the consolation that no charge can be made against their conduct as honourable soldiers.'

But while Churchill was prepared to sacrifice the thirty-nine, others were less committed. His claim that it was necessary to detain submarine prisoners separately, while at the same time insisting that their treatment was in all respects humane and no worse than that of other prisoners, bore the hallmark of sophistry. Why, MPs asked, was it necessary to keep the exact conditions of detention surrounded in mystery – would it not be better to spell these out now in advance of a neutral inspection? Why were German submarine officers more guilty than their compatriots who had bombarded women and children at Scarborough, and who were being held as ordinary prisoners at Donnington Hall?[15] And how could the submarine officers really be culpable when they were simply obeying orders and refusing to do so would have resulted in them being shot? Such questions marked a turning of the tide away from Churchill's position. This was reflected in a leading article in *The Times* the following day. Two days after arguing that there could be no question of giving in to blackmail, the newspaper noted that it was not possible to compete with the Germans in relation to reprisals, 'because they are devoid of scruples and acknowledge no law but their own will'. While accepting that to treat German submarine prisoners in the same way as others would represent tacit acquiescence of the new method of warfare, the leader acknowledged that many people now felt regret at the Admiralty's action.[16] By 29 April, *The Times* was reporting a widespread feeling at Westminster that the differential treatment of submarine prisoners should now stop and that the whole matter should be sorted out after the war.[17]

The fears of Churchill's critics seemed to be confirmed by a report from Gerard on the exact conditions under which the thirty-nine were being held, made worse by the fact that included in these was Lieutenant Goschen, the son of the former British Ambassador to Germany. Goschen had been wounded on capture and placed in hospital at Douai. He and the other officers had now been moved to ordinary jails – a few were held in Cologne and the remainder at Magdeburg and Burg. Gerard had managed to visit these prisoners using his ordinary visitor's pass before the local German authorities had registered the significance. Gerard's report[18] made uncomfortable reading. The men were being held in single cells, some as small as 11ft x 4ft, and were only allowed one hour's exercise a day in the prison courtyards. While the food was acceptable and Gerard had managed to secure a number of minor improvements, it was clear that the overall conditions were far less favourable than those claimed by the British Government to apply to the German submarine crews.

The policy of segregation nevertheless trundled on, causing widespread anger in Germany and a deepening concern to many in the UK. In reporting the sinking of the *Lusitania* in May as 'A Glorious Deed', the German press specifically linked the event to the 'contemptible' and 'furious' reprisals being exacted by the British on captured German submarine crews.[19] On 20 May, *The Times* reported a telegram from HM Envoy to the Vatican stating that the German Government had revoked an agreement to exchange incapacitated civilians because of the treatment of submarine prisoners.[20] This was followed on 2 June by a letter from a correspondent claiming that he had received a letter from one of the thirty-nine British officers expressing 'incredulity' at the Admiralty for allowing the exchanges to be suspended and their ill-treatment to continue, 'only because a member of the Cabinet refused to remove the German submarine crews to ordinary prison camps'.[21] It was in the event Churchill's resignation from the Cabinet in June over the Dardanelles fiasco, and his replacement by Balfour as First Lord of the Admiralty, that finally brought the policy of segregation to an end. The Cabinet debated the matter at length on 4 June and decided that the special treatment of submarine prisoners should be discontinued.[22] On 9 June, in his first appearance before the House as First Lord, Balfour announced that from now on submarine crews would be treated in the same way as ordinary POWs.[23] *The Times* reported that Balfour's statement had been met with repeated cheers and appeared to receive unanimous approval.[24] On 30 June, the government formally announced that the differential treatment of British prisoners by Germany had now ceased.[25] Gerard managed to get most of the British officers transferred back to good camps. And having protested directly to von Jagow over the breach of diplomatic courtesy in exacting reprisals on the son of a former ambassador – made worse by the fact that he had also been a wounded man – Gerard also eventually secured Goschen's return to England as part of an exchange of wounded prisoners.[26]

Like many of Churchill's policies, his decision to incarcerate submarine crews was intensely personal. It ran counter to the established Foreign Office doctrine of treating German prisoners impeccably in order to avoid retribution against British prisoners held in Germany. For Churchill, the power of the policy was in the gesture. It signalled to the German Government, the world and, importantly, the British public that the conduct of the new submarine campaign represented an unacceptable departure from the norms of 'civilised' warfare. Churchill was prepared to accept the consequences, enjoining those British hostages held in reprisal to share in the righteousness of the British position. He was even prepared to order that, in future, German submarine crews would be left to drown in the sea. But it is difficult to believe that either Churchill or anyone else thought that the policy would result in the German Government actually modifying its campaign. The stakes for Germany were too high. Herein lay the obvious weakness of Churchill's policy. Despite the apparently harsh gesture of imposing separate treatment, the repeated statements by the British Government that the incarcerated submarine crews were being treated in all respects humanely and on a par with other POWs invited the obvious conclusion that the policy was, in fact, offering the worst of all worlds. While it was making no difference to the war, and the submarine crews were not actually suffering, the British hostages in Germany were being subjected to a harsh regime of treatment, giving rise to serious concern. The policy continued for as long as it did due to the sheer force of Churchill's personality. In discussing the change of policy by Balfour when it came, *The Times* commented, 'however fair the old policy was, experience showed that it was futile to compete with the Germans in the matter of reprisals'.[27] In a perverse way, this analysis echoes closely that of the *Cologne Gazette* in its own report of Balfour's change of policy: 'It only reveals the powerless anger of the British Government at having to withdraw a bombastically announced measure because its effects recoiled on Great Britain herself.'[28] Churchill had failed and German reprisals had succeeded, leaving the treatment of German submarine crews to remain a vexed question until late in the war, when it was to become a major stumbling block in negotiations over prisoner exchanges (see Chapter 11).

A second major confrontation over reprisals was also provoked by the British Government when it decided in 1916 to send German POWs to work in France. By the beginning of 1916, the demands of the British army on the Western Front were enormous, at a time when shipping capacity was already under severe pressure as a result of the German submarine campaign. To sustain and consolidate its operations, the British army was having to import into France some 21,000 tons of fuel wood each month, 31,000 tons of timber (mainly from Canada) and 3,000 tons of stone each day from

Guernsey.[29] Not only was this putting intense pressure on shipping, but it was also adding to congestion at the French ports. At the instigation of Lord Kitchener, Secretary of State for War, the French Government was approached for help. In response, the French stated that while they would be prepared to make available to the British military forests and quarries, they had no manpower available to carry out tree felling and quarrying; nor had they sufficient railway wagons to get supplies to the British army. To meet these difficulties, an agreement was reached at working level that in return for access to the forests and quarries, the British Government would make available to France 10,000 railway wagons for purchase and would provide labour in the form of German POWs to be transferred from Britain to France. These POWs would be employed on felling and quarrying work as well as on duties to relieve congestion at the ports. Haig, as Commander-in-Chief, at first objected to the scheme – on grounds of the expense of constructing camps for the prisoners, the fear of escapes and the fear of poor performance – but was finally persuaded by Kitchener and Walter Runciman, the President of the Board of Trade, to give it a try.[30]

At the political level, the argument quickly split between the pragmatists, who supported the scheme because of the pressure it would relieve on shipping, and the Foreign Office, whose concern was, as ever, the potential implications for British prisoners held in Germany. At the outset, Lord Newton correctly forecast that the scheme would invite retaliation from the German Government in the form of British prisoners being sent to work 'in very harsh conditions' in either Poland or behind the lines on the Western Front. Newton was also concerned that the scheme might ultimately lead to the German Government withdrawing its agreement to camp inspections. He concluded that the overall suffering caused to British prisoners by the scheme would result in 'considerable friction in this country ... without any commensurate advantage'.[31] The Foreign Office also feared that the scheme contravened the Hague Convention, which specifically prohibited the use of prisoners for work 'in connection with the operations of war' – a further potential cause for retaliation. Despite these arguments, the problem over shipping was so great that Grey was persuaded to agree to the scheme on the basis that it involved 'indirect war work', and was therefore acceptable under the convention, rather than 'direct war work', such as the manufacture of munitions, which this clearly was not.[32] The Cabinet formally agreed to the scheme on 2 March 1916, 'subject to strict conditions',[33] such as that the German prisoners were not to be

employed near the fighting line or on roads, nor on work directly connected with the housing or movement of troops, and that they were to be
entirely under the control of the British military authorities.[34]

Throughout the operation of the scheme, the British Government set out
to minimise any grounds for criticism or retaliation by Germany by ensuring that the conditions under which the prisoners were operating were not
only exemplary but transparently so. Thus, at the very beginning the US
Embassy was told that camps in France would be open to inspection in the
same way as those in the UK, and that the treatment of prisoners in France
would also be exactly as in the UK.[35] The first two batches of prisoners were
sent to Rouen and Le Havre, and were employed under British supervision
clearing cargo ships of goods – other than munitions or on other work
not involving the handling of munitions. Prisoners destined for Normandy
to carry out quarrying and forestry work would not be sent until proper
accommodation and other arrangements had been made. Reports from
the inspectors generally bore out British claims of satisfactory conditions.
The first report on Rouen, received at the end of June, found that the
1,468 prisoners there were housed in clean, tidy and well-ventilated wooden
huts fitted with electric lighting. Mattresses were provided on bedsteads
well off the ground. Reveille was at 5 a.m., with lights out at 9.30 p.m. The
prisoners were given three meals a day, with food being the same as that
provided to the British troops. Some eighty-three prisoners were allocated
work tasks within the camp. The remainder worked outside the camp as
requisitioned by the French authorities. They were accompanied to work
by British soldiers and guards. On the day of the inspection, 558 prisoners
were working outside the camp, discharging ships at the docks, loading and
unloading railway wagons, cutting timber and undertaking specific trades.
The hours of work seem to have been reasonable: from 7 a.m. to 11.30 a.m.
(with 20 minutes' rest at 9.30 a.m.) and 1.30 p.m. to 6.30 p.m. (with a
20-minute break at 3 p.m.). There was no work on Sundays. Pay was at the
standard rate of 40 centimes a day. A report shortly after on Le Havre was
also generally good, though accommodation there was still in the process
of construction. Of the prisoners working at Le Havre, 481 were held on
the steamship *Phryné*, moored beside the quay; 735 were held in wooden
barracks; and 200 in partly completed wooden barracks. Food, health and
sanitation were satisfactory and new accommodation was to be provided
within a few weeks. As at Rouen, the prisoners were employed unloading
ships and loading and unloading railway wagons. They worked an eight-hour

day, six days a week, with Sundays free. By the middle of October, there were some 12,000 German prisoners working in camps in France.[36]

Neither the favourable reports nor the original British assurances of satisfactory treatment influenced the German decision, relayed by Page to Grey on 15 May,[37] to transfer 2,000 British prisoners to Poland by way of reprisal. Nor was the German Government prepared to allow reciprocal inspection rights over the British prisoners held in Poland. The German position appears to have been dictated as much by concern about the conditions under which the prisoners were operating as by the principle involved in returning them to France. While the US inspectors' reports had indeed been glowing, they did include a catalogue of complaints by the prisoners themselves. Some of these related to day-to-day matters such as lack of medicines and soap in the infirmaries, low pay and poor rations, while others touched on matters of principle to which the German authorities were inevitably sensitive. In particular, there were complaints that the prisoners were being insulted in the streets by the local population (a complaint which the local military authorities accepted as being difficult to prevent), that NCOs were being treated and obliged to work as privates, and that some of the prisoners were being directly supervised by French NCOs who were particularly harsh (a matter of special concern to the British Foreign Office since this contradicted assurances given to parliament). At the end of June, the German Government also complained formally that 'educated men' were being required to undertake manual work in France, unlike in Germany where educated prisoners were put on administrative duties – an argument dismissed even by the Foreign Office on the grounds that 'everyone nowadays has a school education', and that there was evidence that the Germans were in any event employing two teachers and four clerks in a coalmine at Moers.[38] A subsequent complaint by the German Government that eighteen German prisoners at Rouen had been sentenced to death for refusing to work on the manufacture of ammunitions was dismissed out of hand as ridiculous.[39]

Throughout the summer the German Government continued to put forward detailed complaints about conditions in France, threatening further reprisals if the situation did not improve, with a final comment that the treatment of British prisoners in Poland was superior ('in sharpest contrast') to the treatment of the German POWs in France, and that this situation would be 'altered' unless the conditions at Rouen and Le Havre were improved by 20 October.[40] Such complaints and threats did have an impact within the Foreign Office, where Newton continued to hold the view that the scheme had been a mistake. But the War Office held firmly to the line that the treatment of German prisoners was satisfactory. While arguing that many of the complaints put forward by prisoners were untrue or exaggerated, the War Office accepted that some were legitimate – this was inevitable – but such complaints had been noted and were being dealt with. On 25 October, five days after the German deadline, a detailed report by the War Office on the German complaints, setting out the remedial action taken where these had proved to be legitimate, was forwarded by the Foreign Office to the US Embassy.[41] There the matter effectively ended. The War Office continued to send German prisoners to France and the German Government continued to ask for details. Meanwhile, the 2,000 British prisoners held in Poland were left to their fate, with Gerard recording that it was many months before the Germans would allow him to carry out inspections there.[42] These prisoners remained in Poland until the British Government ultimately brought the German prisoners back to the UK from France in the spring of 1917.[43]

Unlike the case of the submarine prisoners, the German use of reprisals was not allowed to alter the immediate course of British policy on the employment of prisoners in France. The decision to send German prisoners to France was born out of practical necessity, and although it is possible to construct a number of reasons why the German authorities should dislike this, in principle there was no actual difference between German prisoners working behind the Allied lines in France and, as was already happening, British prisoners working behind the German lines. The British scheme was entirely practical and thus attracted no substantial public or political opposition within the UK. The German decision to send 2,000 British prisoners to Poland was reported in *The Times*, without comment, under the simple headline, 'German Retaliatory Measure'.[44] While the British prisoners sent to Poland undoubtedly suffered harsh conditions, the general mood at home seems to have been to accept this as one of the inevitable consequences of war. The German prisoners sent to France did, on the other hand, make a significant contribution to the Allied war effort. On this occasion, Newton's forecast that the scheme would lead to considerable friction in the country without any commensurate advantage proved to be incorrect.

A surprising incidental postscript to this episode is that it quite unexpectedly provided the occasion for the US Government to reverse its previous policy of allowing the reports of its inspectors to be published.

Gerard notes bluntly that the reason for the decision was that publication provided a major source of irritation to the German authorities.[45] The US State Department expressed things in more neutral terms, arguing that publication had led to recrimination and retaliation on both sides.[46] It seems that the need to avoid appearing partisan was indeed the driving force behind the US Government's decision during a presidential election year, when Woodrow Wilson would go on to secure an increased share of the popular vote on a platform of continuing US neutrality. For the British Government, the decision was a serious setback since it went to the heart of its policy to use the reports as a propaganda weapon and as a means of putting pressure on the German Government to maintain standards. While diplomatic efforts finally secured agreement to the publication of the report on Rouen (the catalyst for the whole argument), the US insisted that this should be regarded as exceptional and that their inspectors' reports should no longer be published in future.[47] Gerard's final reports were eventually published in 1917, just before the US entered the war.

The employment of prisoners in the war zone was also to cause trouble for the rest of the war. At the end of January 1917, the German Imperial Foreign Office formally protested that a considerable number of German POWs were being held behind the lines in France to carry out work in poor conditions, with inadequate food, inadequate accommodation (often only tents) and with irregular receipt of their mails. The work was often unduly harsh and many were employed so near to the front that they were exposed to the fire of German guns and other dangers of warfare, with the result that several had been killed or wounded. The German Imperial Foreign Office claimed that no prisoners held by the German authorities were being similarly treated and demanded that German POWs be immediately moved to a distance at least 30km from the firing line. This was followed by an ultimatum; unless confirmation was received from the British Government by 1 February that this demand had been met, a number of British prisoners would be moved from camps in Germany to 'the area of operations in the Western theatre of war', where they would be treated in the same way as the German prisoners referred to. In addition, new British prisoners falling into German hands on the Western Front would, in future, also be kept in similar conditions within the sphere of operations.[48]

Having originally been reluctant to use POW labour in the battle zone, the British military had now become dependent on it, with around 28,000 prisoners being employed behind the lines at the end of March

1917,[49] of whom some were working as close as 5km to the firing line.[50] The British Government was therefore prepared to accept the threatened reprisals, replying to the German Government in dismissive terms:

> In view of the number of letters which have been sent to Germany from German prisoners of war in France which express gratitude for, and surprise at, the kindly and humane treatment they have received, whether in hospital or employed on labour, ever since they fell into British hands, it is impossible to believe that the German Government are in doubt as to the conditions in which the German prisoners of war are actually employed. The men are given the same rations as British troops, they are warmly clad, receiving over-coats and the same underclothing as the British troops. They not infrequently urge their friends not to send food or clothing, as everything is provided for them. They are by no means overworked.
>
> As regards accommodation, seventy-five per cent are in huts, and the remainder – as in the case of very many British troops – are temporarily in special warmed tents, provided with floor boards, and to all are issued an ample supply of blankets. Consequent on the good treatment they receive, their health is very good.
>
> The only complaint as regards postal arrangements, which has come to notice, was explained on investigation by the fact that the man had communicated a wrong address to friends. It is believed that, with this exception, the arrangements work smoothly and with remarkable expedition.

On the question of the safety of the men, the reply continued:

> Strict orders have been issued that prisoners shall not be employed in handling munitions or within range of the enemy's artillery.
>
> It is much regretted that, notwithstanding these precautions, one man was wounded by a shell which must have been fired at an exceptionally long range. This is the only casualty which has occurred.[51]

The French military was also against giving in to the German demand. General Nivelle, the French Commander-in-Chief, was opposed to any withdrawal beyond 20km. At a joint conference held on 12 and 13 March 1917, Lloyd George pressed French Prime Minister Ribot on whether opposition to the German demand had the support of his War Committee, to which Ribot replied that this was the committee's inclination.[52] But almost immediately afterwards Ribot's administration fell, and without consultation the new French Government caved in to the German demand, leaving the British Government with no alternative but to follow suit at the end of April 1917. As has already been noted in the previous chapter, however, during the last few months of the war the German military were ultimately to renege on the resulting agreement for which they had pressed so hard.

Both sides continued to exact or threaten reprisals throughout the war. One US inspector argued that, 'the reprisal idea is a peculiar mental characteristic of the German'[53] – a view needless to say publicly supported and disseminated by the British Government. Writing after the US had entered the war, Gerard noted that many cases had been brought to his attention where German camp commandants had, on their own initiative, directed punitive measures against prisoners on account of rumours of ill-treatment of German prisoners within Great Britain, and that he had constantly to be on the alert for this so that they could be annulled.[54] He cited as an example the following order issued by the camp commandant at Döberitz on 10 August 1915:[55]

> The unheard of and rough treatment, which, according to reliable infor-
> mation, has been accorded to civilian prisoners, and particularly German
> women and children who remain in England, has caused the withdrawal of
> all privileges formerly granted to English Prisoners of War. On this account,
> permission for all kinds of amusements and games has been cancelled.

There is no evidence that British camp commandants took it on themselves to institute general reprisals in this way. But despite its publicly professed aversion to reprisals, the British Government was in reality no more anxious than the German Government to abandon what was in effect an additional weapon in its armoury. In July 1916 the Cabinet discussed (but discarded) the possibility of exacting reprisals against Germany for the alleged curtailment of British prisoners' rations and interference with their parcels.[56] And as has already been noted in Chapter 5, it rejected a request by the International Red Cross in 1916 for all belligerents to abandon the practice of reprisals on the ground that German atrocities demonstrated that the option was still needed. In February 1918, the government announced in the House of Commons that it was considering reprisals against the alleged German practice of concentrating British POWs in areas subject to air attack.[57] In May 1918, the British immediately threatened reprisals when two captured British airmen were sentenced to ten years' imprisonment for dropping pamphlets over the German lines – an action criticised by the German Government as being outside the scope of acts of war.[58]

When and how to exact reprisals became a frequent item on the Cabinet agenda, which concluded that reprisals for German acts of brutality towards prisoners should be decided on a case-by-case basis. Examples of callous treatment warranting reprisals brought before the Cabinet included: delays by the German authorities in notifying the capture of individual prisoners, causing needless distress to their families; apparently calculated delays in the dispatch of letters by prisoners; and the brutal treatment of prisoners in close proximity to the German trenches.[59] In July 1918, the Cabinet set up a sub-committee comprising Lord Robert Cecil (Assistant Secretary of State for Foreign Affairs), Canadian Prime Minister Sir Robert Borden and Lord Newton, to put forward suggestions for securing effective reprisals.[60] This came to mixed conclusions. It produced a memorandum 'for the purpose of circulation to the Cabinet', drafted by Dame Adelaide Livingstone under the direction of Lord Cecil, who had appointed her as secretary to the sub-committee.[61]

The memorandum reviewed the reprisals taken by both the British and German Governments since the beginning of the war. It distinguished between 'collective' reprisals, such as those taken by the German Government in relation to the detention of submarine prisoners and the dispatch of British prisoners to Poland, and 'individual' reprisals relating to specific and lesser incidents. The memorandum found some examples of success in the case of individual reprisals undertaken by the British. Among these was the case of Captain Blaikie, captain of the *Caledonia*, who had been taken prisoner after trying to ram a German submarine in self-defence in December 1916. The British Government immediately threatened reprisals in the event of Captain Blaikie being executed, as had previously happened to Captain Fryatt for similar action.[62] Blaikie was exonerated. Another example centred on the case of Sir John Irvine, who was transferred from Ruhleben to less satisfactory conditions at Havelberg in July 1917. In response to a threat by the British Government to retaliate by transferring two prominent Germans from Alexandra Palace to Knockaloe, Sir John Irvine was returned to Ruhleben. As far as collective reprisals were concerned, however, the memorandum concluded unequivocally that the results for the British Government had been thoroughly unsatisfactory whenever it had embarked on such an exercise. Indeed, the only example found of the successful deployment of a general reprisal against the Germans related to an event early in the war when the Russian authorities had placed German officers in men's camps in retaliation for the poor treatment of Russian prisoners. The memorandum concluded that this success rested on the fact that the German authorities recognised that the Russians were prepared to be as callous as they were, unlike the British. In an echo of Neil Primrose's comments in 1915, it noted: 'It may ... be safely assumed that Germany will always be in a position to outdo any reprisals which we may undertake, since our people will probably shrink from going to the extreme length necessary to secure success.' And: 'The fact is that the real difference between the two nations is that the British have some regard for prisoners in their power and will not go to extremes in their treatment of them, and the Germans have absolutely no such feeling at all.'

Yet alongside these findings, Lord Newton circulated an 'observation' of his own. This – dated 12 September 1918 – noted that since Dame Adelaide's memorandum had been written in August, the military situation had reversed, with Britain holding more combatant prisoners than Germany for the first time, as well as more civilians. From this, Newton concluded that Germany might be more amenable to threats of retaliation than before, and that the conclusions drawn in the memorandum could therefore 'scarcely be accepted as final'. Thus the way was left open for the continuing use of reprisals.

Newton's comments presaged what was to be the most aggressive stance on reprisals taken by the British Government during the whole of the war. In response to the increasing number of reports being received of brutality towards British prisoners following capture and their employment in harsh conditions near the firing line, Sir George Cave, recently appointed chairman of a new Interdepartmental Committee on Prisoners of War, secured a new agreement from the Cabinet. On 11 October it was agreed to threaten reprisals in retaliation for the use of British prisoners within 30km of the firing line contrary to the earlier agreement, for their use in connection within the operations of war, for grossly overworking them in the salt mines and for general ill-treatment. Reprisals would be directed against German officers whose treatment was a particularly sensitive matter for the German Government.[63] In stark contrast to the line taken by Neil Primrose at the start of the war, Cave told the House of Commons during an adjournment debate on 29 October 1918:

There is one other resource which we have, as to which there is plainly some difference of opinion in the House, as I have no doubt there is in the country – I mean the resource of reprisals. Reprisals are an expedient recognised by all civilised countries. For myself, I have always believed in them, not of course as a method of punishment, but as a means of compelling the enemy to keep to the rules and to cease from crimes which he is committing. It is prevention and not punishment. If reprisals are limited to that, my conscience, at any rate, makes no protest against them.[64]

Thus over the course of the war the argument had switched from practicality and principle to one of simple practicality, though it was clearly too late for this particular initiative to have any practical effect.

There is little evidence that either side paid much attention in practice to any moral discomfort associated with punishing innocent men for the misdeeds, or alleged misdeeds, of others. Some movement towards limiting the application of reprisals did, however, take place in 1917, when Britain and Germany agreed to give each other four weeks' notice of any intention to exact them (see Chapter 11). The parties also agreed in suitable cases to attempt to eliminate the reasons for reprisals by arranging face-to-face discussions at The Hague before they were threatened.[65] Thus, while reprisals could still be used as a weapon, an opportunity had been created for each side to pause before embarking on an exercise that would inevitably harm innocent men and might finally rebound on its own people. Meanwhile, the obvious and moral solution of banning reprisals against prisoners altogether had to await the drafting of the Geneva Convention in 1929.[66]

# 8

# PARCELS, ASSISTANCE & RELIEF

The British Government took steps from the outset to ensure that suf ficient relief, both financial and material, was available to the US Embassy in Berlin to alleviate the hardships being suffered by British prisoners in Germany. But relatives and friends of the prisoners, as well as the public at large, also played their part. Almost as soon as news of the first British pris- oners was received, parcels containing comforts were being dispatched to Germany by the home population. The sheer scale of this private contri- bution ultimately became one of the more remarkable features of the war. One of the US inspectors records that by as early as autumn 1914 British prisoners were receiving practically all their foodstuffs from home.[1] By the end of the war, some 9 million food parcels and 800,000 clothing parcels had been dispatched to British prisoners abroad.[2] In addition, separate per- sonal items, medication, books and sporting equipment had all been sent on a regular basis. After the winter of 1914/15, the provision of relief was managed and financed almost entirely by the voluntary sector and public donations, with the government offering practical support and financial help with administrative expenses only. The machinery for dispatching parcels and other relief was, however, to become carefully regulated by the government as the war progressed.

The initial impetus for providing relief to prisoners had come from friends and relatives of members of the British Expeditionary Force (BEF), who had formed themselves into 'associations of ladies and gentlemen' at

the depots of some of the original regiments of the BEF, under the auspices of the church army. Such associations quickly assumed the formal
title of 'Regimental Care Committees'. Alongside the Regimental Care
Committees, a number of independent associations (which came to be
known formally as 'Local Associations') also quickly sprung up throughout the country to provide relief for prisoners from particular localities
or groups, such as enlisted civil servants or post office workers. By early
1915, the number and diversity of Regimental Care Committees and Local
Associations had grown to such an extent that it became obvious that some
form of co-ordination of their activities was needed. To meet this need,
the government accordingly sanctioned the establishment of a central co-
ordinating committee – the Prisoners of War Help Committee (PWHC),
based at the Savoy Hotel in London – whose role would be to 'assist prisoners of war, as far as that may be done, by facilitating the transmission to them
of money and of comforts and relief in kind'. The committee was to act
under instructions from the War Office, but would have no power to make
representations over the conditions in POW camps and would thus not
cut across the responsibilities of the Foreign Office.[3] The scale of voluntary
effort, meanwhile, continued to grow, with the PWHC reporting in June
1915 the existence throughout the country of ninety-three Regimental
Care Committees and twenty-six Local Associations.[4]

By early 1916, concern was beginning to emerge in a number of quarters
about the apparent waste and inefficiency of the system for providing relief.
On the one hand, the public were worried that sufficient food might not be
getting through to the prisoners, while on the other, the military authorities
and some of the larger relief organisations were concerned about possible
abuses of the system and waste. To get at the facts, a full census of parcels
passing through the Post Office was carried out in June and July 1916. This
found that the overall quantity of food being sent to prisoners was indeed
excessive, but that its distribution was unequal, with some receiving a 'super-
abundance' of up to sixteen parcels a fortnight and others receiving little or
nothing. The military drew a parallel conclusion that greater control was
needed to reduce the risk of articles being sent to prisoners which might be
useful to the enemy and therefore intercepted, and to eliminate the danger
of information useful to the enemy being deliberately included in parcels.
All this argued for more central control, which the government decided
to secure by placing the whole matter in the hands of a new organisation,
the Central Prisoners of War Committee (CPWC), working for the Red

Cross. The CPWC was given direct responsibility by the War Office for authorising, controlling and co-ordinating Regimental Care Committees and Local Associations, and the power to grant financial assistance to Care Committees as required. It was also given the job of itself acting as the Care Committee for civilian prisoners and for prisoners without a Care Committee of their own, and the job of packing and dispatching parcels for Care Committees and Associations on request.[5]

By establishing the CPWC, the government had effectively moved the provision of relief away from being a spontaneous and voluntary matter on the part of those who cared and wanted to help, to being a regulated industry designed to ensure the fair and equal treatment of all British prisoners. But in doing so it failed to consult or properly take into account the views of the existing Regimental Care Committees and Local Associations, who very much resented losing their freedom to help the prisoners on their books in an individual and personal way. In response, some committees withdrew from relief work altogether. Those involved in running the committees and associations were almost by definition active campaigners, often with a close personal knowledge of prisoners' needs. (The records show, for example, that the relief fund for the Second Life Guards was the responsibility of the Hon. Mrs Vandeleur of Burnham, Bucks; the Cheshire Regiment County Comforts Fund was run by Miss Vera Vandeleur of Hatfield, Herts; the Scottish Rifles (Cameronians) Fund included, amongst others, the same Miss Vera Vandeleur of Hatfield and also Mrs L. B Vandeleur of St Lawrence, Isle of Wight.)[6] Such organisers and participants were well able to make their concerns known at the highest levels; concerns which were further exacerbated by a number of publicly obvious teething problems within the CPWC itself. The strength of the public outcry against the new structure finally led to the setting up of a special Parliamentary Joint Committee to investigate whether the CPWC was meeting its objectives in practice.

In its report of July 1917,[7] the Joint Committee was critical of the CPWC for rushing too quickly into introducing new arrangements and in the process creating unnecessary problems. At the same time, it noted that many of the problems which did arise could have been avoided had the experience of the existing Regimental Care Committees and Local Associations been drawn on when the new regime was being set up. To make sure that this experience was not lost in the future, the Joint Committee recommended that the CPWC should now be enlarged to include representatives from the Regimental Care Committees and the

Local Associations – a recommendation readily accepted by both the War Office and the CPWC. The enlarged CPWC was to remain in place until the end of the war, securing the best of both worlds. Regimental Care Committees and Local Associations could continue to flourish (by July 1917, the number of committees had grown to 150 and the number of associations to 160), with the 'tie' between them and the prisoners they served being maintained. At the same time, the central purchasing power of the CPWC enabled it to buy stores on favourable terms, which could be passed on to the local committees and associations, and its central co-ordinating and executive roles enabled it to make strategic decisions about the ideal content of parcels and the frequency of their dispatch.

Even before the CPWC was enlarged to include the Regimental Care Committees and Local Associations, benefits from the new arrangements were starting to come through. By the end of March 1917, the CPWC had become directly responsible for about 8,700 of the 37,700 military and civilian British POWs in Germany and was dispatching about 14,000 parcels a week from its headquarters at 4 Thurloe Place, SW7. According to the Joint Committee, the organisation by then left nothing to be desired: 'Stores are purchased on favourable terms, and we are informed that many Authorised Associations find it to their advantage to make their purchases through the Central Committee in order to get the benefit of their low prices.' Moreover:

> The contents of the parcels are well chosen, and, though mistakes were at first made, notably with regard to the excessive quantity of salt and condiments in the parcels, they have now been corrected. We have the statement of a recently escaped officer, who had made special enquiries among the orderlies in the various camps where he was detained, that the Central Committee's parcels are excellent.[8]

The CPWC's parcels were indeed excellent, both as to quantity and as to quality. The CPWC lay down that each British prisoner in Europe should receive three 10lb parcels and 13lb of bread per fortnight[9] (with the option in the last three months of the war to send one 15lb parcel per week).[10] The contents of the parcels were copious and sustaining. There were four variants to be dispatched by rotation:

A

1lb Beef

1/2lb Vegetables (Cabbage, Brussels
Sprouts, Turnips, Carrots or Onions)

1lb Sausages

1/2lb Cheese (Tin)

1/4lb Tea

1/2lb Nestlé's Milk

1/2lb Sugar

1/2lb Margarine (or Dripping)

1lb Jam

1lb Biscuits

50 Cigarettes (or 2oz Tobacco and Papers)

1 Tin Sardines

Quaker Oats

1 Tablet Soap

B

1lb Tin Rations

1lb Tin Herrings

1 Tin Oxo Cubes or Marmite

1lb Biscuits

1/4lb Cocoa

1/2lb Bacon

1/2lb Dripping

1lb Tin Baked Beans

50 Cigarettes

1/2lb Nestlé's Milk

1lb Syrup

1lb Rice

1 Tablet Soap

C

1lb Tin Beef

1lb Tin Salmon

1/2lb Ration Biscuits

1/2lb Milk

1/4lb Tea

1/2lb Sugar

1lb Tin Fruit (or Dried Fruit)

1 Tin Oxo Cubes

1/4lb Chocolate

1/2lb Tin Beef, Ham, or Veal Loaf

1lb Suet Pudding

1/2lb Margarine or Dripping

Quaker Oats or Grape Nuts

1 Tablet Soap

D

1lb Tin Beef or Rations

1/2lb Bacon

1 Tin Sardines

1lb Tin Baked Beans

3 Soup Squares

1/4lb Tea

1/2lb Nestlé's Milk

1/2lb Tin Ham, Beef, or Veal Loaf

1/2lb Biscuits

1/2lb Dripping

1/2lb Current Biscuits

50 Cigarettes

1lb Tin Marmalade or Jam

Quaker Oats

1 Tablet Soap

While the parcels were sent from Britain, the bread for prisoners was sent separately from specially established bakeries. Initially, most of the bread was dispatched by the 'Berne Bread Bureau', established informally in April 1915 when Lady Grant Duff, the wife of the British Ambassador, began to send bread to three British prisoners in Germany. By the end of 1917, the

Berne Bureau employed some 200 workers and was packing 15,000 loaves each day, sufficient to supply nearly 20,000 men per week. The CPWC itself noted that 'Up to May 1917, the Bureau had sent enough bread to make a pathway from London to Algiers or from Berne to Constantinople'.[11] In March 1918, a prisoner recorded that the bread from Berne '[is] usually 10 to 12 days en route, and arrives so fresh and moist that you can put your finger through the crumb'.[12]

Until December 1916, bread had also been sent directly from England, principally by the 'Bedford Bread Fund', established in April 1915 by a Mrs Picton Warlow whose husband had been taken prisoner. Mrs Picton Warlow had contracted Bedford bakers in April 1915 to send bread to naval and marine prisoners, with interned merchant seamen and military prisoners subsequently being added. By autumn 1916, the Bedford Fund was supplying bread for some 3,600 prisoners, but during the hot summer of 1916 the bread had not kept well, leading the CPWC to close the Bedford Fund in favour of a new Bread Bureau at Copenhagen, to operate alongside Berne. A Mr Slade, together with Mrs Picton Warlow, were accordingly dispatched to Copenhagen to set up the new bureau and to enter into contracts with local bakers initially to supply those prisoners on the Bedford list.[13] Despite a number of early problems, leading to a decision (later rescinded) to close it down completely in July 1917, the Copenhagen Bureau eventually flourished and survived until the end of the war. By 15 July 1917, some 21,626 prisoners had been supplied by Copenhagen with a weekly ration of 4.5lb of bread or biscuits; by 1 January 1918, the supply had increased to 6.5lb per week for 31,000 prisoners. Between 15 October 1917 and 1 February 1918, 785,180kg of bread were distributed from Copenhagen and, out of 103,600 acknowledgement cards received, 98.87 per cent said the bread was satisfactory. The infrastructure supporting all this comprised a factory in Copenhagen, provided free – together with heat and light – by the owner; local bakers contracted to supply 33,000lb of bread each day; and a packing department superintended by one Mr Olsen and secretary, plus thirty-one packers, with a throughput of parcels totalling some 15–16 tons each day.[14]

The comforts supplied to prisoners did not stop at food parcels. A ban by the CPWC on the dispatch of individual parcels by prisoners' relatives and friends caused great resentment. After much wrangling, the CPWC softened its attitude and in October 1917 the War Office sanctioned the introduction of a 'Personal Parcel' scheme, to come into effect from 1 December.[15] The essential features of this scheme were that the next of kin of a prisoner (or someone nominated by him) was allowed to send one parcel each quarter, weighing between 3 and 11lb, to include any of the following contents:

| | |
|---|---|
| Pipe | Hair Brushes |
| Sponge | Tooth Brushes |
| Pencils | Clothes Brushes |
| Tooth Powder | Buttons |
| Pomade | Chess |
| Draughts | Cap Badge and Badges of Rank |
| Shaving Brush | Dominoes |
| Safety Razor | Dubbin |
| Bootlaces (Mohair) | Hobnails |
| Pipe Lights | Sweets (8oz only) |
| Housewife | Medal Ribbons |
| Handkerchiefs (one a quarter) | Brass Polish |
| Shaving Soap (one stick a quarter) | Mittens (one pair a quarter) |
| Health Salts | Mufflers (one per quarter) |
| Insecticide Powder | Combs |
| Braces and belts (if they are made of webbing and include no rubber or leather) | |

Potential senders were warned that the inclusion of any article not specified could result in the offending parcel being confiscated. The CPWC were also intent on countering any illusion that the scheme had been established for the benefit of the prisoners themselves, as opposed to those at home. In response to a question at a meeting of the CPWC in January 1918, the minutes record:

> It was very necessary that the privilege conferred by the Personal Parcel Scheme, which was intended for the benefit of the next of kin and only secondarily for that of the prisoner, should not be abused, otherwise there was reason to fear that the privilege might be withdrawn by the authorities.[16]

Between 7 and 29 January 1918, 5,421 personal parcels were dispatched form Great Britain. During the same period, the Chief Postal Censor returned 244 parcels for failure to comply with the regulations.[17]

As the war progressed, the CPWC also developed an 'emergency parcels' scheme to enable Camp Help Committees (see Chapter 9) to provide basic rations to newly arrived prisoners before their own individually addressed parcels started to come through. The emergency parcel contained sufficient provisions to keep a newly captured prisoner alive for two weeks. At any one time, 24,000 such parcels were located at existing camps throughout Germany, with a CPWC depot at Rotterdam holding some 40,000 parcels in reserve. The CPWC's packers were instructed to keep a further 50,000 parcels permanently available in order to top up Rotterdam. Such immense stocks were needed to keep up with an equally high turnover. From the end of September 1917 to September 1918, some 300,000 parcels were dispatched to Rotterdam, with withdrawals by camps from the depot averaging about 10,000 per week.[18] Pressure also grew for food to be sent to prisoners in bulk, rather than in individually addressed parcels. This move was, however, strongly resisted by some Regimental Care Committees and Local Associations, with the result that War Office permission for it to go ahead was withheld until almost the end of the war.

The amount of relief sent to British prisoners was clearly phenomenal and, until the US entered the war, unsurpassed. The Italian Government set its face against its prisoners receiving relief at all, according to one source, because of the first Battle of the Piave, when the authorities considered that those of their troops who had been taken prisoner were little more than deserters who deserved no help. (While the Red Cross finally persuaded the Italian Government to reverse this position, the Armistice was signed before the new arrangements came into effect.)[19] Russian prisoners generally received few parcels. And while the French received parcels from the beginning via the *Vetement du Prisonnier*, established as a voluntary organisation in autumn 1914 to provide relief to their POWs, and the Germans and Austrians received parcels with the aid of the Red Cross, only the British received them profusely and systematically. As one British prisoner – who received over 400 parcels in twenty months of captivity – wrote after the war:

> We English received parcels out of all proportion to our numbers, when compared with those received by the officers of our Allies. It is as well we did, for we were able in many cases to help the Russians – who were much worse off in this respect than the French – to supplement the food that the Germans provided for them.[20]

The quality and quantity of the food parcels sent to British prisoners caused great resentment in Germany throughout the war, which not surprisingly grew as the Allied blockade increasingly took effect. The standard parcels adopted by the CPWC, together with the separate ration of bread, provided each British prisoner with a food value of 3,345 calories a day, an amount which 'satisfied requirements'.[21] On top of this the prisoners were also being fed, in principle at least, by the German Government, whose regulations at the end of April 1915 prescribed a daily dietary regime for prisoners ranging from 2,430 calories for those doing no work to 2,970 calories for those engaged in heavy labour.[22] Even the CPWC noted in March 1918 that there was a considerable body of opinion in Britain that the amount of bread being sent to prisoners was excessive.[23] In sharp contrast, the average daily intake of every German citizen at the start of the war was only 2,280 calories. By 1917, largely as a result of the blockade (which is estimated to have resulted directly in the death of over three-quarters of a million German civilians),[24] the average daily intake had reduced to 1,000 calories.[25] At one stage Gerard, supported by Bethman-Hollweg and von Jagow, had to specifically secure the agreement of the German military to allow food parcels of unlimited content to continue to be sent to Germany.[26] That the German Government and the military should have allowed this is to their credit – a point acknowledged publicly by Lord Newton, responding to a suggestion that the deteriorating quantity and quality of food provided by the German Government meant that prisoners would die without the food parcels which were being sent from home:

> If the noble and gallant Lord [Lord Beresford] were correct in his assumption that the prisoners in Germany would literally starve to death if parcels did not arrive, let me point out to him that hundreds of thousands of prisoners would be dead already. There are over 1,000,000, if I am not mistaken, of Russian prisoners in Germany at the moment; and if it were literally impossible to exist on the food supplied by the German Government these men would have died like flies. My noble friend must be aware that I am the last person who would desire to give the Germans credit when it was not due; but it would be infinitely more accurate to say, not that our prisoners would die if they did not receive the parcels, but that it is impossible for them to keep in good health if they have to subsist upon the food which is supplied by the German Government.
>
> But I think that the noble and gallant Lord and some other speakers in the debate are rather prone to ignore the fact that Germany is a blockaded country at the moment; and I think the noble and gallant Lord would be the first to denounce the Government if he thought the blockade was not

being maintained with sufficient severity. The plain truth is that there is a general scarcity of food throughout Germany, and if our prisoners unfortunately do not get as much as they ought to have, it has to be admitted that in all probability the vast majority of the German population is in a state of comparative hunger. You might argue that, however hard up a Government may be, it ought at all events to feed its prisoners properly. If Germany cultivated chivalry, that might be the view taken by the German Government. But the German Government does not pride itself so much on being a chivalrous Government as being a practical Government, and that being so there is not much to be expected from them in the way of generosity so far as food is concerned. But personally, I have never been able to see what advantage there is in making out that the case of our prisoners in Germany is worse than it really is. It seems to me to be little short of an act of cruelty to the relations of these unfortunate men in this country to lead them to suppose that our men are not only in a state of misery, but in a state of starvation as well.[27]

To what extent, if any, the German authorities deliberately adjusted the quantity or quality of the food they provided to allow for the receipt of parcels is unclear. Obviously, any overt action of this kind would have exposed them to the risk of retaliation against German prisoners by the British Government (though the impact of this would have been limited since, as food shortages increased in Germany, the dispatch of food parcels to Britain became ever more sporadic).[28] But while there can be little doubt that the position of British prisoners did influence local attitudes, the central German authorities seem to have been punctilious in fulfilling their responsibilities. Responding to complaints about events at Dänholm, for example, Gerard wrote in August 1915:

On inquiry at the Prussian Ministry of War it was ascertained that because of the accumulation of a large number of parcels for British officers at the camp – more than they could use – the Commandant at Dänholm had issued an order to the effect that the prisoners were not to be permitted to receive more than one package a week, but that this order was countermanded as soon as it had come to the attention of the superior military authorities.[29]

Despite the adherence of all sides to the principles, disputes and debates about parcels continued throughout the war. The practical business of securing the dispatch and delivery of over 100,000 parcels each week to over

100 main camps in Germany inevitably gave rise to problems. Until very late, all parcels were individually addressed, resulting in delays in delivery when prisoners moved from camp to camp or when they were working away from their parent camp on *Arbeits Kommando*. And in the early days at least, non-delivery or delays often resulted from rail traffic congestion in Germany due to the fast-moving demands of war.

From time to time there were also allegations of pilfering. During 1917, the British military authorities restricted the allowance of soap which could be sent to prisoners owing to its frequent removal from parcels in Germany, while at the same time there were complaints that meats, puddings, tea and cigarettes were being removed from parcels by camp guards and prisoners in camp post offices. Despite these incidents, however, the Parliamentary Joint Committee set up to investigate the CPWC found no evidence of complicity on the part of the central German authorities in tampering with parcels, and indeed noted that some parcels had even been returned to Britain intact as undeliverable.[30] A report by the British Help Committee at Bayreuth that it had been handed ninety-four tins of conserve by the German police, believed to have been taken from someone caught intercepting British parcels, seems consistent with this finding.[31] Allegations of pilfering were not in any event restricted to Germany. There were complaints by German prisoners at Leigh Camp in Lancashire that their parcels had been opened before receipt, a problem resolved by the authorities by ensuring that in future a German prisoner would always be present to oversee the receipt and opening of parcels.[32]

Other problems arose out of the actual contents of parcels. While the German authorities were prepared to tolerate the inclusion of copious amounts of food, they objected to the inclusion of cigarette packets containing cigarette cards depicting armoured cars and tractors (Wills Gold Flake), and cartoons of the kaiser and others showing Germany in a bad light (Black Cat). The CPWC accordingly asked senders to exclude from all parcels anything that might give offence, reproducing a note from the Imperial Foreign Office which stated that the German Army Administration had given orders that all parcels containing pictures of the nature described were to be confiscated and their contents distributed to 'necessitous prisoners' in the respective camps.[33] For its part, the British Government was concerned to ensure that scarce materials such as leather and rubber were excluded from parcels sent to Germany to avoid them being purloined by the enemy (subject to limited exemptions for footballs, tennis balls and boxing gloves, etc.).[34]

In addition to its work on parcels – the basis of its original remit – the CPWC also gradually took over other schemes which had grown up to improve the welfare of prisoners generally. In February 1917, the CPWC took control of the Invalid Comforts Fund (ICF). Set up in 1916 by Mrs Bromley Davenport in the wake of the typhus epidemics at Wittenberg and other camps, the fund's objective was sending small supplies of simple drugs and bandages to each senior British NCO at every main camp in Germany. On taking over the ICF, the CPWC extended its remit to provide medical comforts for British prisoners in all theatres. By April 1918, the ICF was dispatching some 1,000 cases of medical comforts to camps each month.[35] Even where the local medical provision was adequate – as seems to have been the case in most camps in Germany – such comforts enabled prisoners to look after themselves and to treat minor injuries and ailments without needing to get into the normal camp systems and formally reporting 'sick'. The CPWC also helped with prisoners' recreational needs, dispatching musical instruments, tennis balls and games, etc, at the request of Camp Committees. The CPWC also became associated with the 'Camps' Library', an organisation first established in August 1914 to supply literature to British POWs in Germany and elsewhere.[36] All library stocks were given voluntarily by the public, with regular consignments being sent to every camp where a library existed or was being formed. At the instigation of the CPWC, which made a small grant for the purpose, music and plays were also supplied. By 1918, the Camps' Library was dispatching some 1,000 to 2,000 books every week, sometimes involving over 200 parcels a day. For the educated, or those wishing to become educated, textbooks were also provided under a separate 'British Prisoner of War Book Scheme', operating under the auspices of the Board of Education.

A final service by the CPWC to the relatives and friends of prisoners was the publication from January 1918 to the end of the war of a monthly journal, *The British Prisoner of War*. In its first issue, the objectives of both the CPWC and the journal were defined:

> The Central Prisoners of War Committee is the point on which all efforts made on behalf of prisoners of war are intended to focus, and the Committee has deemed it advisable to issue this journal in connection with its work. No recognised medium for the issue of official regulations or for the exchange of ideas and experiences concerning prisoners and their wants is in existence. Correspondence goes to show that many are working in ignorance of what is

being done elsewhere, and it is hoped by means of this paper to give a more useful and accurate survey of the needs, circumstances, and experiences of British prisoners than would be possible in any other way.

In its last issue, the journal set out some key statistics on the relief provided to prisoners and the CPWC's work. By 11 November 1918, the total expenditure on supplies to POWs, including the work of the Regimental Care Committees and Local Associations, totalled some £6.5 million. Of this, about one-third was provided from the General Fund of the British Red Cross and two-thirds was contributed directly by the public. As far as the CPWC itself was concerned, about 1.16 million communications were dealt with at its headquarters. During its two years of existence, the CPWC Finance Department received some 173,841 letters containing remittances totalling £2.06 million. Of 700 workers employed at Thurloe Place, some 300 worked voluntarily. The CPWC's administration costs were met by a direct grant from the War Office.

In a fitting epitaph, written long before the end of the war, the Parliamentary Joint Committee commended all those engaged in relief work as follows:

we desire to call attention to the organising capacity and the great zeal that have been displayed in creating the establishment at Thurloe Place. It was an undertaking of great magnitude, and the success now attained reflects much credit on all concerned.

We also feel bound to bear testimony to the far-reaching benefits which have been conferred upon the prisoners of war by the Regimental Care Committees and other Authorised Associations throughout the country. These Committees and Associations, in which we desire to include the staff at Thurloe Place, have, with their army of voluntary workers, mostly ladies, rendered services to our prisoners of war and to their friends and relatives which are far beyond any words of praise that we can employ. By their devoted and self-sacrificing labours they have established an enduring claim on the gratitude of the country at large.[37]

The scale and enthusiasm of the voluntary effort to help British POWs was both unique and phenomenal. Its success was enhanced by the light and imaginative touch of the British Government in setting up machinery (the CPWC) to co-ordinate the provision of relief and to ensure equality of treatment, as far as possible, for all prisoners. While British prisoners could obviously not be spared all the discomforts and hardships of the prison camps, the relief provided, both individually and through camp comforts, ensured that these were minimised and, at the very least, that no prisoner should be in want of basic subsistence. To what extent the amount of food provided was actually necessary is open to question, but while Germany was facing ever-increasing deprivation, Britain had sufficient resources to provide relief in the generous way that it did and its prisoners benefited from that.

# 9

# DAILY LIFE IN GERMANY

By 1916, administration of the POW camps had largely settled down Inevitably, a great number of existing sites and buildings had had to be used to house the large number of prisoners taken, as well as new camps specifically constructed for the purpose. In Germany, camps were established in hotels, forts, schools, country houses and traditional barracks. The officers' camp at Schweidnitz, comprising brick barracks sited in a garden of about an acre, had a pedigree dating back to 1870, when it had then been used as a place of internment in the Franco-Prussian War. The officers' camp at Fürstenberg, 50 miles north of Berlin, was based at a well-known summer hotel or convalescent home, *Erholungsheim*, a mile from the town. The hotel offered a good view over the surrounding country and lake, a veranda and considerable grounds. Old castles and forts were popular locations for camps. Celle Schloss, a castle formerly belonging to the King of Hanover, was used to house civilian and ex-officer prisoners; Rosenberg fortress, situated on a hill above the town of Kronach, housed officer prisoners in two wings of the high citadel; and at Beeskow, officers were housed in the old castle of the local bishop, built in the sixteenth century. At Blankenberg, officers were interned in three-storied houses previously comprising 'a home for gentlewomen'.

For NCOs and other ranks, much larger camps were generally needed. As the war progressed, so did the size of the camps. The capacity of the average camp grew to between 10,000 and 12,000 men, though many were even larger. Schneidermuhl had the capacity for 40,000 to 50,000 prisoners. Friedrichsfeld, 60 miles north of Cologne, eventually had the capacity for 35,000 prisoners. This camp comprised barracks with open space in the centre for football and tennis, gardens and flowerbeds between the barracks, and large vegetable and potato fields run by the prisoners. Brandenburg Camp consisted of an abandoned terracotta factory. And particularly unusually, at Danzig the prisoners were housed in barges four deep and four long, moored to a flat stretch of land on the bank of the Vistula. Some of the barges contained between 100 and 500 men, with their holds being lit by electricity. All the administrative and support facilities for the camp, including kitchen, store house and YMCA hut, were located on land. Güstrow Camp, near Mecklenburg, held some 25,000 men in wooden barracks situated in pine woods, while not far away at Parchim Camp, another 25,000 men were held in barracks built on a former cavalry drill ground.

In a number of cases, towns or localities became the home for a cluster of camps. At Senne, the camp of Sennelager actually comprised three camps: Senne I, II and III. Whilst Münster Camp comprised camps I to IV. Camp I was located some distance from the city in open country; Camp II was situated on the racecourse – and hence became known as *Rennbahn* – the grandstand providing space for offices, a chapel and a theatre; Camp III was a block of brick-built barracks intended for German troops; while Camp IV was reserved for Russians. Most of the larger camps had their own hospitals, or 'lazarets'. In other cases, treatment centres were based away from the camps. At Cologne, there were a number of hospitals for prisoners, with the majority of British prisoners being treated at Garrison Lazaret I or Kaiserin Augusta Schule Lazaret IV (there was also within the town a prison for officers undergoing special treatment in the Schnugasse, a massive old military prison). Similarly, in Hamburg there were two hospitals for prisoners – Reserve Lazaret 7, a ward of the central prison at Fühlsbüttel, and Reserve Lazaret 3 at the Eppendorfer Krankenhaus, Veedel, a marine lazaret.[1]

To some degree, the location of the camps was self-selecting. Key factors determining location were the proximity of railway lines and the ready availability of sites. Camps were also deliberately located near manufacturing centres or in agricultural localities because of their potential for supplying labour to local farms. Unlike the British Government, the German Government seized on the value of prisoners as a source of labour from the outset and made full use of the provision in the Hague Convention allowing them to be used in this way. This policy not only freed up German workers for military service, particularly those employed in agriculture, but also made a valuable contribution to the German economy. As early as November 1915, a German banker confessed to Gerard that, 'Prussian landowners were … in favour of continuing the war, because of the fact that they were getting four or five times the money for their products, while their work was being done by prisoners'.[2] (Such was official German embarrassment at this, that when the *Tageblatt* called attention to the story, it was suppressed for several days.)[3] Prisoners were based either in a *Stammlager* (a 'stem' or 'parent' camp) and sent to work outside with an *Arbeits Kommando* (working party), or were based permanently in a working camp attached to a parent camp for administrative purposes. Most of the 100,000 men registered at Neuhammer Camp, for example, never went there, but went straight to working camps under its administration. Similarly, though the physical capacity of Parchim was 25,000 men, at times it had on its books 45,000 men when counting those working outside. And at Soltau, a centre for *Arbeits Kommandos*, only 30,000 men could actually be accommodated within the camp out of a total of 50,000 on the register.[4]

Conditions within the parent camps varied. Camps within Germany were managed by the respective Army Corps Districts. Prisoners were placed in a camp managed by the Army Corps District of the unit which captured them. Different Army Corps Districts had different attitudes towards prisoners and different traditions with regard to such matters as discipline. The effect of this is not to be underestimated. At the outbreak of war, the ultimate power in Germany was transferred from the civil to the military authorities, and the Army Corps commanders were not slow to make full use of this power. The following order, issued by the army's general headquarters in Bavaria in January 1917, is cited by Gerard as a particular example of the all-pervasiveness of military control:

The appearance of many women in Garmisch-Partenkirchen has excited lively anger and indignation in the population there. This bitterness is directed particularly against certain women, frequently of ripe age, who do not engage in sports, but nevertheless show themselves in public continually clad in knickerbockers. It has happened that women so dressed have visited churches during the service. Such behaviour is a cruelty to the earnest minds of the mountain population and, in consequence, there are often many disagreeable occurrences in the streets. Officials, priests and private citizens have turned to the Generalkommando with the request for help; and the Generalkommando has, therefore, empowered the district officials in Garmisch-Partenkirchen to take energetic measures against this misconduct; if necessary with the aid of the police.[5]

Against the background of such far-reaching power, it was by no means easy for the Prussian War Ministry and Imperial Foreign Office always to get the Army Corps commanders to comply with the standards laid down centrally for the treatment of prisoners. The situation was further exacerbated by the fact that the camps themselves were each managed by a high ranking officer, perhaps a general or a civilian equivalent such as a judge, who had even greater influence on the atmosphere within the camps. While many commandants ran their camps with compassion and efficiency, others were less willing or able. The guards also had an influence on the atmosphere within the camps. They operated at the ratio of one guard for every ten prisoners and were usually provided by the *Landstürm* (the older class of reserves) or from younger men physically unfit for active service. Though they operated within the framework laid down by the commandant, there were frequent complaints that the guards displayed a 'nagging and abrasive' attitude.[6]

Individual camps therefore gathered a reputation for good or bad treatment. The US inspectors found Friedrichsfeld to be a good camp. The food was good and there were shops for the prisoners to buy miscellaneous items such as tennis rackets, etc. The mail was regular and there were lessons available. The men were requested to do the work of the camp but NCOs were not. Re-education was provided for wounded soldiers and special equipment was provided for 'correcting deformities'. The inspectors found Parchim, Soltau, Dülman, Wahn and Zossen (Wunsdorf) also to be good camps.[7] By contrast, they found Minden – situated some 40 miles from Hanover – to be a particularly bad camp. While Minden was to grow eventually to house 18,000 prisoners, at the time of their inspection in 1916 it held 8,682 prisoners of whom only 615 were British. The roofs of the huts were found to be leaking, the trench latrines were being emptied only once a week and the 100ft open trough urinal, situated in the open, was heavily encrusted, smelly and dirty. It was alleged by the prisoners that men were being punished by confinement in the *Straf-Baracken* for reporting ill at sick call. There were also complaints that packages and letters were received irregularly and that there was no camp library. The camp lazaret was found by the inspectors to be overcrowded and contained seriously wounded men who were receiving insufficient nursing attention. Moreover, the Church of

England lay reader was refused permission to visit the sick to give religious consolation or to help in the hospital. Within the punishment block, the inspectors found five British POWs, two of whom were there for refusing to work and three who claimed that they had done nothing other than to report sick. The five had been provided with no blankets or mattresses and had to sleep on the bare floor in their clothes. During confinement they were not permitted to receive any packages. The inspectors concluded that Minden was:

> a model of what a camp for prisoners ought not to be. It is built in a relatively unhealthy location, of poor general plan, and as administered, is more of an actual prison for the men, more particularly the non-commissioned officers, than the jail at Cologne, without any of the redeeming features of the latter. The attitude towards the prisoners of war is not only not sympathetic but, on the contrary, a hard attitude of suspicion and repression that appears to us to verge on real intentional cruelty.[8]

The inspectors believed that the harsh regime at Minden was being deliberately used by the German authorities as a punishment for NCOs who refused to work. The Hague Convention stated specifically that men could be used as labour but officers could not. Even this degree of clarity caused problems from time to time due to a widespread mistaken belief among British prisoners that they could not be required to work against their will, often resulting in court martial and, if the protesters formed part of a group, the serious charge of conspiracy. While by implication NCOs could also be required to work under the Hague Convention, both sides recognised early on that this could cause difficulties, and, in order to protect the position of their own NCOs on capture, tacitly agreed not to make work compulsory. Instead, the obvious role for NCOs was to continue to supervise their own men within the camps, a practice best suited to maintaining morale and discipline by avoiding the prisoners having to take orders directly from the camp authorities and guards. Where NCOs could not usefully be employed in this way, it was accepted that they could be invited to volunteer for work. But the insistence of many British NCOs that it was their absolute right not to work and their consequent failure to volunteer increasingly irritated the German authorities, and when the US inspectors found that 357 of the 615 British prisoners held at Minden were NCOs, the suggestion took hold that they had been deliberately sent to the camp as a punishment for refusing to work and as an incitement to get them to do so. Further evidence of deliberate provocation at the camp was the practice of requiring NCO prisoners to drill under a German private and to accept commands in German, accompanied by the argument that a German common soldier outranked all POWs. This caused a breakdown of British military discipline, with the British NCOs considering the practice simply as a punishment for them refusing to volunteer for work.[9]

German denials that NCOs had been sent to Minden for disciplinary reasons failed to convince the inspectors, who noted following a further visit in April 1916 that while there was no direct persuasion to induce NCOs to work, there was a considerable amount of indirect persuasion, including the refusal of facilities for recreation and amusement, and a refusal to allow musical instruments in the British compound. The inspectors concluded that the German authorities were in breach of the Hague Convention at Minden by operating a punishment regime for NCOs which went beyond holding them simply as a measure of safety.[10] By 1918 the situation had changed with NCOs no longer being concentrated there.

Another point of contention between the two sides was the German use of guard dogs, in particular at Minden, Wittenberg, Langensalza and Stendal. The British Government saw the use of guard dogs as further evidence of deliberate repression, its concern being exacerbated by reports of the actual misuse of dogs against prisoners.[11] One report alleged that a prisoner had been dressed up in sacks and used as bait for the dogs in order to train them. Other ex-prisoners relayed stories of dogs being set on prisoners 'for fun'. Two attempts by Grey to resolve the matter failed. Following one reported attack on a prisoner by a dog at Stendal in 1916, Grey formally asked the US to make representations. The response of the German Imperial Foreign Office (IFO) was dismissive, merely stating that the use of dogs at Stendal was 'necessary' and that in the particular case in question the dog had simply 'slipped its lead'. Further, the injuries to the prisoner, if any, could only have been slight, since he had failed to present himself to a doctor. Later the same year, Grey made a more general attempt to get the use of dogs abandoned, noting that they were never used in the UK. He argued that the practice was open to strong objection, 'not only because it exposes the prisoners to serious bodily harm, but also because it places men entitled to honourable treatment on the same footing as criminals'. But while Grey was attempting to introduce the question of principle into the argument, the IFO continued to maintain that in some camps the use of police dogs was simply a 'military necessity', and that it was 'impossible to regard this measure as a breach of the principles of the humane and reasonable treatment of prisoners'. The dogs were not 'particularly savage', and the fact that dogs were needed in Germany and not the UK merely reflected the larger number of prisoners held in Germany.

While conditions at many of the worst camps were to improve during the course of the war, harsh conditions at others remained until the end. The repressive regime at Brandenburg came to the fore in early 1917, following the death there on 9 March of Able Seaman John Player Genower, aged 24, and seven other prisoners.[12] The case of Able Seaman Genower, late of HMS *Nestor* and captured at Jutland on 1 July 1916, was first brought to the attention of the British authorities by the Netherlands' Government, which had taken over as protecting power following US entry into the war. According to a report by eight Spanish seamen captured from the SS *Gravine*, sunk by a U-boat on 7 February 1917, the incident started in a hut at Brandenburg used as a 'dungeon'. At the time of the incident, the hut contained six Russians, one Frenchman and one Englishman (Genower). The hut caught fire and despite the prisoners calling out for release, it was alleged that the guard remained 'unmoved'. The Englishman then broke a window and leaned out and was bayoneted by a guard in the chest. Other men tried to get out and were also bayoneted. The fire could not be extinguished and all the men died. The Spanish seamen said that the commandant subsequently issued an order saying 'sorry'. Coffins were made by Russian prisoners at the camp, and '10,000 marched with them to the cemetery'.

This version of events was backed up by Captain C.V. Fox, DSO, of the Scots Guards, an escaped POW. He had arrived at Brandenburg after the incident had taken place, but his report of what had happened was essentially the same as that of the Spaniards, with the exception that instead of all the prisoners in the hut being burned to death, the Frenchman and three of the Russians had got out alive. Further substantiation was subsequently provided by two other prisoners who had been at Brandenburg. According to them, when the fire started the prisoners were not allowed to help. The guard would not open the doors to the hut, being afraid to do so without the authority of an NCO. Then the key was lost. Genower had tried to get out and was bayoneted – five Russians, one Frenchman and Genower were burned to death. They also gave the background to Genower's confinement. According to them, when the barge carrying Genower and other prisoners to Brandenburg had arrived there, the men were told to make it secure. Genower had jumped off before it stopped and was hit by a German with the muzzle of his rifle; he had then gone to a doctor to have his face dressed and had been placed in the cells.

The German Government denied the version of events put forward by the prisoners, stating that a thorough investigation had shown that no blame for what had happened could be attached to the German staff. The investigation had established that the fire had started at 12 noon on 9 March, and that although everything had been done to save the prisoners the fire had spread too fast. The guard had done his best to save the men and it had been possible to save all those who had shown themselves at the windows. They confirmed, however, that Able Seaman Genower, who was awaiting trial for insubordination, was among those who had died. It had not been possible to establish the cause of the fire, though the remains of a packet of tobacco had been found in one of the cells and it was possible that a prisoner had smoked, against orders, and that he had fallen asleep with his pipe alight, setting fire to his mattress.

Both versions of events were reported in the press – the 'British' version being carried by Reuters while the official German version appeared in the *Norddeutsche Allgemeine Zeitung* on 9 August 1917. It is clearly not possible from this distance to determine which of the two versions was closer to the truth, though in the chaotic circumstances of a fire the events narrated by the prisoners seem distinctly credible, in particular the proposition that the guards were not prepared to let out the prisoners, and hence save their lives, without superior orders. This was certainly the view of the British Government and is consistent with the generally harsh regime of the camp. Further evidence of the harsh regime is to be found in the report of a US Red Cross Deputy to Switzerland, charged with overseeing the conditions of American POWs in German camps, who visited Brandenburg on 2 October 1918. According to this report, the prisoners complained of having to do unnecessarily hard work and of petty officers being required to undertake inappropriate work; the parcels service was poor, with parcels being frequently lost; no soap and towels were being provided by the camp authorities; and there was no cinema. Things were even worse by the time of the next visit on 1 November, when the inspector reported that the huts housing the prisoners were leaking and there was no coal for heating. There were only two blankets for each prisoner; there was only one (insufficient) light in each hut; and there was no hot water for washing.[13]

In direct contrast to the harsh conditions of the 'repression' camps, a number of camps were established by the German authorities with the

1 British POWs being marched through the streets of a German town (IWM Ref. Q 83667)

2 Döberitz Camp, general view (IWM Ref. Q 83666)

3 Dorchester Camp, general view (IWM Ref. Q 56588)

4 Douglas Camp, IOM, civilian internees on parade (IWM Ref. Q 83947)

5 Douglas Camp, IOM, brush making workshop (IWM Ref. Q 83970)

6  Dyrotz Camp, British barracks and church (IWM Ref. Q 83672)

7  Dyrotz Camp, cemetery with cross made out of beaten tins by Russian POWs (IWM Ref. Q 83673)

8 Güstrow Camp, Allied POWs in parcel store (IWM Ref. Q 84029)

9 Wittenberg Camp, memorial stone and graves (IWM Ref. HU 105480)

10 Stobs Camp, near Hawick, POWs receiving parcels from Germany (IWM Ref. Q 56593)

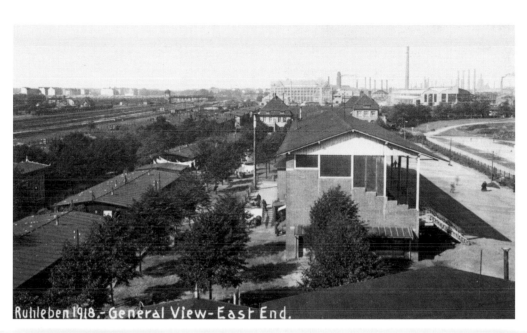

11 Ruhleben Camp, general view, 1918 (IWM Ref. Q 102937)

12 Ruhleben Camp, 'Marine Parade and Clubland', 1918 (IWM Ref. Q 102953)

13 British POWs repatriated from Germany, 1918, accompanied by Dutch Red Cross nurses (IWM Ref. HU 105476)

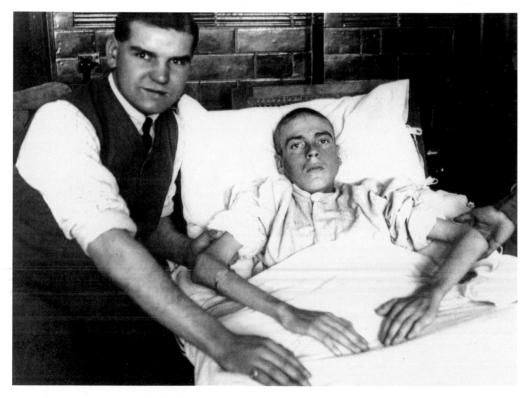

14 Private Thompson, Durham Light Infantry, repatriated 1918, employed on tree felling behind the German lines (IWM Ref. HU 65894)

specific objective of 'seducing' prisoners to change sides through the provision of comforts accompanied by propaganda. One such 'seduction' camp was Zossen (Wunsdorf), which was set aside for Muslims, Indians and black prisoners. The regime within the camp was particularly comfortable, with a mosque being built in the centre 'at the Kaiser's command'. Other facilities were also provided to facilitate the practice of religious rites, including the provision of livestock to enable prisoners to meet the requirements of religious slaughter. The German officers at the camp were selected from those who had served in India and the East and who had an understanding of local language and customs. Some success was reported in weaning prisoners away to fight for Turkey.[14]

An attempt to seduce Irish prisoners away from the British cause had been much less successful during the winter of 1914/15. Following a declaration by the German Government in favour of Irish independence, some 2,500 Irish prisoners had been concentrated at Limburg, near Frankfurt am Main. There they were given special treatment with a view to persuading them to join the 'Irish Brigade', whose declared purpose was to fight 'solely for the cause of Ireland'. Over the winter of 1914/15 the prisoners were visited at the camp by Sir Roger Casement, ostensibly to give lectures on historical subjects. When his true purpose of recruiting for the Irish Brigade became clear he was met with widespread antagonism. Of the total prisoners in the camp, only fifty-four volunteered for the Brigade. A Cabinet memorandum circulated during the progress of Casement's subsequent trial noted that the remainder 'indignantly refused his tempting offers of freedom and a German uniform, with harp and shamrock on the collar, and hissed and booed when he spoke'.[15] Casement himself could have hardly disagreed with this, having written to a friend following his final visit: 'I will not return to Limburg to be insulted by a handful of recreant Irishmen.'[16] The prisoners recruited hardly formed a platoon, let alone a brigade. The fifty-four – comprising one sergeant-major, one deputy sergeant-major, three sergeants, three corporals, three lance-corporals and forty-three privates – quickly disappeared from Limburg and were subsequently found at another camp near Berlin, following an urgent US request to inspect them. They were subsequently moved again to Zossen (Crescent Camp) in June 1915, where they were treated as 'comrades in arms' rather than prisoners.'[17] Only two of the Brigade landed in Ireland during the war. The first accompanied Casement in the submarine landing giving rise to Casement's arrest. However, the Crown offered no evidence against him at Casement's subsequent trial and he was allowed to continue his service in the army. The second was dropped off by a German submarine in April 1918, arrested and sentenced to death. His sentence was subsequently commuted to penal servitude for life and he was finally released from prison in 1924. The consequences for the vast majority at Limburg who refused to join the Brigade were unpleasant, with food and comforts being substantially reduced. There were reports of actual ill-treatment and even of two prisoners being shot, leading to US intervention. A Roman Catholic priest at Limburg (Father Crotty) who refused to co-operate in the seduction was ordered out of Germany, though following intervention by the Vatican was allowed to stay.[18]

The record indicates that it was Casement, rather than the German Government, who first put forward the idea of an Irish Brigade and initiated the events at Limburg.[19] The German Government were, nevertheless, fully behind the process of 'seduction'. In contrast, the German military had serious misgivings about being involved in what they saw as a dishonourable and possibly illegal practice, as the following extract from a secret note by the War Office, Berlin, dated 9 May 1916,[20] makes clear:

As for the view put forward that the work of German officers and soldiers in propaganda camps is incompatible with the sense of duty and honour of a German soldier, it may be remarked that the first suggestion to undertake such propaganda came from the highest quarters in the Empire, and, *moreover, with the knowledge of His Majesty the King Emperor.*

As for the officers, all they have to do is to supervise the propaganda, whereas it is left to the professional propagandists to influence the opinions of prisoners-of-war ...

As to the question of international law, the War Office has the honour to submit that in a life-and-death struggle such as that which we are compelled to wage, and in which our enemies, disregarding international conventions, shrink at nothing, *Germany must likewise make the utmost use of every means of defence at our disposal.*

And on the inspection of seduction camps, a regulation issued by the War Office in Berlin, on 2 February 1916, stated:

Propaganda camps may likewise be visited by the protecting Powers without notice, but on condition that they contain subjects of a nation whose interests are confided to the delegate soliciting admission to the camp in question. In general, it shall be left to the Commandant *to prevent unpleasant discussions aris-ing in such camps.*[21]

For the vast majority of prisoners based in the main camps, daily life focused largely on how to relieve boredom. Sport inevitably featured strongly in the list of recreations. The British Government's decision to allow the limited export of leather and rubber materials in sporting goods for prisoners made a major contribution to raising morale. Under the exemption, the export of rubber and leather in footballs, boxing gloves and tennis balls was allowed at the rate of one football per hundred men, one pair of boxing gloves per man and six tennis balls (or other small balls) per man.[22] It was not only the sport itself which provided a useful diversion. The arrival of sports equipment at Bayreuth in early 1918 prompted the establishment of a Sports Committee, whose task was to allocate equipment (including draughts and playing cards) to those not working outside the parent camp and to control the system for the loan of equipment within the camp. This could be an intricate and time-consuming activity, as one of the reports of the committee shows:

> On the 25th of May 1918, a meeting was held to discuss the availability of converting the Rugby balls, of which we have received four, into Association balls. A French Adjutant, who had previously made the experiment, informed us that from two Rugby balls, one Association ball (full size) could be made; or, if preferred two Association balls from the Rugby balls. The feeling of several men in the camp was broached, and after consideration, and in view of the fact that the only available ball in the Camp was a French one, it was decided to accept the Frenchman's offer, and to permit the conversion of one Association ball from two Rugby balls.

This decision was so successful, especially in facilitating England v. Scotland international games, that there was soon pressure for a second association ball, with the decision to be made by a general meeting. The report con-cluded: 'the Committee ... express its approval that the English have shown themselves, as they always have been, the greatest sporting nation of the world, and hope for the continuance of the sporting interest so vitally nec-essary as a preventative against disease in the Camp.'[23]

Amateur dramatics and theatricals also represented a common diver-sion in the camps, as did the cinema. In contrast to the early complaints of squalor at Döberitz, the prisoners there were granted the use of a large wooden building for use as a theatre in 1917, with the camp motto '*Dum vivimus vivamus*' emblazoned across the base of the stage. The inmates of the officers' camp at Freiburg, based in the old university building, established FADS – the Freiburg Amateur Dramatic Society. FADS was started by the first group of prisoners at the camp in 1917, holding weekly impromptu 'smokers' after their evening meal. These programmes 'with a liberal allowance of cheap wine enabled us to pass many pleasant evenings'. Costumes and wigs were at first forbidden by the camp authorities on the ground that they might be used to aid escape, but were finally permitted. Next came a stage and the installation of a 'Cinema instrument'. The resulting twice-weekly film shows usually comprised a German comedy ('which nobody laughed at') and a German drama ('at which everyone did'). The film shows in turn gave rise to satirical skits written by the members of FADS, the first of which was entitled *Purplepazionheit*. Eventually, FADS was so successful that an advance booking office was set up and shows had to be run on consecutive nights to accommodate all those who wanted to see them.[24] Many of the larger camps also had their own prisoners' newspaper. Münster II had three newspapers: the *Rennbahn Review* and the *Church Times*, as well as the *Echo du Camp*, which was printed in French and English, and was described as the 'highbrow' newspaper, containing articles on such matters as, 'the social role of the individual in a prison camp'.[25] The newspaper at Treves (or Trier) was called *The Barb*.

For officers, a major breakthrough came in 1916, when the British and German Governments agreed to allow walks outside the camps. Since it was accepted as being almost the duty of officers to attempt to escape, those allowed out were first required to be photographed and to give their parole. The prisoners at Treves had to sign and deliver to the camp authorities a card bearing the following before leaving the camp:

> By this card I give my word of honour, that during the walks outside the camp I will not escape, nor attempt to escape, nor will I make any preparation to do so, nor will I attempt to commit any action during this time to prejudice the German Empire.
> I also give my word of honour to use this card only myself, and not to give it to any other prisoner of war.

Prisoners at Torgau were allowed out on two or three days a week, in groups of fifty or sixty, accompanied by a German officer. It was made clear that the German officer's function was to deal with any hostile reaction by local civilians (though none was experienced) and not to act as a guard. A number of different trips had been arranged to provide variety.[26] The representative of *The Barb*, who was allowed out on the first walk of twenty officers on a Sunday afternoon at Treves, wrote, 'Trier viewed the strange sight of British officers walking her streets, unguarded, without any great demonstration of surprise or hostility.' The accompanying German officer gave them 'a guided tour'.[27] Similar equanimity on the part of the local population was evident at Crefeld. Following an inspection of the camp on 19 March 1916, the US inspectors reported:

> The walks on parole, which have lately been arranged, have been entirely successful. The officers go out in sufficient numbers to allow each officer two walks a week. The only complaint as to these was that the German, accompanying the party, was a non-commissioned officer instead of a regular officer. This will, however, be rectified at once, as I was informed by the Department office at Münster. There is no trouble of any kind with the inhabitants on these walks, but the children, so I was told, often approach the officers to beg, generally with success, for chocolate.[28]

The system of outside walks made a major contribution to the morale of officer prisoners, adding, for many, to an already fairly tolerable existence, as the following extract from an article in *The British Prisoner of War* on Pforzheim Camp makes clear:

> British officer prisoners were housed in an hotel on the outskirts of the town. One officer told us that excellent arrangements had been made for study and occupation of all kinds. Games had been planned, and the days passed fairly quickly for a prison camp. Prisoners had the use of a football field and of tennis courts. There is a yard behind the hotel in which small trees grew, but the photograph [not reproduced here] shows it to be restricted for exercise. Officers, however, were allowed to go for long walks in the Black Forest, which they enjoyed, and they described the country round and the views from the camp as beautiful.[29]

Aside from recreation, camp duties such as cleaning, maintenance and camp building works also occupied the time of prisoners. Many became involved in the work of 'Camp Help Committees', which gradually became established in many of the larger camps. Help Committees embraced prisoners of a particular nationality and were set up by the prisoners themselves. Their usual role was to channel through to the camp authorities concerns or complaints by the prisoners, to monitor the handling and distribution of parcels, and to act as a distributing point for bulk supplies of clothing, food and books, etc. sent by relief organisations. They were often allowed to communicate directly with the relief organisations about the prisoners' particular wants and needs.

The work of the committees could become time-consuming and all-pervasive, as a report by the Secretary of the British Help Committee at Bayreuth for the period 16 February to 30 May 1918 indicates. During this period, some 220 newly captured and wounded British POWs arrived at the camp and were given help by the committee; the committee sent full details of these men to the Red Cross at Berne, Copenhagen and London the day after their arrival; some 10,073 parcels were distributed within the camp and 32,606 were sent to working parties outside; and letters had been sent to Care Committees on behalf of men who had not received clothing. During the period three British prisoners had died and the committee had made repeated requests to have crosses erected over their graves. Letters of condolence had also been sent. One of the prisoners had been killed by a fallen tree and full details were to be sent to the relatives and friends of the prisoner on request. A Dutch inspector had visited the camp on 27 March, and complaints put to him by the committee had included the small size of the recreation ground; a prohibition by the camp authorities on concerts; no place set aside for religious services; objection to an order requiring prisoners to salute German corporals; the failure of the camp authorities to hire a piano for the prisoners; lack of accommodation for the committee's stores; the bad state of the latrines and washing places; and the striking of one Private Pike by a German civilian. The committee had also pressed the case of Private West, who the prisoners wanted to have recognised as the British chaplain but whom the authorities had refused to allow to preach. The secretary also reported that the committee had had to consider and adjudicate on a matter of principle, as follows:

> In April, when new prisoners began to arrive in numbers, the President of the French Committee offered to give us assistance with biscuits, etc. and he personally attended a meeting of our own Committee. At that meeting, it was decided gratefully to decline the French offer, but on their President

stating that his collection had already been made in two of the Companies it was arranged that two of our members should attend a meeting of the French Committee. The Grafenwöhrer French whose representatives number five, pressed us to accept their offer, stating that it had always been their custom to help our wounded comrades who arrived at Grafenwöhr Lazarett. Our members felt that it was a matter which was too weighty for them to decide, and accordingly a special meeting of the Company was held on 1st May, when the new men were asked for their opinions. They were unanimous in declining the kind offer on the assurance that the Committee and old members of the Company would do their best for them.[30]

Another potential for collaboration between the national Help Committees took place at Chemnitz in 1917, when the French POW Committee there gave British POWs arriving back from Poland 1,772kg of biscuits, as these prisoners had received nothing for Christmas owing to their move.[31]

The control of the men by their own NCOs, together with their participation in running the camps through Help Committees, played a major part in reducing potential grievances. Yet despite measures to make daily life run as smoothly as possible, there were inevitably problems over discipline, often accompanied by complaints about unduly harsh punishments. An inspection of Villingen identified the case of a Lieutenant Vaughan, who was given six days' arrest for having written the word 'Boche' in his diary. He considered this excessive. For their part, the camp authorities justified the punishment on the ground that Lieutenant Vaughan *always* used the word Boche in his diary.[32] Punishments for escape attempts were a particular cause of concern. During a visit to Berg, the US inspectors found three officers awaiting prison in relation to an escape attempt – one was charged with bribery (he claimed that his £3 cheque for a guard was out of gratitude); the other two were charged directly with attempted escape and also for 'destruction of Government property', in relation to the tunnel they had cut.[33] There were also often problems over the length of time it took to bring prisoners to trial, thus involving inordinately long periods of confinement. Throughout the war, the Allies tried unsuccessfully to secure immediate notification of the arrest and charging of prisoners, and for the involvement of the protecting power in the trial itself. Allegations of summary punishment were also common, though not always substantiated. In February 1916, for example, *The Times* carried reports that two British POWs at Güstrow had been bayoneted by the Germans for smoking in a 'forbidden vicinity' and that one had died while the other was in hospital. A US inspector arrived at the camp unannounced and spoke to prisoners privately. He also visited the camp lazaret for signs of a bayoneted prisoner. He found nothing to substantiate the report and concluded, 'On the whole the camp struck me as being as nearly as ideal as it is possible for a place of detention of this kind to be.'[34]

The harshest conditions were, in fact, experienced by prisoners when working outside the camps. By far the majority of prisoners in Germany either worked outside the parent camps during the day or were permanently based in outside camps. According to one source, out of the 1.6 million combatant POWs in Germany in 1916, at least 1.2 million (75 per cent) were employed in production industries, especially agriculture.[35] Another source states that at least 1.1 million POWs were at work at the end of 1916, of whom 340,000 worked in industry and trade, and over 630,000 in agriculture.[36] The conditions in agriculture were generally good and the work popular with the prisoners. In the smaller farming communities, notices were posted making it an offence for German civilians to communicate with the POWs, and the farmer would then be made officially a military guard of his prisoner workers. In most cases, the prisoners would actually live in the assembly hall of the village inn rather than on the farm. Typically, between thirty and 200 POWs would be housed at night under a guard comprising an NCO and from two to six men. The arrangements were so popular that POWs rarely attempted to escape or requested a return to the parent camp. Those employed on other work were often less fortunate. Work on land reclamation projects was generally carried out under private sector contracts, where the employer had every incentive to complete the work quickly, at the expense of the welfare of prisoners.[37] As one inspector records:

> Then there were the marshes, where men stood in water knee deep all day long. I have authentic reports of large groups of men working in the open, who were not allowed to attend to the calls of nature for the entire day, on the pretext that a guard must be sent with each man and that guards could not be spared.[38]

Undoubtedly the least fortunate were those employed in the German coal and salt mines. Few would volunteer for the unpleasant and dangerous work of mining in civilian life. Prisoners working in the mines had to be pressed to do so – 'beaten into submission' according to the Government Committee, which commented:

> There is no doubt that in fact, though not ostensibly, work in the mines is inflicted as a punishment, and that when the selection of prisoners for these *Kommandos* is made at the parent camp, the choice falls first on those who have incurred the displeasure of the commandant or his subordinates.[39]

In addition to the work being hard and the conditions being inevitably unpleasant, a particularly nasty practice in the deep mines was for the military guard to remain on the surface while the civilian foremen, or *Steiger* (who were armed), took their place below. Assaults and physical ill-treatment were common. Although inspections by the German military should have been able to curb any excesses, such inspections were usually announced in advance and their impact thus rendered ineffective. Men were also frequently asked – and British prisoners frequently refused – to work on munitions. In some instances they were punished for this refusal but in most cases their views were respected. The US inspectors nevertheless found POWs stamping shell cases and working for explosives manufacturers. In one case reported by the inspectors, prisoners refused to work on the construction of a Zeppelin hangar and were tried and sentenced to twelve months in prison.[40] These and similar cases clearly breached the Hague Convention prohibition on employing prisoners in connection with the operations of war.

While the US and subsequent neutral inspectors undoubtedly had some impact in curbing the worst excesses of the working camps or working parties, the task confronting them was formidable. Some civilian employers tried to resist inspections by claiming that 'trade secrets' were at risk, resulting in endless to-ing and fro-ing between the inspectors and the Army Corps Districts, with the inspectors taking the general view that if an inspection was being resisted it was because the employer had something to hide.[41] They tried to counter this by increasing the frequency of inspections in those specific cases. But the biggest problem was the sheer number of places to be visited. At one stage, in the 6th Army Corps District alone there were 18,000 working camps, of which 3,000 contained British POWs.[42] The US inspectors considered, nevertheless, that the use of prisoners for labour was in their best interests and that over time the problems would be ironed out:

On the whole the effect of work on the prisoner of war was for good. Conditions for the great majority of prisoners were reasonably good, and the prisoners both mentally, morally and physically better for having some purposive work to do. Evils that grew out of the peonage system would have been corrected in time by frequent inspections by neutral embassies, and the desire on the part of the military authorities to be relieved of the criticism and trouble which protests from the above sources would involve.[43]

Unlike combatant POWs, civilian internees were not required to work. But many of the problems they faced in everyday life, especially the tedium, were otherwise the same. The plight of British internees in Germany, all of whom were ultimately held at Ruhleben, particularly captured the imagination of the British public and press, partly because as civilians they were regarded as the innocent victims of war, and partly because many of those detained were especially well-to-do and articulate. Ruhleben Camp was situated on a racecourse some 6 miles from Berlin and was almost exclusively British. For a large part of the war about 4,500 internees were held there, though this reduced to about 2,500 towards the end, following exchanges. The internees comprised about 42 per cent business and professional classes, 23 per cent unskilled and other, and 35 per cent captured merchant seamen.[44] While the conditions were not unduly harsh, they were far from comfortable. The prisoners were accommodated in stables on the racecourse, the grandstand being unsuitable for this purpose. There were continual complaints in the early days about poor conditions and overcrowding, with prisoners being accommodated six to a loose box 11ft square. Not only did the men have to sleep in these loose box 'dormitories', but they also had to live and eat in them as well.

As in the case of the camps for combatant prisoners, the quantity and quality of food was also the cause of recurring complaint. The British Government, and the US on its behalf, pursued this question doggedly, with the German Government typically responding with attempted, albeit irritated, reassurance. In reply to an approach by the US Embassy in Berlin in January 1915, the German Government pointed out that the diet provided centrally was supervised by the camp doctor, examined daily by an officer and prepared by experienced cooks; while not inspiring, the diet was adequate:

> The annexed general bill of fare, which covers the first three weeks of January, is not perhaps as varied as one would wish in normal times; but it will

certainly be admitted by every discriminating British inmate of the camp at
Ruhleben that, in the face of the attempts of his own Government to starve
the German people, the bill of fare offered is above criticism.

The reply also pointed out that though alcohol was forbidden throughout
the camp, milk, mineral waters, butter and other things eaten with bread
could be purchased. And prisoners certified by the doctor to be suffering
from stomach or intestinal diseases were also permitted to cater for themselves at the casino within the camp, where the prices were moderate 'and
the food, of which the officers and non-commissioned officers in charge
of the camp also partake, is good'.[45] Reporting in March 1915, two British
internees released from Ruhleben as unfit added further comfort by noting
that conditions at the camp had improved considerably following the sack-
ing of the catering contractor and the bringing of the catering in-house:
'The German authorities provide the bread which is better quality than
formerly. The allowance is over half a pound per man per day, i e more than
the civil population is allowed'; and:

> The meat is inspected by two of the prisoners, one a veterinary surgeon and the
> other a butcher; it is cooked by ships' cooks who are interned, and served by
> men chosen from among the prisoners. The food is said to be well cooked and
> the meals quite appetising, at any rate when compared to the previous régime.[46]

Despite this, the Ruhleben diet continued to cause concern within the UK
to the extent that in April 1916, the US arranged for Dr Alonzo E. Taylor,
a food expert from the University of Pennsylvania, to visit the camp and
report back. Dr Taylor produced three reports, one dated 1 May 1916,[47]
and two others dated 24 May and 1 June 1916, following a sharp reduction
in the amount of foodstuffs allotted to the camp.[48] The nub of Dr Taylor's
findings was that, on its own, the quantity of food provided by the camp
authorities would have been insufficient to provide an adequate diet if
shared between all the prisoners. Many of the men, however, received food
parcels from outside – there were some twenty-three British organisations
sending food into the camp. Thus, without knowing how the food parcels
from outside and the food provided by the camp authorities were actually split between the men, it was impossible to know whether individually
they were receiving adequate nourishment. Dr Taylor suggested that the
two governments should agree how to deal with this between them, leading

the British Government to try, unsuccessfully, to secure agreement to sending bulk food supplies to the camp. For their part, according to Gerard, the German authorities were so incensed at Taylor's suggestion that they were providing a 'starvation diet' that they forbade him to re-enter the camp.[49] But as to complaints about the quality of the food provided, rather than its quantity, one US inspector at least had no doubt about where the real truth lay:

> The objection of some of the men, usually stokers, and men of the labouring
> class, to some of the food appeared to be unreasonable. The kitchen com-
> mittee, who had control of the preparation of the food, was composed of
> exceptional men. What these men had to put up with in scurrilous criticism
> from some of the lower orders in the camp in return for their unselfish
> devotion to their self-imposed task, I am afraid, will not be included in the
> tales of Ruhleben.[50]

The organisation of daily life within the camp was left very much to the men themselves. The prisoners elected a captain for each of their various barracks and the captains collectively elected one of their number as camp captain, or *Obmann*. The camp captain acted as the link between the camp authorities and the prisoners, and the camp authorities also allowed him to visit the US Embassy at least once a week.[51] Gerard records that uniquely among the prison camps, the internees at Ruhleben refused to carry out the daily cleaning and other domestic work of the camp, leaving the camp captain having to pay a number of the poorer prisoners to do this out of funds provided to Gerard by the British Government. Gerard was also able to pay poorer prisoners 5 marks a week to buy additional food and luxuries from the camp canteen.[52] Without the distractions of work and outside visitors – the German Government refused to allow women visitors, and men only with special sanction[53] – the need to make camp life tolerable on a day-to-day basis became even more pressing. The efforts of the internees to achieve this in accordance with 'the spirit of Ruhleben' became legendary. An internal postal service was set up, with prisoners paying for stamps, and thoroughfares were given names from home. 'Bond Street', for example, housed a number of stores such as a tailor's shop, a watchmaker's and a shoemaker's. Gentlemen's Clubs were formed, with one of the poorer prisoners paid to act as steward, and newspapers and magazines were established, such as the *Camp Daily News* (nicknamed the *Daily Daily*) and the monthly *Ruhleben Camp Magazine*. The more educated prisoners within the camp held classes for the less educated; the camp library held over 5,000 books; and there was a reading and meeting hall provided by the YMCA.

As elsewhere, theatre, cinema and sport also provided major diversions. Early on a dramatic society was formed, its first performance (of Shaw's *Androcles and the Lion*) taking place at the beginning of 1915. Admission was free, with seats costing between 20 and 40 pfennige, not according to their seat but according to the means of the purchaser. Another society gave plays in French and a third put on operas in conjunction with the camp orchestra. (On New Year's Day 1916, Gerard attended a performance of *Cinderella*, and in early 1917 a performance of *The Mikado*.)[54] Another popular pastime was walks in the country, though for a time this privilege was withdrawn because of unfavourable reports given by the internees to the press about conditions within the camp. Sport inevitably occupied the time of many, with a number of prominent sportsmen among the internees playing a key role in organising events. Association football was the most popular game, the 'Ruhleben FA' having been formed by F.B. Pentland, of Middlesborough and international fame, who was its president. Other professional footballers involved were Stan Wolstenholme, Everton; Jack Brearley, Spurs – both internationals – Percy Hartley, Preston NE; and Steve Bloomer, Derby. The league comprised two divisions, each of twelve clubs. International matches were tried but had to be dropped because Scotland, Ireland and Wales had too few players to contend against England (not, however, before Scotland had defeated England 3-2 on New Year's Day, 1916). There were nine tennis courts, rented at £50 a season. A club was formed with 200 members, including Logie of Dresden, who had British parents and who had played for Germany at Wimbledon before the war. The Ruhleben golf course was laid over three football pitches and consisted of five holes, 'barren of grass', the longest being about 200 yards, the shortest being not more than 30. The putting greens were all sand, rolled as hard and level as possible. Membership of the club grew to over 500, of whom 'very few save the 38 original members had seen a real course let alone played on one', and all of whom were 'golf fiends, of which, strange to say, sea captains and engineers were the most fiendish'.[55] Other sports included boxing, fencing, wrestling, gymnastics, hockey, baseball and cricket.

Nothing could fully alleviate the unwelcome and uncomfortable conditions of camp life for men who were forced to stay at Ruhleben, sometimes for years. For some, food and housing continued to be a problem. But despite the undoubtedly genuine concern of the British public, press and government, there is little evidence of any deliberate attempt by the German Government to make life more uncomfortable than necessary for the internees. To the maximum degree possible, the men themselves were allowed to control daily life within the camp, even to the extent that the military guard was ultimately moved outside to guard the perimeter, leaving internal policing in the hands of the camp police department under the charge of the camp commandant and committee.[56] The camp commandant, Graf Schwerin, and his deputy, Baron Taube, were sensitive to the needs of the prisoners and played a full part in the life of the camp, including, for example, making a point of being present at all entertainments organised by the prisoners and making a short speech of thanks at the end. According to one of the inspectors, Graf Schwerin 'not only did everything possible under the circumstances to mitigate the lot of the interned, but co-operated in every way in carrying out any suggestion from the men or their committee which would make for their peace of mind or for their comfort'.[57] For his part, Gerard commented that it was 'impossible to conceive of better camp commanders than Graf Schwerin and Baron Taube'.[58] The consensus seems to be, as another author put it, that despite the adverse propaganda, the internees at Ruhleben survived adequately, if not comfortably.[59]

# 10

# DAILY LIFE IN THE UK

There was no direct equivalent to Ruhleben in the UK. Sheer numbers ruled out concentrating all civilian internees in one camp. The two largest camps for interned civilians were both located on the Isle of Man: at Knockaloe near Peel, and at Douglas. The remaining internees were held in camps around the country, sometimes (on a segregated basis) in camps also occupied by combatant POWs. Knockaloe was the principal civilian camp. It was purpose-built, eventually having accommodation for 25,000 men.[1] By the middle of 1916, the camp housed about 20,500 prisoners allocated between four 'camps' within the main camp. Of these, some 17,000 were German and 3,500 Austro-Hungarian, with a small number of Turks and others making up the remainder.[2] As in the case of the other civilian camps, the Home Office was responsible for administration and the War Office for security. Day-to-day management was made easier by the internees being formed into companies, the members of which elected their own 'captain', whose job it was to maintain order and to act as a liaison between the men and the camp commandant. According to one source, the internees at Knockaloe comprised 10 per cent 'bourgeoisie' and 90 per cent 'proletariat'. (One compound – presumably included in the latter – was set aside for a large number of German pimps who had accompanied their prostitutes from Hamburg to London before the war. The prostitutes themselves had been repatriated with the other women and children shortly after the war began.)[3]

A report by the Army Council dated 7 August 1915 discussed problems at Knockaloe.[4] The report noted that it was not yet possible to find accommodation at the camp 'for those who consider themselves of superior class'. The report also referred to the forthcoming introduction of a 'new scale of dietary', to bring Knockaloe into line with other camps. As far as canteen prices were concerned, these were 'no higher than IOM generally'. The report concluded by referring to 'a great deal of trading and gambling among the prisoners'. Some had apparently openly sold articles given charitably. Bulk supplies into the camp were accordingly to be restricted in the future. The Austro-Hungarians seem to have been particularly affected by the shortcomings. In November 1915, one Frederick Nettel wrote directly to US Ambassador Page comparing Knockaloe unfavourably with a camp for British prisoners at Grossau, Lower Austria.[5] Nettel alleged that instead of being given a proper mattress, pillows, blanket and a sheet, about half the prisoners at Knockaloe were still lying on the floor on straw sacks. No pillows or sheets had been supplied, only three shabby blankets. The heating was inadequate, with half the huts having no heating at all; bathing space was too cramped, with only shower bathing possible; the floors in the bathing area were concrete with no boards; vegetables were practically non-existent; and exercise provision was inadequate – the prisoners being allowed on to the recreation ground only two or three times a week. The huts had been built on a newly ploughed field which rain quickly turned into a quagmire; the camp was also seriously overcrowded, with ninety prisoners being housed in each hut and, 'Whereas the British prisoners at Grossau are segregated, we have in some instances to share huts with niggers, who are neither our countrymen nor our allies'. Further complaints were received during November, some via US Ambassador Page and some from the internees directly. Amongst other things, these alleged that the huts were not waterproof and that some had no heating fuel.[6] At the end of November, thirty-four Austro-Hungarians from Compound V at the camp sent a petition via the American Embassy to the FO, which concluded: 'The statement made in the press that we are treated according to the rules laid down by the Hague Convention is not a fact and the treatment meted out to us leaves in every way much to be desired.'[7]

While clearly attempting to offer comfort, a report by the Lieutenant-Governor of the Isle of Man, also at the end of November, seems to indicate that there was substance in at least some of the internees' complaints.[8] This stated that water drainage existed throughout the camp and 'adequate' latrines were provided; it went on to say that new lavatories for fifty POWs to wash at one time were being constructed. Similarly, unlimited coal was supplied for the water boilers, which were under the charge of the prisoners. But the report then continued that the existing two large stoves in each hut were to be replaced by six smaller ones, indicating a need to improve the heating. The shortage of beds also seems to have been acknowledged by a statement in the report that new beds were presently being made by the prisoners themselves at the rate of 2,400 per week. By mid-1916, there had clearly been some improvement, with the US inspectors noting that not only the accommodation but also the sanitary provision was better than at the last inspection. In particular:

> The incinerator for refuse has been done away with. Refuse is now thrown into the sea from a high cliff at a short distance from the camp, where it is rapidly carried away by the tide, and the garbage is carted far away into the countryside and used for purposes of manure.[9]

Catering was also now satisfactory:

> The canteens are run by the Isle of Man Government, which gives a certain percentage of the profits to the interned men ... This money is turned back into the kitchens for extra food at the rate of £2 per week per compound. The kitchens and the food were examined and we found nothing to criticize.

But faults did still exist:

> In the isolation hospital we found only one bath and one tap for all the patients who are suffering from various sorts of contagious diseases. We took this matter up with the proper authorities, who assured us it would receive their attention. The sanitary arrangements in all the hospitals might be improved, except, possibly, in the hospital in Camp I, which was originally the main hospital for the camp.

All in all, the inspectors found that things were now much better: 'The whole tone of the camp is much better than it was at the time of our last visit ... There were fewer complaints, and the prisoners seemed much more contented.' Despite this, Knockaloe continued to attract attention. In October 1916, Mary Pankhurst submitted a petition to the government on behalf of the internees about the continuing poor conditions there.[10]

Conditions at Douglas seem to have improved considerably after the riot there in November 1914, discussed in Chapter 4. On 1 May 1916, there were 2,744 internees held at the camp – 1,968 German, 759 Austrian and 17 Turkish and other. By then, Douglas had been split into two 'camps' – the upper camp, consisting of two compounds, and the lower, or 'privilege' camp. The privilege camp housed some 500 men who had the advantage, amongst other things, of being allowed to have servants. The servants were obtained from the poorer men in the upper camp. There were 100 men acting as servants in May 1916. The men in the privilege camp contributed financially to their own maintenance. The tariff was 12s 6d per week for board and half of a tent; 12s per week for board and a third of a hut; and 10s per week for board and a third of a tent. The US inspectors noted that those men occupying tents in the privilege camp did so 'at their own desire'. They also noted that the camp library now held 5,000 to 6,000 books. There were no serious complaints. About 85 per cent of the internees at Douglas worked as servants, cleaners, tailors, dentists, gardeners and artists; a large number also went out every day to work as labourers on neighbouring farms.[11]

In contrast to Ruhleben, encouraging civilian internees to work became a widespread practice in the UK, with organised industries eventually being established for this purpose. Brushes were made at Douglas and Islington, employing 600 people at industrial rates, which they were allowed to keep less a reduction for maintenance. Sewing machines were made at Hackney Wick, designed to drive out cheap German imports. In 1917, a scheme was introduced at Knockaloe under which furniture was made for the inhabitants of recaptured areas of France.[12] A unique arrangement operated at Libury Hall German Farm Colony at Ware in Hertfordshire. The colony had originally been founded by Germans in England to provide temporary work and shelter for unemployed and destitute German-speaking men, in order to give them a fresh start or to enable them to earn sufficient money to return home, as an alternative to 'habitual begging, with its concomitant, moral degradation'. During the war, the Home Office interned civilians at the colony while allowing it to continue to run along the original lines. For each of the men interned there, the Home Office paid the charity a fixed sum for board and lodging. There was no military guard at the camp and the men were given every opportunity to work on the farm in return for a wage. At the time of a US inspection in mid-1916, the camp comprised nine staff, twenty-nine original pensioners and colonists (many of whom had their wives and children in the camp) and 159 wartime interned civilians. The interned civilians were mainly older men, most with wives in England and not wishing to return to Germany. All the prisoners were found by the inspectors to be content and in good health.[13]

Civilian prisoners elsewhere also seem to have been treated well. In early 1916 the camp at Cornwallis Road, Upper Holloway, north London, which held 714 prisoners, was given a very clean bill of health by the inspectors. The entire camp was run by the prisoners themselves through a camp committee, assisted by sub-committees on canteen, kitchen, workshop, bedroom, wages and relief. Sleeping accommodation was neat and clean, well lit, well heated and well aired. The kitchen was served by one chef, one assistant, four carvers, six potato peelers, twelve washers-up, six bakers and two turnspits – all German. The kitchen was found to be neat and clean, and the food excellent. There were 600 men at work at the camp, of whom some 500 were paid. Their work included tailoring, shoemaking, making international postbags, carpentering and woodcarving. Some acted as waiters, hairdressers, cleaners, general managers of the camp, musicians, painters, lecturers and teachers. For recreation and exercise there were 3¼ acres of ground for walking, skittles, a gymnasium and three billiard tables. The inspectors found no complaints of any kind, observing:

> There seems to be no criticism to be made of this camp, and the fact that the only guard consists of a sergeant and four policemen, and of there having been no attempts to escape, shows that the prisoners appreciate their comfort and good treatment here ... There are no cells at this camp, as none have been needed.[14]

There were no problems either at Alexandra Palace, housing nearly 3,000 civilians: 'The men are now very busy making arrangements for Shakespearean performances to celebrate the tercentenary of Shakespeare's death, and these are to take place before long.' And: 'Work is constantly being done to make the life of the men interned here more agreeable.'[15]

It is clear that, overall, civilian prisoners in Great Britain were treated reasonably, if not always well. Work and recreation opportunities helped relieve the boredom and, unlike Ruhleben, visits were permitted, though this facility was far from generous. War Office instructions allowed each prisoner two visitors a month at the same time for fifteen minutes. This rule could be varied by camp commandants and, in recognition of the particular travelling difficulties to the Isle of Man, special arrangements allowed each visitor on to the island every three months, during which stay they could make three camp visits, each of a half-hour's duration. Such hardships as did exist for civilian prisoners were most likely to be those inevitably associated with internment or simply the result of poor management within the camps. In fact, many outside the camps thought that the internees were being treated too well, being shielded from the restrictions, discomfort and food short-ages increasingly faced by the indigenous population, and being better fed than British prisoners held in Germany.

The locations used to house combatant POWs varied greatly. Unlike Germany, accommodation availability, rather than close proximity to manu-facturing or other 'work' centres, was originally the sole determining factor. It was not until 1916 that combatant POWs were used as a matter of policy to provide labour to aid the war effort. There had been a consistent reluc-tance to do this for a number of reasons. The number of prisoners held by the British was far less than that held in Germany, and the potential contribution they could make to the economy was correspondingly less. Though the War Office claimed to support the idea of using prisoners for labour, the British military, which controlled the camps, were in practice reluctant to get involved in non-military activities. Private sector employ-ers did not want to get involved in the management of prisoners, and the public did not want to see jobs that had been vacated by enlisted men filled by the enemy. The trades unions saw prisoner labour as a general threat to jobs and established terms and conditions. There had been a number of attempts to make progress, but with little success. In reply to a parliamentary question on 24 April 1915, the government reported that schemes had been put forward with the assistance of the Local Government Board for work in the neighbourhood of camps, but the local authorities themselves were reluctant to start non-urgent schemes. They wanted to keep such schemes for 'times of distress'. The reply noted that a number of prisoners were, nev-ertheless, employed on clearing ground and making roads in the south of England, and on the Isle of Man and near Hawick they were engaged in preparing the ground for their own hutments. A suggestion that prisoners might be used to construct the Clyde canal was simply noted for subse-quent investigation.[16]

Little progress appears to have been made nearly a year later when, in March 1916, the government admitted that of the 13,821 German military and naval prisoners held in thirteen camps in Great Britain at the time, only 'some' were employed in their local neighbourhood and were paid at the same rate as British soldiers, while 'others' made mailbags for 6*d* a bag. It was hoped to employ 'large numbers' shortly on forestry clearance and quarry-ing.[17] Later the same month, however, against the face of mounting disquiet over the failure to use prisoners to plug the growing labour gap, the government admitted that there were still no central rules on the employment of POWs. Apart from some minor works on roads and, for example, the erection of barbed wire around the camps, little use was made of them. Newton vented his own frustration about this in the House of Lords on 22 March:

> I am quite prepared to confess that in my opinion the situation generally as regards the employment of prisoners is by no means satisfactory, and I agree with my noble friend that it would be difficult to conceive a more ludicrous spectacle than that which is afforded to us at the present moment. Here we are, with an alarming scarcity of labour throughout the country, imploring women to come to our assistance, whilst there are thousands of able-bodied prisoners in this country who are doing very little work at all ...
>
> I have been informed that in the past the Government did endeavour to employ these men and made proposals with regard to their employment. I believe they approached the railways, but the reply of the railway people was that they did not want to have anything to do with prisoners. They tried mining. I believe they were told that the miners would have nothing to say to them at all. Then they fell back on the docks, and when the question of employing them was raised I believe that petitions were received by the Admiralty and by the War Office, and that as a climax the men who represented the Dockers' Union said that the men would have nothing to do with them. Then, again, it was suggested frequently that they should be employed on public works, but in every case there has been opposition proceeding from either the employers or from the trade unions ... But I am not at all satisfied that sufficient efforts have been made to employ these men.[18]

Newton's comments were inevitably met with questions about who was running the country – was it the government or the trades unions? But he was right in replying to these that the matter was more complicated than that. As late as September 1916, the Adjutant General placed before the Cabinet a memorandum reporting that some 5,332 combatant prisoners were now employed in the UK, mainly on timber cutting and quarrying, out of a total of 17,694 available for work; this compared to 8,097 employed in France (see Chapter 7). The memorandum set out a number of reasons why employing POWs in the UK was difficult, most of which from this distance, seem hardly convincing. In comparison to employing prisoners in France, which had been done since earlier in the year, the memorandum argued that the population density in the UK meant that there was less space for employing prisoners on the land. It argued that the hostile attitude of the population towards Germans also worked against their employment. Guarding requirements were excessive – a recent party of 135 prisoners employed on timber felling had required a guard of seventy men. And then there was the 'feeling' of the Labour Party. While the Adjutant-General saw scope for the employment of large numbers of prisoners on national land reclamation and road-building schemes from the following spring, the overall tone of his memorandum was markedly less than enthusiastic.[19] The rapidly deteriorating manpower position nevertheless provided the final impetus for positive action. At the end of the year the government decided to allocate all suitable POWs to agricultural labour. A Cabinet paper records that, in view of the urgent need for agricultural labour, the 'Prisoners of War Employment Committee' had resolved at its meeting on 22 December that 'all suitable prisoners of war, both military and civilian, who have had any experience of agricultural work should be allotted to the Board of Agriculture and Fisheries unconditionally except for the approval of the War Office on points of technical detail'.[20]

The subsequent 1917 harvest was accordingly assisted by a labour force of 30,000 POWs, under the supervision of 350 agricultural committees.[21] By the end of 1917, the total available POW labour force had grown to 70,000, including 2,000 NCOs (officers and senior NCOs were exempt). Those not employed in agriculture were given jobs mainly on construction works, timber cutting, road building and land reclamation (especially in the fens). Within the parent camps, those not capable of heavy work manufactured such items as mailbags, thermometers and brushes. (There was even an experiment in getting prisoners to manufacture glass eyes, but this had to be stopped when the only colour available was a bright blue which was not popular among the POWs.) Despite the major shift in policy on the use of POWs for labour, by the end of the war the number in work remained at about 67,000, leaving almost 97,000 POWs in the United Kingdom still unemployed.[22] In terms of economic efficiency, this remains in poor contrast to the more proactive policy adopted by the German Government from the outset.

Daily life within the parent camps mirrored closely that in Germany. As in Germany, the prisoners were given a great deal of autonomy in controlling their own day-to-day affairs, thus enabling efficiency and morale to be more easily maintained. At Leigh, in Lancashire, a US inspector was particularly impressed at the role played by the German NCOs in securing the smooth running of the camp:

> This camp seems to me to be noteworthy on account of its great neatness and cleanliness, and on account of the general good health of the men consequent thereon, and also on their regular exercise in the open air.
>
> It is conducted on strictly military principles, but the men, being soldiers, seem to understand this. They are under the charge of their own Feldwebel, who are trusted by the Commandant, and who have an excellent influence over the men under them.[23]

Camp recreation, also like Germany, featured sport and exercise heavily.[24] At Leigh, there were two fields in which the men were 'obliged' to drill and do exercises three times a week. Sports included 'fistball', football and baseball. There was also a 'tank' for swimming in the summer. At Shrewsbury, route marches took place four days a week. There was also a field of 90 square yards and a compound of 50 x 40 yards for hockey and football. Gymnasium equipment was provided for exercise, with parallel and horizontal bars, dumb-bells and boxing. Officers at Dyffryn Aled had 4 acres of 'playground', which were unrestricted from 9.30 a.m. to 12.30 p.m. each day, and also from 3 p.m. to 5 p.m. on Sundays, Tuesdays and Thursdays. On the other four afternoons, the field was opened to the servants for exercise: 'On these afternoons, a certain number of interned officers may teach their servants games, if they feel so inclined.' The officers also had available to them an enclosed compound of about 3 acres, available from 9.30 a.m. to 6 p.m., and a bathing pool. The new system of outside walks introduced at the beginning of 1916 also provided a particular pleasure and source of satisfaction for officers. Unlike Germany, however, the walks were not always well received by the local population and often had to be taken early in the mornings to avoid confrontation. At Holyport in Berkshire, some twenty-five prisoners were taken out on 'each clear day', conducted by an unarmed British officer and a British orderly. On passing The Eagle, a public house on their return route, the practice grew among the prisoners to salute the inn sign in recognition of the eagle as the German national emblem. This practice annoyed the local population to such an extent that they finally changed the name of the public house to 'The Belgian Arms', which it has retained to the present day.

Camp life was punctuated by the usual concerts and opportunities for study. In the larger camps, there were also camp newspapers produced by the prisoners themselves. At Handforth, the *Handforth Camp Prisoner of War Newspaper* seems to have been issued every few days.[25] The newspaper was produced by the prisoners in manuscript and contained remarkably detailed and up-to-date information about the progress of the war – such as tonnage and other details of U-boat sinkings and detailed maps of Verdun. The issue dated 23 March 1918 even contained reports of the Spring Offensive launched only two days earlier. The newspaper also contained articles on policy and economics, etc., as well as day-to-day information such as the ending of summer time. The series included a Sunday newspaper, given out by the *Christliche Verein junger Männer* (YMCA). In contrast to Germany, and like civilian internees, captured officers also enjoyed the privilege of being able to receive visitors, a privilege often exercised in a surprising way, as elicited by a parliamentary question about Donnington Hall in April 1915.[26] Asked whether inmates there were allowed visits from 'English girls', the government replied that:

> any prisoner may, with the permission of the commandant, be visited once a month by not more than two persons at a time. These visits take place in the presence of a member of the staff. No rules have been laid down as to the age or the sex of the visitors.

A subsequent parliamentary question elicited the information that between 1 January and 19 April 1915, thirty-four passes for male visitors and thirty-five passes for female visitors had been issued at Holyport; six passes for male visitors and ten for female visitors at Bevois Mount; four passes for male visitors and four passes for female visitors at Donnington; and at Dyffryn Aled five passes had been issued to males and seven to females.[27]

None of this is to say that there were no complaints. Some of these were fairly humdrum and easily dealt with. Prisoners at Leigh, for example, complained to the US inspectors about the heating (which was subsequently improved); about the practice of them being shut in their dormitories from 4.30 p.m. until morning (which would be changed with the onset of lighter evenings); and about parcels being opened before delivery (dealt with by ensuring that a German prisoner would in future be present to oversee their opening). Specific incidents also gave rise to individual complaints. At Stobs, near Hawick – regarded by the US inspectors as one of the better camps along with Leigh – one 'A. Schierling, POW 5253, Camp A, Hut 2', was moved in April 1916 to write the following:

To the American Embassy

The undersigned ventures to lay the following complaint to the American Embassy. On January 28th last for reasons unknown to me a sentry standing outside the camp fired into the camp. I was already in bed so cannot have been the cause of the firing. Through the carelessness of the sentry in question my suit and overcoat were riddled. The coat had 2 holes, the waistcoat likewise 2 and the overcoat 7 which rendered my suit entirely unwearable. I at once complained to the Commandant here and was informed after a long enquiry that my claim for damages of £6 was refused. I was not satisfied with this decision so with the consent of the Commandant I sent a written complaint direct to the War Office who however rejected my rightful claim and advised me to arrange to have my clothes repaired.

I should be grateful to the American Embassy if they would approach the British Government on my behalf and secure the recognition of my assuredly justified claims.

My unwearable garments are meanwhile at the disposition of the British Government.

The War Office reply to this complaint, dated 3 May 1916, merely observed: 'this matter was thoroughly investigated at the time of the occurrence and the [Army] council decided that justice in this case would be fully met by repairing the prisoner's clothes at the public expense.'[28]

Some of the complaints were much more serious. Just as Minden in Germany attracted a reputation for being a 'repression' camp, so did Brocton, Staffordshire. One ex-prisoner wrote after the war: 'I don't think England was ever more roundly cursed than at Brocton. It is known among all the prisoners as the worst and the most hunger-stricken. We lay in barracks where the dampness ran down the wall, with the thermometer down to freezing, without coal.' And:

At Brocton … fifteen of us, all on crutches, came together in a barrack. The commandant, who had himself been in German captivity, tormented us to the utmost. We men on crutches had to scrub and carry water just like the others. And if we didn't he would lock us up … The Commandant sometimes shot into the floor next to us. When he felt like doing so, he would furnish no coal, or post a notice 'Meals will be omitted today'. Our mail would be held back until the contents of the packages were spoiled.

Another wrote about the punishment facilities at Woking:

> A cell with stone floor, whitewashed walls and a small barred window. A small table, a chair, shelf and bench were the furniture.
>
>   Not a sign of heating apparatus. And next the window was a kind of air hole, an opening through which the icy January wind could whistle unhindered ... When the English believed they had caught a particularly hard boiled sinner, they would have a special remedy ready for him, the so-called special cell. It was of such size that one could not lie down in it, only crouch, and instead of a door was barred with iron so that the inmate was fully exposed to the weather. Handcuffs and manacles were used according to the whims of the men in charge, quite like in the middle ages ... Some of our guards came from English prisons, criminals mostly, whose character could be read on their faces ... if they did not report a certain number of offenders each day, they themselves would be punished ... The commandant was a German-hater, unscrupulous and brutal.[29]

To what extent, if any, these claims are exaggerated is not possible to determine now, but the collective evidence suggests that what is alleged to have happened at Brocton was far from typical. For the most part, prisoners in the United Kingdom – both civilian and combatant – appear to have been treated humanely, if not always to the highest standards. Like British prisoners in Germany, there were undoubtedly lapses and some cases of hardship and ill-treatment. As one German ex-prisoner noted:

> Naturally, there was much to find fault with [in the British camps], but it was generally due to lack of organisation, not to hatred, and except for isolated cases, was not caused by brutality or the desire to vent one's spleen on individuals who were in no way responsible for the war.[30]

Or, as observed by *The British Prisoner of War* magazine in its final edition: 'We should never forget that whether the prisoner is treated in strict justice or with gross cruelty and injustice, his lot is a miserable one.'[31]

# 11

# EXCHANGES, INTERNMENTS & AGREEMENTS

The question of exchanging incapacitated combatant prisoners first arose just four months into the war. While stipulating that the sick and wounded should be treated as POWs, the Geneva Convention provided for belligerents to agree (if they wished) arrangements for their repatriation or, with the agreement of the government concerned, their internment in a neutral country. Such arrangements made obvious sense in the case of seriously sick or wounded prisoners whose condition made them unfit for further service and, at the prompting of the US Embassy in London, the British Government formally proposed an exchange of military and naval prisoners in this category in December 1914.[1] At about the same time the Pope proposed independently the exchange of prisoners incapable of further service.[2] From this arose a scheme covering both combatant and civilian prisoners which provided for prisoners to be selected for exchange on the basis of a detailed list of qualifying injuries and conditions agreed by the medical authorities on both sides. The practical arrangements for the exchanges were to be made by the Red Cross, which would accompany the German prisoners to the place of handover and then return with the British. The scheme met with only modest success. The first exchange, securing the return of 107 British prisoners, took place via Switzerland in February 1915.[3] A second exchange took place at the end of June. The scheme then effectively stalled, with only a few exchanges subsequently taking place, at least in part because of the practical difficulties involved. Apart from the practicalities, a particularly unsatisfactory feature of the scheme was that tuberculosis was excluded from the list of qualifying conditions. This exclusion was decided on the basis that prisoners might subsequently recover and become fit for further service. But the fact remained that while in the camps sufferers could not be fed or looked after to the standard required by their condition.[4]

The Pope intervened again in the summer of 1915, this time suggesting the internment in Switzerland of prisoners who were only partially inca-pacitated. While the British War Office was opposed in principle to such a scheme on grounds of practicality and the opportunities it presented for escape, this position was undermined when France and Germany adopted the proposal and carried it forward under a bilateral agreement, with the first internments under the scheme taking place in January 1916.[5] This ena-bled the Foreign Office to override War Office opposition and to reach agreement with Germany on a similar basis in late March. Like the Franco-German scheme, the Anglo-German agreement provided for the respective costs of internment to be met by the parent government. The first group of 304 British internees, including thirty-two officers, reached Switzerland on 28 May 1916. According to *The Times* they were met all along the way by large crowds, with nearly 10,000 people there to meet them when they arrived at Lausanne at 5 a.m.[6] To deal with the problem of possible escapes, the Anglo-German agreement provided for prisoners to go to Switzerland 'on parole', with the respective governments agreeing to return to Switzerland any of their interned prisoners who might escape. And like the earlier scheme for the repatriation of incapacitated prisoners, eligibility for internment was based on a detailed list of agreed qualifying conditions. Again tuberculosis was excluded from the list, as were psychiatric conditions.

Decisions on who could be sent to Switzerland initially rested with a roving commission of Swiss physicians (the 'Itinerant Commission') who visited camps to assess possible candidates, with prisoners themselves being free to apply for consideration. Those selected were then sent either to Lyons or Constance for examination by a Control Commission, which included representatives of the detaining power – two medical officers and an official.[7] Those rejected by the Control Commission were periodically re-evaluated. In contrast to the earlier repatriation scheme, the scheme for internment was highly effective. By the end of 1916, there were some 26,990 prisoners interned in Switzerland under the combined Franco-German and Anglo-German agreements – 8,487 German and Austrian, 16,637 French and Belgian, and 1,866 British. This number effectively stabilised throughout the rest of the war, with some 27,077 being held in internment at the end of 1917 and 25,614 at the Armistice.[8]

Internees in Switzerland were generally housed in hotels, boarding houses and sanatoria. British internees were sent to Murren and Chateau d'Oex, as well as to a number of other camps scattered elsewhere. At Chateau d'Oex, the officers occupied cottages and were allowed to be joined by their families – there were no guards. The object of internment was seen to be twofold, first to get prisoners back to health and then to ensure that when they returned home after the war they were able to play a full part in the social and economic life of their community.[9] To this end they were expected to work and were categorised by the Swiss authorities according to their skills and physical abilities: Category 1 prisoners were those deemed to be incapable of any work; Category 2 were capable of light work around their own accommodation – barbers, tailors, shoemakers, etc.; Category 3 prisoners undertook similar grade work outside (often in small shops set up by the relief organisation *Pro Captivis*, which manufactured slippers, shoes, tags, etc.); Category 4 were deemed to be capable of resuming their pre-war professions and were often employed in private concerns regulated by the Swiss Government; Category 5 were appointed to learn a new trade; and Category 6 (very few in number) were allowed to attend classes at secondary schools or universities.

In practice much of the work allocated via the Swiss authorities was strongly criticised by British internees on grounds that it was excessive, tedious and unpaid – effectively that they were being used as cheap labour. One author has suggested that the reason for this was the very large pro-German element in Switzerland.[10] The reality seems to have been more complicated, since the initial operation of the scheme attracted much criticism beyond that relating simply to working conditions. Some internees took the view that they should not be required to work at all, though all the governments involved considered this essential for their morale and general mental and physical wellbeing. Other complaints ranged from allegations of generally poor medical treatment and lack of cleanliness in hospitals, through to unduly harsh disciplinary punishments handed out by the Swiss military authorities. Reports were also received of widespread drunkenness among the British internees.

Such was British concern about all this that Colonel Lord Edward Cecil visited Switzerland between 23 March and 15 April 1917 to investigate. Cecil's subsequent report dealt comprehensively with the conditions he had found there.[11] He noted that while the Swiss Government had done its utmost to assist, the large number of internees arriving in the country had caught them to some extent unprepared. The fact that the camps were widely scattered had caused management difficulties, while their location was not always ideal. The camps at Murren and Chateau d'Oex, for example, had been chosen because these locations were frequently visited by British tourists and the local population was therefore more likely to be able to understand the needs of British internees. But in practice the sites were not suitable. They were steep and impractical for many of the crippled and injured, and were snowbound for many months of the year during which the internees had little to do. These factors tended towards discontent, depression and intemperance. Cecil found that problems over medical treatment had often arisen because local doctors had no military experience, while hospitals in Switzerland were generally less clean than those in Britain. There was no suggestion that internees were being singled out and Cecil recommended that British nurses should be sent to Switzerland to help. As far as punishments were concerned, Swiss military discipline tended to be harsher than that in the British army. Resentment caused by this had now been largely overcome by British officers recommending appropriate punishments in individual cases. These recommendations were generally endorsed by the Swiss authorities. Cecil found that the amount of drunkenness among British internees had been exaggerated. While there was undoubtedly too much drinking, the situation was not alarming when considered against the background of loss of morale due to confinement followed by a sudden easing of conditions, idleness and large amounts of money now being received from home.

Overall, the tone of Cecil's report was sympathetic to the Swiss authorities, laying the cause of many of the problems at the feet of the internees themselves: 'Though for the most part the patience and pluck of the interned are admirable, as one would expect after all they have gone through a proportion of the officers and men are not in normal condition and they are irritable, inclined to exaggeration, and difficult to deal with.' And at a meeting on his return:

> It was quite evident that the mentality of the majority of the prisoners was not normal. They had suffered so long and so severely that many had become self-centred, irritable, and had lost their sense of proportion. Their complaints, therefore, require to be received with a certain amount of reserve.[12]

Cecil pointed out, nevertheless, that all those involved would still have preferred Switzerland with all its defects to staying in Germany. He also agreed with the internees that some of the work that they had been required to undertake had been unsatisfactory – for example, 'making useless articles fit only for a charity bazaar'. He noted that the position had now improved, with better co-ordination being studied by a Dr Garnett, late technical instructor at the London County Council.

Within the UK the Ministry of Pensions and the War Office were also looking for improvement, pressing for the extension into Switzerland of the network of training centres that had been set up in 1917 for maimed or disabled men discharged from the services. When they were unable to secure Treasury finance for this, the Red Cross agreed to take things forward on their behalf. The resulting scheme managed by the Red Cross, though modest in terms of numbers, was well supported by British industry. Firms offered to train men at their own expense and then to employ them at union rates. By 1918, firms supporting the scheme included Brinsmead, the pianoforte manufacturers; Worrall, leather manufacturers of Birmingham; and Davis, leather bag manufacturers of Hackney. The Watch Section of the London Chamber of Commerce donated money and undertook to provide work. A school for motor mechanics was established, with the magazine *Autocar* meeting the entire costs. The range of skills being covered by training included carpentry and piano work (34 men), cabling, telephone and switching work (18), leatherwork (84), watch repairing, painting and drawing (20) and motor mechanics (43).[13]

How to deal with physically fit combatant POWs was much more difficult. In previous wars it had often been the practice to exchange prisoners, either head for head or on the basis of agreed formulae which weighted the numbers exchanged according to their rank. There were a number of factors inhibiting this approach in the present war. One of the US inspectors put the blame squarely, if not entirely accurately, on Germany. He argued that the prisoners held by Germany represented too valuable an asset as a source of labour, especially for food production, to give up lightly.[14] This was particularly important for Germany because the war effort had soaked up a large proportion of its own agricultural labour force at just the same time as the Allied blockade was putting evermore pressure on it to increase its internal food supply. An all for all exchange would clearly be to Germany's disadvantage because it held the greater number of prisoners. A head-for-head exchange would also be to Germany's disadvantage because a greater proportion of the men held in Germany were trained than vice versa, and the British Government was reluctant anyway to use prisoners as a source of labour. On top of all this, as has been noted previously, the food of the British POWs in Germany was largely provided by food parcels from Britain, while POWs in Britain were well looked after by the authorities.

Views within Britain were, as ever, divided. Papers advocating an exchange, circulated by Asquith to the Cabinet in December 1915, picked up on the point that British POWs in Germany were largely supported by food parcels from home and that the practice was likely to increase, while German prisoners in the UK were mainly fed and clothed 'at the expense of the British taxpayer'. Extending the economic argument into a case for exchanges on humanitarian grounds, the Foreign Office expressed concern that the conditions for British prisoners in Germany would become intolerable as the blockade strengthened its grip, noting that currently their treatment from the point of food was better than that of the German civil population. The Foreign Office was also concerned about the incidence of tuberculosis among British prisoners, citing a 90 per cent death rate in one German sanatorium. In response, the War Office simply told the Cabinet that the military authorities were firmly opposed to any exchange of prisoners in good health, thereby ensuring an end to any immediate prospect of progress.[15]

The Cabinet again returned to the theme in June 1916, when Grey circulated a Foreign Office paper analysing the current position of British prisoners in Germany, this time proposing a scheme for the internment of physically fit combatant prisoners in a neutral country.[16] The paper noted that the quality of treatment of British prisoners in Germany was mixed. Those employed in mines and coal yards were being treated with brutality. Those in agriculture or the parent camps were being treated reasonably well, but even then German NCOs could be rough and brutal and were responsible for whatever ill-treatment took place. These considerations argued for the internment of all prisoners in a neutral country. But the Russian and French Governments were also likely to want to join in a scheme of this sort, which would result in numbers too great for a small neutral country to accommodate. The paper then acknowledged the more obvious point that the German Government would in any event be unlikely to agree any large scheme because of the use they made of prisoners for labour. Even if they did agree to a large scheme, it was likely that it would only be on a 'head-for-head' basis which, at the time of the paper, would result in them holding a residue of 10,000 British prisoners whom they could treat as hostages. For all these reasons, the Foreign Office concluded that the best chance of success would be to propose a more modest scheme involving only those prisoners who had been wounded or had recovered from a serious illness such as typhus, and those who had suffered the privations of captivity the longest, say those who had been captured in 1914. Like the earlier one, this initiative also failed to make progress, becoming enmeshed in the Cabinet with the question of civilian exchanges. It was effectively buried by being referred to a small committee for decision.[17]

The problem continued to run on, with the Foreign Office sustaining their search for ways to secure relief for British prisoners and the War Office persisting to obstruct any suggestions. In September 1916, for example, the Foreign Office reported to the Cabinet that the War Office had at first looked encouragingly at a recent proposal to intern 5,000 of the longest held prisoners on each side in Denmark; only for this to be turned down finally by the Secretary of State for War. Some progress was made in the first part of 1917, when agreement was reached with the German Government to repatriate from Switzerland any interned prisoners found to be unfit for further military service. Even at this stage, however, the War Office held firmly to the view that in a war of attrition any exchanges and repatriations would do nothing but help the enemy (see also Chapter 1). In a letter dated 11 June 1917 to Colonel Picot, the officer in charge of British POWs in Switzerland, Lt Gen. Sir Herbert Belfield wrote rejecting a Swiss proposal for the repatriation of internees cured of tuberculosis in the following terms:[18]

As a matter of principle we are opposed to all these exchanges, repatriations and such like on the broad grounds that we regard this very largely as a War of attrition, and every man we send back to Germany, unless seriously incapacitated, although not perhaps himself able to fight will release someone for the front.

It may be said that we shall score equally with Germany, but we consider that our business is to put as many Germans as possible out of action as we can, and to keep them out of action, and that any other course is, in fact, most inhumane, as it means a prolongation of the War. If after you have got three parts of the way through a game of chess each can agree to put back on the board a similar number of pawns it may be that neither side has gained any advantage, but it unquestionably prolongs the game, and when that game is a War of the present magnitude it means a vast amount of misery and death. From our point of view it is eminently unadvisable that this should be allowed.

It is for this reason among others that we do not accept the Swiss proposal for the repatriation of those who have been cured of tuberculosis, and it is for this same reason that we always hesitate to adopt any step which, although seemingly [replacing 'ultimately', crossed out by original author] humanitarian, is, we believe, in effect exactly the reverse.

I must ask you not to make any official use of this letter, but it is just as well that I should explain to you the general lines of the policy that we have adopted. It may be that if the French and German Governments come to some definite agreement opposed to our views on the subject we may have to give way, but I must say I hope that will not be the case.

Despite these firm sentiments, a major and astonishing breakthrough was to occur a little time later when, in an extraordinary development, the British and German Governments agreed to face-to-face discussions to be held at a specially convened conference at The Hague. For the belligerents to meet in this way, not for the purpose of securing an armistice or peace but in order to progress the daily business of war, was inevitably controversial; arousing considerable opposition and bewilderment in the UK. In an exchange in the House of Commons on 28 June 1917, Bonar Law tried to take some of the steam out of the opposition by arguing rather pointlessly that the people attending the conference were not representatives of the government, but 'representatives of the official staff'. Nor had it been necessary to give them special instructions as to how to treat the German representatives there or what the 'civil relations' should be, leading Commander Wedgwood MP finally to ask: 'Were they to kiss them on both cheeks?'[19]

Despite its controversial nature, the Hague Conference, which lasted from 25 June to 2 July, was surprisingly successful in moving things forward and tidying up along the way a number of issues that had been troubling the two sides. The British delegation comprised Lord Newton, Lt-Gen. Sir Herbert Belfield and Sir Robert Younger. They negotiated with General Friedrich, head of the German POW Department, assisted by Major Draught and Dr Eckhart. The conference was chaired by the Netherlands' Foreign Minister. The resulting agreement covered both civilian and combatant POWs and provided for a more lenient approach to be taken towards prisoners suffering from disabilities.[20] New and more relaxed schedules were to be drawn up of ailments or disabilities qualifying for repatriation or internment in a neutral country. These were to include a very new category of mental illness attributed to the effects of long periods of incarceration. Acknowledgment of this new form of illness had been growing for some time as initial concerns about the physical well-being of prisoners gradually gave way to concerns about their mental well-being. A doctor attached to the Swiss Legation in London, Dr A.L. Vischer, who visited the camps at Knockaloe and Douglas in May 1917, found that prolonged internment had caused in many prisoners what he called 'barbed wire psychosis', a condition characterised by 'a gradual loss of memory, irritability and continued concentration of the mind on certain aspects of camp conditions'.[21] The condition had also been identified elsewhere, and was sometimes referred to as 'barbed wire fever'.

The name which stuck, however, was 'Barbed Wire Disease' – described by another contemporary observer as 'a well-recognised form of neurasthenia caused by confinement for long periods in barbed-wire enclosures'.[22] Under the agreement, prisoners suffering from Barbed Wire Disease who had been in captivity for at least eighteen months became eligible for internment in a neutral country. If a considerable improvement was not discernible after three months of internment, they would then become eligible for full repatriation. To make room for the influx of new internees which would result from the agreement, those already interned who would need a long time to recover were to be repatriated following examination by Swiss doctors. A proviso was also included that anyone repatriated under the agreement would not be employed 'on any front of military operations or on the lines of communication or within occupied territory'. In another major breakthrough relating to fit combatant POWs, it was agreed that all officers and NCOs who had been in captivity for eighteen months would be interned in a neutral country. (Other ranks were excluded at the insistence of the German negotiators, as presaged by the British Foreign Office in its paper to the Cabinet the previous year.) Finally, in order further to ease the pressures of internment in Switzerland, the Netherlands agreed to take 16,000 German and British internees at the expense of the captor governments. As before, Britain and Germany agreed to return to the Netherlands any internees who escaped. Ratification of the Hague Agreement by both governments was announced in the House of Commons on 27 July 1917.[23]

Prisoners returning to the UK under the 1917 agreement became a major focus for celebration. The February 1918 issue of *The British Prisoner of War* reported the arrival of the second batch of prisoners at St Pancras on 20 January 1918, to the sound of sirens, horns and cheering. The prisoners were met by a collection of dignitaries and subsequently handed individual cards by the 'Prisoners' Reception Committee' conveying a message from the king: 'The Queen and I send our heartfelt greetings to the Prisoners of War of my Army on your arrival in England. We have felt keenly for you during your long sufferings, and rejoice that these are ended, and that the New Year brings you brighter and happier days.'

There then followed a speech by Lord Sandwich about the opportunities being developed for the prisoners' rehabilitation, such as the training in diamond cutting already underway in Brighton for servicemen who had lost their legs. The proceedings were concluded by a distribution to the men of chocolates and cigarettes and in addition, for the Australians, 'little bunches of wattle'.[24] The ceremony for returning prisoners further developed. For the third batch, arriving at St Pancras on 23 February 1918, the GOC London District gave permission for the Guards' Band to play on the platform. As before, the men were greeted with motor horns, sirens and cheers, against the fear that the proceedings might be interrupted by an air raid. The band played 'patriotic tunes and familiar airs, such as "Home Sweet Home"', and the men were presented with 'little bunches of primroses, the most English of wild flowers', along with the King's Card of Welcome.[25] On 26 February, HRH Princess Mary visited recently returned prisoners at King George's Hospital, handing out chocolates and cigarettes. She was accompanied by Adeline, Duchess of Bedford and Chairman of the Prisoners' Reception Committee, who made a speech welcoming the men home. A little later in the year, the newspapers were given permission to disclose in advance the time of arrival of British prisoners from Germany, which on Whit Sunday evening resulted in a large crowd gathered to welcome them, forming 'an avenue of human beings' stretching from St Pancras to the Tottenham Court Road.[26]

Despite the progress made under the 1917 agreement, pressure continued within the British parliament, the public and the Church, for a full-scale repatriation. This was to a great extent born out of concern for the civilians held at Ruhleben, but not exclusively so. The government resisted this pressure, arguing amongst other things the need to remain in step with France over repatriation. This position was undermined in early 1918, however, when the French and German Governments reached a further bilateral agreement on exchanges. The main features of this latest agreement were an 'all for all' repatriation of NCOs and men between 45 and 48, and all those between 40 and 45 with three children; and a 'head for head, grade for

grade' repatriation of NCOs and men who had been in captivity for eigth-
een months. Officers in the categories covered by the agreement were to be
interned in Switzerland rather than repatriated. In all, some 330,000 French
and German prisoners were affected. This development forced a change
in the British Government's position, and on 28 May 1918, Lord Newton
told parliament that negotiations were now about to begin at a new Anglo-
German conference at The Hague, with the objective of reaching a similar
agreement to that secured by the French. Discussions would be conducted
urgently, but the issues were complex, not least because of the practical
difficulties of transporting prisoners across the sea. Almost as if to reinforce
the point, one of the ships accompanying the British delegation to the
conference – the hospital ship *Koningin Regentes* – sank during the cross-
ing on 6 June. There were thirteen persons injured but all on board were
saved and transferred to the hospital ship *Sindoro*, on which the delegation
itself was travelling, in order to complete their journey. Though it was never
established whether the *Koningin Regentes* had struck a mine or had been
deliberately torpedoed, its crew believed the latter.[27] An ironic side-effect
of the incident was that it resulted in the immediate stoppage of all repatriation sailings. The Dutch line concerned only agreed to reinstate them
shortly before the Armistice.

The British delegation to the 1918 conference comprised Sir George
Cave, the Home Secretary, Lord Newton and Lt-Gen. Belfield. As before,
the delegation was supported by Dame Adelaide Livingstone, secretary
to the Government Committee.[28] The conference lasted from 8 June to
14 July. The event caused something of a stir locally, with a 'Concert for
Legations of the Entente' being staged at The Hague by interned British
prisoners, on Ruhkhen, on 17 July. The programme unselfconsciously
included Bach's *Double Violin Concerto* and works by Schumann. A stir was
also created at the conference itself by the behaviour of Cave. In an address
to the British prisoners interned in the Netherlands, Cave made comments
which caused offence to the German delegation and led to a suspension of
the negotiations. These were only resumed after the issue of an 'explanatory'
communiqué. The conference also coincided with an upsurge of anti-alien
agitation in Britain, leading Lloyd George to recall Cave to London early
The official reason given for his departure was the need to deal with a
number of important questions in London, and the need for him also to be
on hand to take the Cabinet's views on the discussions as they proceeded
and to relay their instructions to the delegates. There were suggestions that

these events created an unhelpful atmosphere and that the terms of the final agreement suffered as a result.[29] The agreement was, nevertheless, more far reaching and comprehensive than any that had gone before.[30]

The 1918 agreement at long last got to the question of able-bodied other ranks. It provided for NCOs and men who had been in captivity for eighteen months to be repatriated, 'head for head, rank for rank'. The earlier provision in the 1917 agreement for the internment in a neutral country of officers and NCOs who had been in captivity for eighteen months henceforth applied only to officers. Excluded from this new provision were petty officers and men of submarine crews, who were to be interned in the Netherlands rather than repatriated. All combatant POWs who were currently interned in the Netherlands and Switzerland were to be repatriated 'all for all'. There then followed elaborate provisions to ensure the repatriation of a further batch of British combatant POWs, should this be necessary to secure an overall balance of British and Germans repatriated, taking into account the separately agreed 'all for all' exchange of civilians. As far as sick and wounded prisoners were concerned, the new agreement at last recognised tuberculosis, with those suffering 'curable' tuberculosis qualifying for internment and those suffering from 'incurable' tuberculosis qualifying for repatriation. The schedules of qualifying conditions and illnesses also now required the medical authorities to take a lenient view of cases of nervous debility ('psychasthenia'). To give effect to its provisions the agreement then set out, in elaborate detail, the arrangements to be made for transporting all the prisoners concerned and the order of their internment or repatriation. The further day-to-day planning and administration of the transport arrangements was then delegated to a Transport Commission, meeting at The Hague, and comprising one Dutch representative and two representatives of each of the contracting governments.

The Hague Agreements of 1917 and 1918 together went further than simply dealing with exchanges and internments. Face-to-face meetings presented the ideal opportunity to discuss many other issues which had become contentious. Procedures agreed at the 1917 conference for giving notice of the intention to carry out reprisals have already been recorded in Chapter 7. Also at the 1917 conference consideration was given to reducing delays in the delivery of parcels. In response to a complaint by the British delegation that delays were often caused in Germany by excessive censorship, with parcels sometimes being examined as many as three times on their way to prisoners working away from the parent camps, the German delegation argued that such censorship had become necessary because many parcels contained items of sabotage. As a way forward they suggested that both governments should publish simultaneous and mutually agreed statements in their national and in the neutral press to the effect that 'the including of articles of sabotage in the parcels addressed to combatant and civilian prisoners of war is deprecated and disapproved of by the Government as being contrary to the interests of the whole body of prisoners of war'. This would minimise the need for censorship and enable the standard practice in future to be for all parcels to be censored only at their final destination. For its part, the German delegation raised concerns about the treatment of 'youthful prisoners', proposing that, subject to reciprocity:

> those British subjects who are youthful and who are captives in German hands, shall be separated from the rest of the prisoners of war and put in a separate block in one camp by themselves. They shall be kept away from all unfavourable influences to which they might be subjected by being brought in contact with adult prisoners of war. Their further education and instruction shall also be provided for.

The question of punishment for escape attempts and other offences had become a matter of particular concern to the Allies and occupied time at both the 1917 and 1918 conferences. The legal principle was clear. The law to be applied in dealing with offences committed by prisoners was to be the army law of the capturing state. The practical problem was that the provision had an unduly harsh effect on Allied POWs because of the inordinately strict German military tradition. Sentences inflicted on many British prisoners in Germany were far in excess of those imposed for corresponding offences in the UK, giving rise to much public concern. There were also concerns about the length of time it often took the German authorities to bring offenders to court, with the effect that the sentences ultimately handed out were in practice substantially extended by the time already spent on remand. In line with a similar agreement reached between Germany and France, the German delegation at the 1917 conference agreed to a British proposal to deal with the immediate problem by remitting all existing punishments on either side from a date to be agreed. Although the British proposal related specifically to combatant prisoners, the final draft of the 1917 agreement provided for the remission until the conclusion of peace of all punishments inflicted on both civilian and combatant prisoners for offences committed between the date of capture and 1 August 1917. A note annexed to the agreement also recorded a commitment by General Friedrich to instruct the various commands on his return to avoid delays in bringing prisoners to trial. The specific question of punishments for escape attempts was looked at in detail at the 1918 conference. The Hague Convention provided that unsuccessful escapees could be punished (though successful escapees should not be punished for their escape if they subsequently returned to the front and were captured again). The punishments meted out to unsuccessful escapees in Germany were often harsh, with additional punishments also sometimes being inflicted for attempted escape during arrest by the civil authorities. Agreement was therefore reached at the conference to set the maximum period of detention for a single escape attempt at fourteen days, or twenty-eight days for escapes attempted in concert with other prisoners. In the case of attempted escapes involving or giving rise to damage to property (e.g., tunnelling), the maximum period of confinement was set at two months. The agreement also provided specifically that:

> Prisoners of war recaptured after an attempt to escape shall not be subjected to any unnecessary harshness. Any insult or injury to such prisoners shall be severely punished. They shall be protected from violence of every kind. In particular, officers recaptured after an attempt to escape shall be treated in a manner suitable to their rank.

Finally, the agreement specifically forbade collective punishments on account of the misconduct of individuals.

The 1918 conference went on to address the thorny question of prisoners working in the war zone. With both sides clearly unwilling to give up the benefits of such labour, they agreed instead to send officers from their respective War Offices to examine the conditions of POW labour in the war zone. These officers were to talk to the local commandants with a view to rectifying abuses and improving the lot of the prisoners. 'Detailed and conscientious' reports of the conditions discovered during the inspections would then be prepared by both sides and exchanged via the protecting power. Other more detailed issues were dealt with in the annexes to the 1918 agreement. The British Government had for a long time expressed concern about the treatment of officer prisoners held in the German Tenth Army Corps district.[31] In contrast to the generally satisfactory treatment of officers by the German authorities at that stage of the war, those held at

Clausthal, Ströhen, Schwarmstedt and Holzminden were alleged to have been subjected to an 'organised system of coercion'. The fault was laid by the British Government at the door of General von Hänisch, who had been appointed GOC Tenth Army Corps at the beginning of 1917. Hänisch and other officers under his command – Niemayer at Holzminden and his twin brother at Clausthal – were described as arrogant and offensive British haters. There were complaints that their prisoners were subjected to harsh and punitive regimes, overcrowding and 'the removal of their furniture'. Excessive punishments were introduced for attempting to escape. Claustal had been a good camp but was no longer; at Ströhen the bayonet was used to intimidate, not in consequence of any insubordination; Schwarmstedt was unsanitary, with poor food; and at Holzminden 'there were many hardships'. For their part, the German authorities had their own complaints about the conditions at the British camps at Dyffryn Aled and Kegworth, and other camps for officers. Following discussion at the conference, the German delegation agreed to remove British officers from Holzminden and Clausthal to camps outside the Tenth Army district, and to cease using these camps for British officers in the future. The British delegation agreed generally to meet the causes of the complaints by the German authorities and to allow any German officers at Dyffryn Aled to move to other camps if they wished to do so. (A subsequent report by the British Government Committee on the treatment of prisoners noted that following the agreement the camps at Ströhen and Schwarmstedt were eventually closed and that General von Hänisch was ultimately removed from his command.)

The bold and unorthodox step of holding face-to-face discussions with the enemy clearly paid dividends in breaking the logjam of arguments over repatriation and internment, as well as enabling major points of contention to be discussed and resolved. But an equally or perhaps even more important outcome from the historical perspective is that the belligerents also used the opportunity of the Hague conferences to set out a comprehensive and agreed set of rules for the future treatment of prisoners. Effectively, they rewrote the Hague and Geneva conventions, filling in the gaps and removing the ambiguities that had become apparent in the light of experience. Their starting point was a statement of the basic rights of prisoners in more specific terms than hitherto. Prisoners were to be treated humanely and protected from violence, insults or public curiosity; they had the right, if they chose, not to give information about their army or their country; objects of value were not to be taken from them; and on first capture they were to be brought back as quickly as possible to a collecting camp at least 30km from the firing line. Prisoners could not be compelled to do any work directly connected with the operations of war (though deliberately or otherwise the parties still failed to define 'operations of war', and in appearing to permit such work in the absence of objection actually weakened the provisions of the Hague Convention). Conditions of work were also amplified. Prisoners were henceforth not to work more than ten hours a day, six days a week, with Sunday being given as the day off wherever possible; in arriving at the ten-hour maximum, travelling time to and from work had to be included when the journey was over 1km; and prisoners were to have one hour for lunch. In allocating work, only prisoners who were physically fit and whose previous occupations did not render them unsuitable were to be employed in mines and quarries. And those working in mines and quarries were to do so under the same conditions as civilian workmen. Similarly, prisoners employed in operational areas were also to be physically fit and their general conditions were to be the same as those applying to prisoners held in the home territory.

The agreements also dealt with the procedures for running the camps, the physical standards of accommodation and the food clothing, and equipment to be supplied to prisoners. In outline, these provisions were very similar to the detailed regulations adopted by the German authorities early in the war. Agreement was reached on the minimum daily standard for rations – 2,000 calories per day for non-working prisoners, 2,500 calories for normal workers and 2,850 for heavy workers. (It is worth noting the comparison between these figures and the 2,700 calories +/- 10 per cent set out in the German regulations of April 1915.) The daily ration of bread was to be no less than 250g, with an additional 100g for ordinary workers and 150g for heavy workers. As to the quality of diet, the agreements stated, 'The daily rations of prisoners of war shall be sufficient in quantity and quality, especially as regards meat and vegetables, regard being had to the restrictions imposed on the consumption of food by the civil population of the country.' And, 'Combatant prisoners of war shall receive as far as possible the same allowance of the rationed articles of food as the civil population'. Every prisoner was to be given a full set of clothing – underclothing and boots, together with spares and, where appropriate, overalls – according to a detailed schedule laid down. Accommodation standards were set out in the greatest detail. Officers were to be given a minimum floor space per head of 12 square metres for general officers, 10 square metres per head for field officers and 6 square metres for captains and subalterns. Every general officer was to have one servant. Field officers were entitled to one servant between four, and captains and subalterns one between seven. 'Men employed as servants shall be physically fit in every way for the work and shall only work for officer prisoners.' And, 'The rations and other rights of the servants shall not be diminished on account of any gratuities or gifts in kind which they may receive from the officers'. For other ranks, 3 square metres per head were prescribed for dormitories or 2 square metres where bunks were utilised. A whole range of other detailed issues were also covered, from heating and lighting, sanitary provision, the establishment of Help Committees in all camps with over 100 men, games and exercise provision, to dental and medical provision. Agreement even stretched to the conduct of roll calls and the provision of graves, and to the position of camp personnel who had abused their position.

The regime agreed between the parties represented the cumulative experience of nearly four years of war. It was clearly established in a constructive spirit with a view to securing clarity and the humane and equitable treatment of prisoners on both sides. But ironically it was to fall at the last hurdle. On reaching the final stages of discussion on the 1918 agreement at The Hague, the German delegation introduced the bizarre reservation that in their 'personal opinion' the agreement should not be ratified except on terms securing a satisfactory settlement of conditions for Germans in China, where the Chinese Government was threatening internment or deportation. Since Britain had no direct involvement in Chinese affairs, the British delegation insisted that this was not relevant to the discussion. Nevertheless, after the agreement had been signed by both delegations the German Government made it clear that ratification would not take place until the Chinese question had been settled. This decision caused anger in Britain, with some blaming Newton and Belfield for allowing the muddle to develop.[32]

But while the British Government was content for Germany to take the blame, it had its own problem over ratification which was not made public. This related back to the vexed question of submarine crews. As has already been mentioned, submarine crews were excluded from the repatriation provisions of the 1918 agreement, in favour of internment in the Netherlands. At the same time, all combatant prisoners already interned in the Netherlands and Switzerland were to be repatriated. Included in these were twenty-five German submarine officers interned in the Netherlands.

The British delegation held that this was a mistake, and that in the original draft of the agreement submarine crews had been specifically excluded from repatriation. This had been lost in the final version due to a 'printer's error'. When the agreement came before the Cabinet for agreement to ratify on 30 July 1918, the Admiralty objected. The First Sea Lord argued that the return of the submarine officers would give Germany a 'tremendous advantage': 'the return of twenty-five experienced submarine officers, available as instructors, would exercise an effect out of all proportion to their numbers.' The Cabinet decided that correction of the error should be pursued but that, if the German Government failed to concede, the agreement was so important that ratification should nevertheless go ahead.[33] It then took two months before a reply from Germany was received. In this the German Government not surprisingly refused any amendment to the agreement with regard to submarine crews, but at the same time reduced its demands over China following a decision by the Chinese Government not to proceed with internment or deportation. These were now reduced principally to asking for a general declaration by the British Government that it would allow Germans in China to return home if they wished.[34] At the ensuing Cabinet meeting on 11 October, the First Sea Lord again resisted ratification on the ground that the repatriation of the twenty-five submarine officers would have the effect of giving Germany an additional fifty submarines. This would result in Germany having about 183 submarines by the end of the year – more than ever before. However compelling this argument, the Cabinet again came down in favour of offering ratification of the agreement as it stood, not least because of the strength of public opinion. The minutes record that Bonar Law put in the ultimately decisive argument:

> Mr Bonar Law said that the House of Commons felt very strongly on this matter, and, should the Agreement not be ratified, the Government might find itself in a difficult Parliamentary situation. He understood that there were some 60,000 prisoners involved in the exchange on each side, and, if the Agreement was not signed, every relation of every prisoner in England would say that the Government had stopped 60,000 men coming home for the sake of twenty-five men.[35]

At last, naval and military considerations had to take second place to those relating to prisoners. But it was, of course, too late for the decision to have any effect. The role of the new regime was by now simply to provide a legacy for the future. In this respect it would sit alongside a similar agreement reached between the US and German Governments during a face-to-face conference held in Berne from September to November 1918. According to one observer, the US–German agreement represented 'the most thorough guide [on the treatment of prisoners] yet written'.[36] Ironically, this agreement was finally signed on 11 November 1918.

# 12

# THE ARMISTICE & REPATRIATION

Concern about the treatment of British prisoners increased substantially during the final months of the war. Reports coming before the British press, parliament and the government indicated that conditions were becoming worse and the treatment of prisoners more brutal. In the fast-moving battles following the Spring Offensive, and in the chaos and disorder of the final German retreat, this is perhaps not surprising. As already discussed in Chapter 7, concern within the Cabinet about the employment of prisoners within 30km of the firing line, their use in connection with the operations of war and their gross overworking in the salt mines, led the British Government to take its most aggressive stance in favour of reprisals throughout the whole of the war. In parallel with this, action was taken to ensure that any armistice with Germany would include provision for the immediate release of all British prisoners.[1] Cave announced this intention in the House of Commons on 29 October 1918.[2] When it came, the Armistice accordingly required the German Government to carry out the immediate repatriation, without reciprocity, of all Allied and US POWs. The detailed arrangements were to be prescribed later. All civilians interned in Germany were to be repatriated within one month. The return of German prisoners was to be settled 'at the peace preliminaries', though the repatriation of those interned in Holland and Switzerland would continue as before.[3] All agreements and treaties in conflict with the Armistice were annulled.[4]

The immediate effect within the German camps varied. In many, the authorities simply gave up and released the prisoners. In one camp, the guards took the prisoners to the local beer garden to celebrate. In others, the authorities tried to maintain discipline and carry on as before. This was often difficult because of disaffection amongst the guards, many of whom by this stage had donned red armbands out of sympathy with the Bolsheviks. Other more ingenious means were deployed to allow prisoners to go free, such as connivance in 'mass escapes'. The decision by many Germans to let their prisoners go free was not only borne out of an attitude of mind: Germany on 11 November 1918 was starving – the fewer prisoners there were to feed, the more food was available for the local population. In some instances, news of the Armistice took time to get through, or for practical reasons prisoners were forced simply to carry on as before. In one particular case, an ex-prisoner who had been working in a German mine reported that when the prisoners refused to carry on working after 11 November, they were told that unless they worked they would not get fed. Germany was desperate for coal just as much as for food, and the prisoners continued to work as paid labour until late December.[5]

At Ruhleben, the camp was already effectively under the control of prisoners at the time of the Armistice, following the appearance of red armbands among those guarding the camp. On hearing rumours of the Armistice, the camp 'captain', Joseph Powell, set off for Berlin, without any interference from the camp authorities, to consult the Netherlands Delegation as protecting power. On receiving details of the terms of the Armistice, Powell returned to Ruhleben and announced the news midway through a performance in the camp theatre. Following loud cheering, the audience allowed for the performance to continue.[6]

A flood of released, or 'self-released', prisoners quickly spread across Europe. Stories abounded of prisoners walking through their own lines in organised columns or catching public transport to the nearest French or Belgian town where they mixed freely with the local population before making for the coast. Such prisoners, if anything, hindered rather than helped the formal arrangements being developed for repatriation. Indeed, the scenes of released prisoners wandering towards freedom brought their own criticism of the German authorities, however culpable they actually were in individual instances. The situation near the front lines following the Armistice was described by *The Times History of the War*:

far more pitiable were those blue – and khaki-clad refugees who, after the armistice, staggered along the roads in passing to the rear. At every town on the front, from the far north of Belgium southward to where the mountains of Alsace overlook the Rhine, these thinly clad, shivering warriors, whose arms had not the strength of a child's, and who, if they could swallow a morsel of bread, thought themselves fortunate, crowded together in search of warmth and food. They had been let loose by their captors the Germans, who having underfed and maltreated them for months, cared nothing whether they ever reached the Allied lines or died on the way.

A more melancholy and wistful procession, men seldom saw. French, British, Belgians, Italians, Americans and Russians, all shared the horrors of that march. With sunken cheeks, with shoulders bent with fatigue and ill-treatment, with shrunken frames that made their uniforms look ridiculously ill-fitting in their abundant largeness, dressed in amazing collections of coats and caps, no distinction of nationality or speech was recognised, for the helpless helped the helpless whether Russian or Italian.

And:

They all told a similar story of hardships, of cruelty, and of underfeeding. The British had been mocked with the retort that if they were hungry the blockade was the cause, and towards them, the prisoners said, the Germans evinced a spite and malice which caused intense suffering. Many had come hundreds of miles from distant camps by boarding the trains, and many had walked 40 miles to reach the Allied lines.

The situation became so bad that action had to be taken: 'weeks passed before the stream of refugees began to slacken and then finally ceased, and it was only after Sir Douglas Haig had addressed a vigorous wireless demand to the Germans that the inhumanity of turning these men adrift came to an end.'[7]

Responsibility for the formal repatriation arrangements had been given by the Allies to a sub-commission on Prisoners of War of the Permanent International Armistice Commission. The sub-commission met quickly at Spa, with Major-General Sir John Adye representing the British. The German authorities were also represented. Details of the resulting scheme were published on 28 November. The sick and wounded were to be repatriated first. Germany was divided into four zones, with POWs being held at collection centres until Allied troops arrived to take custody. Five collection camps were established at Friedrichsfeld, Limburg, Darmstadt, Mannheim, and Rastatt. Prisoners in north and central Germany were to be sent to the Baltic and North Sea ports, such as Danzig, Hamburg, Bremerhaven, Rotterdam or Antwerp. They were then to be handed to a Commission of Reception of Prisoners of War, which allocated prisoners to individual transport vessels. POWs in southern Germany were to be sent by rail to Switzerland, where they were again to be met by Commissions of Reception. Those on the left bank of the Rhine were released to advancing Allied soldiers.[8]

The arrangements for the repatriation of British prisoners were further refined during discussions between the British Naval Attaché in Copenhagen and the Central Prisoners of War Committee (CPWC) representative there. Agreement was reached on the following targets for the repatriation of prisoners west of the Elbe: through Copenhagen and the Baltic Ports, 50,000 men; through Rotterdam, 50,000; through Switzerland, 4,500; and through the British lines and France, 41,000.[9] By 10 December 1918, over 70,000 prisoners – combatant and civilian – had reached Britain, with repatriation being carried out at the rate of 4,000 a day. The true scale of the task can best be seen in the European context. According to German records, there were 937,000 non-Russian Allied POWs in German custody at the end of the war. Of these, 476,000 were repatriated by 19 December 1918, and 576,000 by 30 December 1918. By 1 February 1919, repatriation was fully complete.[10]

Immediately following the Armistice, the CPWC had stopped packing individual parcels. At that stage, most camps in Germany indicated that they had enough by way of food supplies. But this was undoubtedly based on too optimistic a forecast of when individual repatriations would be carried out. By December, more food needed to be sent to the camps. Given that Germany was starving and that the Armistice had specifically provided for the Allied blockade to continue, the following – if generally known about – would clearly have been particularly galling to the civil population:

The Red Cross representatives in Berlin have arranged for the despatch from Rotterdam of complete trainloads of food supplies under an armed escort, and similar arrangements are being made for trainloads of bread and biscuits from Berne and Copenhagen. Very recent news received from Rotterdam shows that 14 or 15 car loads of foodstuffs are sent forward to the Camps and are, we trust, reaching the men.

The CPWC also reported at the same time (December 1918) that Mrs Bromley Davenport, who was in Holland, had with her some £30,000 worth of medical supplies and comforts, which were being distributed as required.[11]

Most returning British prisoners landed at Dover, Leith or Hull, where they usually received a rapturous reception. They would then be taken on to dispersal (or 'Reception') camps at Dover, Canterbury or Ripon, where they were 'entertained and given the largest amount of liberty that is compatible with the object of the authorities, which is to get them registered and "boarded" and despatched to their homes in the shortest possible time'. They were kept at the reception camps for about forty-eight hours, and then sent off on two months' leave.[12] Either on arrival at the docks or at the reception camps, all returning officers and men of the army, navy or mercantile marines were given the following message from the king, written in his own hand and lithographed:

The Queen joins me in welcoming you on your release from the miseries and hardships which you have endured with so much patience and courage.

During these many months of trial, the early rescue of our gallant Officers and Men from the cruelties of their captivity has been uppermost in our thoughts.

We are thankful that this longed-for day has arrived, and that, back in the Old Country, you will be able once more to enjoy the happiness of a home and to see good days among those who anxiously look for your return. GEORGE R.I.

For men who had already returned, the king 'had specially desired that this message should be sent to them through their own Care Committees, who were the bodies which had done most for their prisoners throughout the war'. For civilian ex-prisoners, the king ordered that his message of welcome should be read to them on landing by the mayor of the seaport town at which they disembarked.[13]

The CPWC also reported that the Prisoners' Reception Committee (Chairman, Adeline, Duchess of Bedford) had done its best to meet all trains with invalid prisoners coming into London – sometimes involving three or four trains a day, arriving at stations as far apart as Cannon Street, Addison Road, Charing Cross and King's Cross. There were also committees of ladies at both Hull and Dover, organised under the main Reception Committee. Lady MacDonnell was in charge at Dover and Lady Nunburnholme at

Hull. These committees provided 'amusements and comforts' for the men.[14] Such reception arrangements had a lasting impact on many of the prisoners. Private Cecil Bacon, who returned to Leith on a hospital ship from Copenhagen, recalled sixty years later how he had never forgotten being greeted at Leith by Princess Alice, with the words, 'I hope you will be all right soon my boy.'[15]

Returning civilian prisoners were also to be offered practical and financial help. Lord Sandwich, Chairman of the CPWC, told the House of Lords on 20 November 1918 that a 'strong' committee was being formed by the British Red Cross Society and the Order of St John to arrange relief and find employment for repatriated civilian prisoners. He noted that:

> This Committee will not in any way conflict with the excellent work now being carried out by the Central Charities Committee and Local Government Board. It is felt, however, that many of these men need further assistance than the existing organisations have power to provide. The new Committee will consist of a member of the Central Prisoners of War Committee, representatives of ex-prisoners of war from Ruhleben, one representative of the Mercantile Marine, and it is hoped one representative from each of the Government Departments concerned.

Funds for the scheme would be provided by the Red Cross and out of the profits from the 'Ruhleben Exhibition'.[16]

Plans for the 'Ruhleben Exhibition' had been in existence for some time. *The British Prisoner of War* reported in May 1918 that the CPWC had been asked by the POW Department to organise an exhibition of articles made by POWs at Ruhleben. The Chairman of the Handicrafts Committee at Ruhleben had written, 'hoping that the exhibits will make everyone in England realise that the Britishers at Ruhleben are full of courage in spite of terribly depressing surroundings and the unending character of the war.' (At the time of this approach, there was already an exhibition of drawings on display at the Carfax Gallery, Bury St James', by a Mr Wiggin, who had recently returned following three years' imprisonment at the camp.) Plans for the main exhibition took shape with a view to its opening at the RIBA in October. This had to be postponed following the detention in Berlin of eighty-nine cases of exhibits. The exhibition was finally opened at the Central Hall, Westminster, by Princess Patricia and the Duke of Connaught on 14 January 1919. The exhibition lasted for a month.[17]

The exhibition itself comprised hundreds of books bound in the camp school, utilising old gloves, boots and corduroy trousers; model ships – destroyers, submarines and cruisers – all in working order, with a dynamo installed at the exhibition so that the models could be seen actually running; and much hammered silverwork and bags and purses made from leather, some of which had been made from the skins of rats killed in the camp. In addition to the artefacts, a full model of Ruhleben Camp was on display:

> which has been executed and designed by a distinguished artist, an ex-prisoner, Mr Nico Jungman. He has taken immense pains about the construction of this model. Every building is exactly reproduced, thousands of miniature prisoners have been modelled by Mr Wiggin, trees have been made and planted, and barbed wire has been set up. Nothing could possibly give people who are unfamiliar with the look of a prison camp a better idea of its appearance.

The exhibition also included a full sized replica of one of the loose boxes which housed the men at the camp, including life sized wax figures donated by Mr John Tussaud of Madame Tussaud's. Refreshments were provided and music put on. To give those working during the day a chance to visit the exhibition, it was open from 11 a.m. to 9 p.m. each day. In encouraging maximum attendance, *The British Prisoner of War* noted:

> We ... hope that everyone who can will come to the Exhibition if only to show their interest in, and admiration for, the courage of their fellow coun-trymen, the civilian prisoners who, though prevented by circumstances from taking any glorious part in the war, or making the sacrifice of their lives, nevertheless have by their constancy and faith upheld the name of England to a hostile and contemptuous people.[18]

For German POWs, the circumstances following the Armistice were quite different. They had nothing to celebrate and had to remain in captivity until the coming into force of the peace treaty. During the intervening period they continued to be used for labour. Some of the work would cer-tainly have been questionable under the Hague Convention. For example, German POWs were often employed by the American military after the Armistice on the disposal of old munitions. This is in stark contrast to the high moral stance taken by the US during the war, when the general head-quarters of the AEF had issued an order – GO No 106 – that no enemy prisoners were to be kept in the war zone. This, according to one of their own inspectors, had been strictly enforced: 'While on a visit to the General Headquarters I was present when word was received that a few German prisoners were being employed within the forbidden zone, and orders were issued immediately to remove them.'[19] There was no such sensitivity after the fighting was over. On 18 June 1919, an explosion occurred during the course of munitions removal by prisoners, although on this occasion no one was injured. A more serious incident took place shortly afterwards, on 9 July, when an explosion killed twenty-five of forty POWs employed on munitions disposal, as well as one American soldier. A further eight POWs were injured. There immediately followed a strike by the prisoners, ultimately involving some 463 men, who argued that the work contravened international law. The imposition of a bread and water diet and confinement to barracks quickly quelled the rebellion.[20]

The peace treaty was finally signed at Versailles on 29 June 1919. The treaty provided (Article 214) for the repatriation of German POWs to take place as soon as possible, and for it then to be completed as quickly as possible. It required the German Government to meet the whole cost of the repatriation and to provide the necessary staff and transport. Subject to the agreement of the Allies, those who did not wish to go to Germany could be excluded from the repatriation, and the treaty forbade the German Government from taking 'exceptional or vexatious proceedings' against such prisoners or their families on this account. The treaty also stated that, 'The High Contracting Parties waive reciprocally all repayment of sums due for the maintenance of prisoners of war in their respective territories'. The balance of numbers worked overwhelmingly to the disadvantage of Germany in this respect, though the impact was fortuitously lessened by the arbitrary decision of the German Government during the war not to pay captured officers at full rates of pay, as required by the Hague Convention. The German delegation at the Peace Conference had, of course, simply to accept these provisions along with all the other terms being imposed on them. They had tried to negotiate the terms relating to prisoners, even to the extent of requesting that prisoners should be returned with new clothing because of the economic situation in Germany, but all such efforts had been unsuccessful.[21]

By mid-1919, those POWs held by Britain and the US had become a burdensome expense. In contrast, the French authorities had found the prisoners they held (some 350,000) to be a particularly useful source of labour, especially in clearing up the battlefields. Clemenceau, the French Prime Minister, accordingly proposed in August 1919 that Britain and the US should 'lend' their POWs to France to help out. Neither country thought that they could legally do this and argued instead for early repatriation. Clemenceau finally conceded and Balfour, the British Foreign Secretary, announced on 28 August that the repatriation of POWs held by the British would take place immediately, before ratification of the treaty (which ultimately took place on 10 January 1920). The first POWs were moved on 30 August and the exercise was completed by the end of October 1919. Those POWs held by the US (41,000) were repatriated in late September 1919.[22] The repatriation process was itself not without incident. The first trainloads of German POWs passing through Belgium were pelted with stones by the civilian population. Thereafter such transportation was only undertaken at night.[23]

# 13

# LEIPZIG: THE AFTERMATH

On numerous occasions during the war, the British Government threatened to bring to justice those committing war crimes. But privately it remained ambivalent about the practicality and the principle of achieving this. When Churchill wanted to threaten that the activities of captured submarine crews would be fully investigated after the war, and that 'no effort will be spared to bring home to the proper quarter the responsibility for the acts referred to', this was resisted by the Foreign Office.[1] Instead, Churchill acknowledged publicly that the situation was 'not free from difficulty', because the crimes committed by the submarine crews had not been foreseen in international law[2] (see Chapter 7). Towards the end of the war, the Cabinet rejected a suggestion that it should be made a condition of peace that anyone who had been responsible for the ill-treatment of British prisoners should be tried by a court of law. This was on the grounds not only that it would in practice be difficult to fix responsibility, but also because 'no nation, unless it was beaten to the dust, would accept such terms. If England had been badly beaten in this war, we should never agree to our officers being tried by German tribunals.'[3] In the event, for all practical purposes Germany was 'beaten to the dust', providing the opportunity to impose provisions that had otherwise been unthinkable. Article 228 of the peace treaty stated that: 'The German Government recognises the right of the Allied and Associated Powers to bring before military tribunals persons accused of having committed acts in violation of the laws and customs of war.'

This represented the first attempt to deal with war crimes through an international system of justice. Perhaps surprisingly, the German Government appear to have had no quarrel with the concept of bringing those alleged to have committed war crimes before international tribunals of neutrals; though it did try unsuccessfully during negotiations to mitigate the full effects by arguing that 'violations committed by nationals under the strain of war' should be forgotten, on the ground that such an amnesty had traditionally been included in peace treaties. It did, however, understandably take the view that any provision for dealing with war criminals should apply equally to both sides, which Article 228 clearly did not. This was to cause long-term resentment in Germany, both in principle and in its ultimate application. But from the point of view of the Allies the article formed part of the general desire to make Germany pay for all the ills of a war for which it was held to be solely responsible, including a determination to bring to justice all those who had committed war crimes. Public expectations in this regard had been conspicuously stoked by the British Government's repeated threats to bring war criminals to justice.

As soon as the treaty came into force, the Allies drew up a list under Article 228 of 900 people accused of committing such crimes. The list was presented to the German Government on 3 February 1920 – some fourteen months after the Armistice. Largely at the insistence of the French Government, the list included the names of many of the principal German naval and military leaders, such as von Tirpitz and von Hindenburg, as well as those accused of operational crimes or the mistreatment of POWs. The presentation of the list gave rise to an immediate protest by the German Government that if it were in practice to secure the surrender of many of those accused, the political consequences in Germany could be sufficiently grave as to bring down the government. Tempers had by this time cooled down, with many people now expressing concern about the general severity of the treaty itself. The Allied governments therefore agreed momentously to a compromise; a German proposal to try the cases against non-political alleged offenders themselves before the 'Supreme Court of the Empire' at Leipzig. This agreement was subject to the caveat that: 'If it should be shown that the procedure proposed by Germany did not result in just punishment being awarded to the guilty, the Allied Powers reserved in the most express manner the right of bringing the accused before their own tribunals.'[4]

In early May 1920, the Allies accordingly presented a shortened list of forty-five names for trial by the German authorities. Further difficulties were then faced. Some of those on the list had fled and could not be found (there had been attempts during the drafting of the treaty to introduce measures to arrest suspects, but these had failed). Also, the German Government pointed out that much of the evidence against the accused was actually in records held by the Allied and associated powers and was thus unavailable to them. At a General Conference held at Spa on 9 July 1920, the Allies and the US agreed to collect such evidence and to hand it to the German authorities. As far as the British cases were concerned, a volume of evidence was subsequently presented to the German Ambassador in London on 26 October 1920.[5]

The British Government chose to proceed initially with six cases from the list presented to the Germans. Three of these related to incidents involving German submarine commanders: the sinking of the hospital ship *Llandovery Castle* and its lifeboats containing the survivors (total loss: 234 lives); the firing on the hospital ship *Dover Castle*, resulting in the loss of six lives; and the killing of the crew of the SS *Torrington* by submerging the submarine which had sunk their ship while the crew was on its deck. The other three cases related to the ill-treatment of British POWs. Because some of the witnesses in these cases were either unwilling or unable to travel to Leipzig, arrangements were made for them to be interviewed before the Chief Magistrate at Bow Street, where the German Government was represented. In the POW cases, fifteen witnesses were interviewed at hearings which took place from 26 to 29 April 1921. The trials themselves then took place before a court of seven judges in Leipzig from 23 May to 16 July 1921. Although the British Government played no direct part in the proceedings, a British mission was attached to the trials, led by Sir Ernest Pollock, KBE, KC, MP, Solicitor-General. The accused had legal representation.

The first case to come before the court was the British case against Karl Heynen. Heynen had been in charge of British POWs at the Friedrich der Grosse coalmine in Herne, Westphalia, from October to November 1915. In civil life he had been a master cooper. He had also served in the army from 1895 to 1897, and then in the reserve. He had been called up at the outbreak of war to the Landsturm as an NCO. He was wounded in Russia and transferred from active service to look after POWs. The charge against him was that he had consistently ill-treated prisoners by knocking them about with the butt end of his rifle and his fists. While he was at the mine, complaints had already been made about his conduct, as a result of which he had been removed from the camp and court-martialled. He had been found guilty and sentenced to fourteen days' 'medium arrest', suspended until the end of the war. This sentence was set aside by the Leipzig Court, pending its own judgement. Though not the most serious of its kind, the case had been selected by the British as one of the first test cases because: 'it seemed probable that if a German Military Court during the War had found Heynen guilty of the charges made against him, the Supreme Court at Leipzig could hardly fail to do the same.'[6]

Sixteen witnesses testified against Heynen at Leipzig, and three at Bow Street. The main case against him related to events on 13 and 14 October 1915. On 13 October, Heynen was put in charge of 200 British and 40 Russian POWs at Münster and told to take them to Herne. He had as his draft one lance corporal and twelve Landsturm men. Heynen was told to keep quiet about the fact that the POWs were going to work in a coalmine, but they expressed discontent because this became clear on the journey. There was no interpreter, so Heynen had difficulty making himself understood. After arrival at Herne, he found an Englishman – Parry – to interpret, though Parry had little knowledge of German. On the night of 13 October, the British POWs agreed among themselves that they would refuse to work – partly because they did not like mines and partly because they thought the work constituted helping in the operations of war. On 14 October, only some reported for work and less still had put on their mining clothes. The rest refused to put on these clothes when requested to do so. The accused was under strict orders to see that the work was undertaken, so his position was difficult. He ordered his men to load their rifles and to fix bayonets in front of the prisoners. This did not work, so he then arrested some of the prisoners. This did not work either, so the pickets showed clearly that they intended to use their bayonets and rifles. This still did not work, so Heynen was obliged to use force. The POWs were struck and kicked by both Heynen and his men. They were then divided into small groups and forced to put on miners' clothes and to work in the pits. Even then, however, when the POWs had been forced to work, they were assaulted in the mine and the camp.

Another major accusation was that Heynen had driven prisoner Cross (who had since died) insane through cruelties. It was alleged that Heynen had thrashed Cross and forcibly put him in a shower bath – hot and cold – for half an hour. A further example of Heynen's alleged cruelties related to POW McDonald who, together with another prisoner, escaped and was recaptured. Apart from his legitimate punishment for this, it was testified that Heynen had hit him with his rifle butt, knocked him down and kicked him. In November 1915, there had also been problems over prisoners reporting sick in the camp. The doctor was some way away and required prisoners to report to him at his surgery; this gave rise to prisoners missing a whole shift when reporting sick and thus encouraged many to do so for this purpose alone. Often twenty or thirty POWs reported sick when only one or two cases were genuine. Heynen was therefore told to take the temperature of those reporting sick and to send to the doctor only those who had a temperature and showed signs of fever. This caused resentment and gave rise to accusations of ill-treatment.

During the trial, Heynen denied most of the incidents. General von Fransecky defended Heynen's actions on the ground that it was his job to secure discipline, 'in keeping with the German Army's finest traditions'. This attracted much criticism in the United Kingdom. The State Attorney had some sympathy with General von Fransecky's comments, but asked for two years' imprisonment. The court's overall view was that the conditions at Heynen's camp had been satisfactory. Heynen himself, however, had been overworked and could not cope. He worked from 4 a.m. to midnight. The court commented that, 'In carrying out his duties he spared himself least of all'. No continuous intention to ill-treat was found; instead, his conduct was due to momentary annoyance or excitement. Also, he had received no adequate instruction or training. The court also had regard to Heynen's overall record and character, noting that following his court martial on 5 April 1916, he had been sent back to the front, where he had earned the Iron Cross, 2nd Class, and promotion to sergeant on 17 April 1918. As far as individual incidents were concerned, the court found that although prisoners had the right to complain, they did not have the right to refuse orders. Heynen had acted properly in securing compliance by force. This included using his rifle butt. But force should not exceed the minimum necessary. There was no evidence that Heynen had gone beyond this with regard to the events of 14 October 1914, and so he was acquitted of this charge. As regards the other accusations, he was found guilty of ill-treating Cross (though not necessarily of driving him insane because Cross had already been showing signs of 'derangement'); he was also found guilty of ill-treating McDonald and a number of sick men. In all, Heynen was found guilty on fifteen charges of brutality unconnected with the refusal of POWs to obey orders. The treatment of Cross was the most serious of these. He was also found guilty of three charges of insulting POWs (calling Parry a *Schweinhund*). In passing sentence, the president of the court commented:

One cannot help acknowledging that this is a case of extremely rough acts of brutality aggravated by the fact that these acts were perpetrated against defenceless prisoners against whom one should have acted in the most proper manner, if the good reputation of the German Army and the respect of the German Nation as a nation of culture was to be upheld.

And: 'There can be no question of detention in a Fortress in view of the nature of his offences, especially those committed against prisoners who were undoubtedly sick. On the contrary a sentence of imprisonment must be passed.'[7] Heynen was sentenced to ten months' imprisonment with the period of detention during the inquiry to be counted as part of the term of imprisonment.

The second of the British cases involved Captain Eric Müller, in civilian life a barrister living in Karlsruhe. In April 1918, Müller had been a captain in the reserve and was appointed to take command of the prison camp at Flavy-le-Martel. His duties comprised housing, feeding and supervising prisoners, and providing troops requisitioned for outside work. He took over an empty camp, previously used by the British as a temporary reception camp. The camp was in a wretched condition: it lay in a marshy and completely devastated district immediately behind the firing lines. During the time that the camp had been run by the British it had not been fit for human habitation. It had suffered from overcrowding (600 instead of 300 being accommodated), it had muddy unboarded floors, no beds – instead, rotten wood-wool infected with vermin – leaks, insufficient heating, primitive latrines, an absence of cooking and washing facilities, and no rugs. Many had been sick with influenza and intestinal problems, especially dysentery. Many had died. There had been a plague of lice, even affecting the guards. The camp doctors had tried in vain to rectify all this. The British camp commandant had, despite everything, behaved very well and German prisoners usually only stayed at the camp for three or four days, or occasionally a fortnight.

The German use of the camp as a working camp housing over 1,000 men doing heavy work was quite different. In these circumstances the camp quickly became a 'large cesspool'. The 1,000 men were herded into three huts of 60 square feet by 20 square feet, each of which could only satisfactorily hold 100 men. There were no floorboards, and no bedding or camp utensils were supplied. The men had to sleep on wet ground with no room for them all to lie down. Sanitary and washing facilities were primitive or non-existent; food and medical provision was wholly inadequate. Men were soon starving, verminous and filthy. Dysentery appeared and men started to die rapidly. Moreover:

> In spite of the terrible condition of the men, they were forced to engage in heavy work behind the lines at long distances from the Camp, and practically no excuse of weakness or sickness was accepted as relieving them from work. Men in the last stages of dysentery were driven out to work and fell and died by the road.

Müller was charged with causing or presiding over this state of affairs, together with carrying out a number of specific acts of personal violence. A key issue which influenced Müller's trial was how many of the events described took place while he was actually there. Müller had been in charge of the camp from the beginning of April 1918 to 5 May 1918 – a period of only five weeks. On 4 May, he had been given leave as he needed treatment for 'neurosis of the heart'. He left on 5 May, never to return. It proved impossible for witnesses to recall whether events took place before or after his departure. Another key issue was that immediately on his arrival at the camp Müller had set about trying to secure improvements, writing many memoranda to his superiors describing the situation there; he had 'made emphatic demands for what was wanting'. Indeed, he had secured many improvements: he had obtained medical supplies, had wells sunk, had stoves installed, proper latrines laid out, cooking and washing places provided, fought lice plagues with powder, and then established a disinfecting station. He had also improved the food and secured supplies of soap. This all worked in his favour, with the result that in relation to the main charge the court found that: 'So far, therefore, as the general conditions in the prisoners' camp at Flavy-le-Martel are concerned the accused must not only be acquitted of any blame, but it should be placed on record that the zeal with which he carried out his duties deserves high praise.'[8]

The court found that the dysentery epidemic at the camp, which had claimed 500 lives in less than a month, had developed after Müller's departure. Müller's attitude and behaviour towards the prisoners was, on the other hand, quite another matter. The court commented that, 'instead of earning the prisoners' confidence, he got a reputation among them of being a tyrant and a nigger driver'.[9] And:

His attitude towards the prisoners was hard and over severe, sometimes even brutal, and in other cases it was at least contrary to regulations. He treated them not as subordinates, and it was as such that he ought to have regarded his prisoners, but he treated them more like convicts or inmates of penitentiaries. His methods were those of the convict prison or such like institutions, although even on this standard his conduct could not be tolerated. The Court has heard of his ill-treating of prisoners by hitting and kicking them. He allowed his staff to treat them in the same manner. Insults were hurled at the prisoners and there was other ill-treatment which was contrary to the regulations. He habitually struck them when he was on horseback, using a riding cane or a walking stick.[10]

During the trial, one observer noted that:

The Court showed a tendency to attribute Captain Müller's conduct to his nervous state due partly to his heart affection, partly to his inexperience in dealing with prisoners of war, and partly to the great difficulties in which he found himself in a camp so ill-equipped to receive such a large number of men.

Be that as it may, the final judgement of the court was that nine instances of deliberate personal cruelty had been proved; that in addition there was one case in which Müller had allowed one of his subordinates to ill-treat a prisoner; that there were also four instances of minor breaches of regulations; and two cases of insults. A sentence of six months' imprisonment was passed, the period of detention pending and during trial to be considered as part of the term awarded.[11]

The last of the British cases was brought against Sergeant Heinrich Trinke and Private Robert Neuman in relation to alleged offences against British POWs employed in a chemical factory at Pommerensdorf. Trinke and his subordinate Neuman had been in charge of a detachment of POWs at the plant from March to December 1917. The detachment comprised between 150 and 200 men, of whom about fifty or sixty were British. They were engaged in filling, weighing and loading phosphate. Trinke could not be found by the German Government, so Neuman – the lesser offender – stood trial at Leipzig alone. As in the other cases, the charges against Trinke and Neuman turned on accusations of physical abuse and ill-treatment. In Neuman's case, some incidents involved the defence of acting under orders from Trinke. In other instances, however, Neuman was found to have committed acts of violence under his own initiative. The court found that twelve out of seventeen instances of assault had been proved: 'The accused kicked, struck, or otherwise physically ill-treated prisoners who were under his charge and were his subordinates. He did this deliberately and intended that his blows should hurt the prisoners. In doing this he had absolutely no justification.'[12] Neuman was sentenced to six months' imprisonment, the four months which he had already spent in prison awaiting trial to be counted as part of the sentence.[13]

It was left to the French Government to bring a test case relating to the handling by the German authorities of typhus epidemics in the 'plague' camps. Lieutenant-General Hans von Schack and Major-General Benno Kruska were brought before the court in relation to events at Cassel. The background to the case was that in September 1914, the acting German general in Cassel received a telegram from the Ministry of War inform-ing him that it was intended to form a POW camp for 15,000 men there. At first tents were set up, then construction started of wooden barracks. The newly built camp was at first placed under the control of Lieutenant-General (retired) Hans von Schack. As soon as there were 5,000 POWs, Major-General (retired) Kruska was appointed camp commandant. He took command on 5 October 1914. The camp contained French, Belgian and Russian POWs. By March 1915, the camp totalled 18,300 men. At first, the health conditions were good, but in mid-February 1915, spotted fever (typhus) broke out as a result of the Russian influx. In April 1915, the dis-ease escalated, with the number of new cases per day fluctuating between 50 and 200. On 5 May 1915 (the highest point) the number rose to 349. Of the 18,000 POWs, 7,218 fell ill with typhus. Of these, 1,280 died, of whom 719 were French. The epidemic died down in July 1915. The French Government held that the accused were responsible for the conditions which prevailed and for their consequences. They were therefore accused of murder.

The court gave the case short shrift. It noted that out of eighteen German doctors at the camp, all except two were attacked by spotted fever and four had died. Also, two German officers and thirty-two sergeants and NCOs had fallen victim to the disease:

> General Kruska in no way spared himself. He personally visited the prison
> camp by day and by night, even when the epidemic was at its height, in order

to see that all was right. Against all the warnings of the doctors, he went in and out of the disease stricken hospital barracks, in order to bring confidence to the sick.

As far as negligence by the accused was concerned, the court found them free from blame:

> It may be, as some of the French witnesses state, that all the sick could not be immediately taken into the overflowing hospitals, and that several of them were carried to the hospital on overturned table tops which were later on used again for meals. This was forbidden, but was excusable at times when occasionally, on one day, hundreds of prisoners fell ill and the available stretchers were insufficient to meet the demands.
>
> The accused admits the incident described by Leroux in his evidence. Leroux states that dead and sick prisoners were left lying side by side for a time. This, however, proves nothing against the accused. General Kruska, owing to the vast extent of the camp, could not be everywhere. It was out of his power to prevent such neglect. In such neglect, the medical staff were mainly to blame.

The court held that, 'what most contributed to the outbreak of the epidemic was the order of the Camp Commandant that the Russians were to be placed with the other prisoners'. But:

> The responsibility for this, however, rests exclusively with the High Command of the Army. An order for this was given by the War Office on 18th October 1914, and this order stated that it was advisable to place the Russian prisoners with their Allies, the English and French. From the medical point of view, the doctor at the camp made representations against this ... The higher authorities obstinately insisted on their order, and the parties concerned had nothing else to do but obey.

The court gave weight to the argument that typhus was practically unknown in Germany before the outbreak of war, and that as soon as sufficient knowledge was gathered, steps were immediately taken – at great expense – to combat the disease. In acquitting both the defendants, the court concluded that: 'General Kruska, as well as General von Schack, is, as the State Attorney has himself said, to be acquitted absolutely ... the trial before this Court has not revealed even the shadow of proof for these monstrous accusations.'[14]

The French also took up the question of the illegal killing of prisoners in a case against Lieutenant-General Karl Stenger and Major Benno Crusius. Stenger was accused of issuing an order in August 1914, as commander of the 58th Infantry Brigade, to the effect that all prisoners and wounded were to be killed. Crusius was accused of having passed on Stenger's order, of killing French prisoners and of inducing his subordinates to do the same. The court reviewed events at Saarburg on 21 August 1914 and in a wood near Sainte Barbe on 26 August 1914. As far as the events of 21 August 1914 were concerned, the accusation that Stenger issued such an order was refuted and he was found not guilty. Crusius admitted carrying out the order in the mistaken belief that such a command had been issued and was therefore guilty of killing by negligence. As far as the events of 26 August were concerned, Stenger was found not guilty of issuing an order to kill. Crusius did not deny passing on and carrying out 'the order', but the court found that:

> The medical experts have uniformly and convincingly demonstrated the possibility, nay, the overwhelming probability, that, already at the moment when the alleged brigade order was passed on in the afternoon of 26th August (not merely at the time when it was executed), the accused was suffering from a morbid derangement of his mental faculties which rendered impossible the exercise of his free volition. These experts do not hold that this was already the case on 21 August. The court shares this view.

And so: 'As in accordance with practice, reasonable doubt as to the volition of the guilty party does not allow of a pronouncement of guilt, no sentence can be passed against Crusius as regards the 26th of August.'[15] In relation to 21 August, allowing for previous good character, Crusius was sentenced to two years' imprisonment and to deprivation of the right to wear an officer's uniform. The period of detention on remand was to be deducted from the sentence.

The final case involving POWs related to the killing of French Captain Migat, allegedly by First-Lieutenant Adolphe Laule. The circumstances here were that Captain Migat had fallen asleep while his contingent marched off. The Germans came upon him but he refused to be taken prisoner, shaking off those who attempted to restrain him. He made towards the French troops, whereupon he was summarily shot. The court found that Migat was drunk (though it is not clear on what evidence), that Laule did not himself fire the shots nor issue an order to shoot, and that Migat was killed by German soldiers of their own accord as he would not cease struggling. Laule was acquitted.[16]

The Leipzig Trials were widely regarded outside Germany as a travesty because of the apparent leniency of the court. Including the cases not related to the treatment of prisoners, the court had heard six cases brought at the instigation of the British, which resulted in five convictions; five prosecutions by the French, which resulted in one conviction; and one case brought by the Belgians, which resulted in an acquittal. *The Times* correspondent at Leipzig described the results of the Heynen case as a 'scandalous failure of justice'.[17] This was a view shared by a number of MPs, one of whom called for the remaining trials to be moved to London, while another considered that the 'contemptible' sentence awarded to Heynen had reduced the whole process to a 'judicial farce'.[18] The interpreter in the Neuman case was criticised for being so incompetent as to cause some of the gravest charges made in testimony being 'passed onto the judges in an incomplete fashion', with 'acts of cruelty being whittled down in consequence to meaningless acts of horseplay'.[19] And such was the anger at the acquittal of General Stenger that Briand, the French Prime Minister, ordered the recall of the French Mission sent to oversee the trials. In reporting this development, the correspondent of *The Times* was moved to ask, 'How are the Germans to be shown that justice cannot be flouted with impunity?'[20]

In sharp contrast, the prevailing mood within Germany was one of anger at what was seen as the harshness of the penalties imposed and the fact that, of all the belligerents, only German citizens had been singled out for trial. German opinion was particularly incensed at the reaction to the trials abroad. The *German Gazette* commented on the Heynen case that, 'The first verdict in the series of Leipzig trials has agitated public opinion in two great countries, Germany and England, in apparently sharply contrasting ways. The degree of punishment has been criticised in England in a manner that is in the highest degree wounding to German susceptibilities.'[21] Sympathy went to Heynen himself, regarded as an ordinary soldier simply doing his best in trying conditions. His defence that he had done nothing which went beyond the accepted norms of the German army – citing as an example his own experience as a recruit when his sergeant had often pelted him with stones – attracted much support. The *German Gazette* noted that, 'many Germans, in complete contrast to the English conception of it, find the sentence too hard. They think of the extraordinary difficulties of war, to cope with which the accused, a simple man, was not competent.'[22] Another newspaper noted that Heynen would no doubt feel the victim of a cruel accident, while the *Tageszeitung* considered that, 'the bringing of the charges illustrates the depths to which the morality of Germany's enemies has sunk'.[23]

Despite the widespread criticism of the trials from outside Germany, the British Government consistently defended the process. Sir Ernest Pollock, Solicitor General and leader of the UK delegation to Leipzig, told the House of Commons on 23 June that from the point of view of those in court, the sentences handed out did not appear derisory.[24] This view was subsequently expanded upon by Claud Mullins, a member of his team. Mullins argued that the sentences needed to be looked at in the context of the German attitude towards authority and the need to obey orders: 'I always think that it is significant that there are notices in many German railway carriages that "in case of dispute as to whether the window should be opened or closed, the guard will decide." Germans have a respect for authority which we British can scarcely understand.'[25]

Mullins argued that the court's decision to impose sentences of imprisonment, rather than the usual army punishment of detention in a fortress, made the sentences much harsher in reality to the Germans because of the shame attached: 'Six months in a civil jail thus meant far more than three years' detention in a fortress, which is the usual military punishment. The Germans always have had strange ideas about service "honour", and this "honour" was deeply wounded by a sentence of imprisonment, such as mere civilians received.' And while accepting that there were some weaknesses about the trials, he concluded:

none the less the fact remains that these trials were neither 'a travesty of justice' nor 'a farce'. There was throughout a genuine desire to get to the bottom of the facts and to arrive at the truth. This and the fact that a German Court severely condemned the doctrines of brutality, which General von Fransecky and Admiral von Trotha applauded, are the important results that will live in history long after the miserable offenders have been forgotten.[26]

In the event, history has failed to provide the forecast vindication, since not only have the 'miserable offenders' been largely forgotten, but the Leipzig Trials as a whole have been confined to a footnote along with them. On

15 January 1922, a commission of Allied jurists, appointed to inquire into the trials, reported unanimously that it was useless to proceed with further cases, holding that some of those acquitted should have been condemned and that the sentences of those condemned were not adequate. The commission recommended that the remaining accused should be handed over to the Allied governments for trial.[27] No attempt was made to do this. The Allied governments had lost their appetite. In the case of the British Government, in particular, it is clear that the decision to defend the results of Leipzig Trials was taken simply to bring the whole matter to an end, the desire for retribution having passed. Its public claim that the results of the trials were satisfactory was in fact a sham, as is made clear in the following extract from a record of a conversation between Sir Eyre Crowe, Permanent Under-Secretary at the Foreign Office, and the German Ambassador on 3 February 1922:

> The Ambassador thought it was not his duty to discuss the alleged leniency of the sentences. He could not go behind the judicial decision. The sentences were in accordance with German law, which had to be impartially applied.
>
> I remarked that although this was not the point immediately at issue, I felt it impossible to refrain from observing what a mistake had apparently been made by the Allied Governments when agreeing to the trial of the culprits by a German court, and accepting the assurances of the German Government that they could absolutely rely on full justice being done. It was impossible, I thought, to convince opinion in this country that the sentences imposed by the court represented justice.[28]

Handing over the judicial process to the German authorities had indeed been a mistake. The decision to do so had directly negated the first attempt to deal with war crimes through an international system of justice. But the seeds had been sown and the lessons were learnt. When it came to dispensing justice at Nuremberg following the next war, the pitfalls were avoided. Sadly, however, the crimes to be tried there would also be that much more widespread and serious.

# NOTES

## Preface

1    Richard B. Speed III, *Prisoners, Diplomats, and the Great War: A Study in the Diplomacy of Captivity* (1990), pp. 76, 101, 195. Speed estimates a total of 6,637,000 prisoners held in 1918, made up as follows. Germany 2,500,000; Russia 2,250,000; Austria-Hungary 916,000; France 350,000; UK 328,000; US 43,000; Other 250,000.

## Introduction

1    Ibid., pp. 1–2; Ronald F. Roxburgh, *The Prisoners of War Information Bureau in London: A Study* (1915), pp. 3–4; Manual of Military Law, War Office (1914), pp. 244–5.
2    'Convention for the Amelioration of the Condition of the Wounded in Armies in the Field', Geneva, 22 August 1864, International Committee of the Red Cross.
3    Ibid., 6 July 1906.
4    'Convention (III) for the Adaptation to Maritime Warfare of the Principles of the Geneva Convention of 22 August 1864', The Hague, 29 July 1899, International Committee of the Red Cross.
5    'Convention (II) with Respect to the Laws and Customs of War on Land and its annex: Regulations concerning the Laws and Customs of War on Land', The Hague, 29 July 1899; superseded by 'Convention (IV) respecting the Laws and Customs of War on Land and its annex: Regulations concerning the Laws and Customs of War on Land', The Hague, 18 October 1907, International Committee of the Red Cross.
6    James W. Gerard, Speech to the Ladies Aid Society of St Mary's Hospital, New York, 25 November 1917, at http://www.firstworldwar.com/audio/loyalty.htm [accessed 9 February 2009].
7    See Charles Seymour (ed.), *The Intimate Papers of Colonel House* (1926), 1, p. 190; and Binoy Kampmark, *James W Gerard: His Image of Imperial Germany, 1913–1918* at http://www.unc.edu/depts/diplomat [accessed 8 July 2008].
8    *The Times*, 23 March 1942, p. 6, cited in *The Oxford Dictionary of National Biography*.

## I Civilians: The Innocent Bystanders

1  Richard B. Speed III, *Prisoners, Diplomats, and the Great War: A Study in the Diplomacy of Captivity* (1990), p. 143.
2  L. Oppenheim, in Introduction to Ronald F. Roxborough, *The Prisoners of War Information Bureau in London: A Study* (1915), p. vii.
3  Manual of Military Law, War Office (1914), p. 236.
4  Oppenheim, pp. vi–viii; and Speed, *Prisoners, Diplomats, and the Great War*, p. 143.
5  James W. Gerard, *My Four Years in Germany* (1917), pp. 141–2.
6  Ibid., pp. 139–40.
7  Letter dated 14 November 1914, Foreign Office file, FO 369/714, National Archives, Kew.
8  House of Commons: Parliamentary Debates (Hansard), 5 August 1914, Cols 1986–7.
9  Cabinet Paper, CAB 37/122/182, 7 December 1914, National Archives, Kew.
10  Hansard, 13 May 1915, Cols 1841–2.
11  Robert Jackson, *The Prisoners 1914–18* (1989), p. 138.
12  Gerard to Page, 8 November 1914, 'Correspondence between His Majesty's Government and the United States Ambassador Respecting the Release of Interned Civilians and the Exchange of Diplomats and Consular Officers and of Certain Classes of Naval and Military Officers, Prisoners of War; in the United Kingdom and Germany Respectively', Misc. No 8 (1915), HMSO CD 7857 April 1915, p. 19.
13  Grey to Page, 9 November 1914, ibid., pp. 15–6.
14  FO Memorandum dated 4 October 1914, ibid., p. 1.
15  See Grey to Page, 20 January 1915, ibid., p. 49–50.
16  Grey to Page, 8 October 1914, ibid., p. 12; and Page to Grey, 22 October 1914, ibid., p. 13.
17  Letter dated 17 November 1915, War Office file, WO 32/5371, National Archives, Kew.
18  Cabinet Paper CAB 37/139/50, 30 December 1915.
19  Cabinet Papers CAB 37/142/19, 9 February 1916; CAB 37/143/18, 22 February 1916; and CAB 37/148/3, 16 May 1916.
20  Cabinet Paper CAB 37/154/17, 24 August 1916.
21  Grey to Laughlin, 24 August 1916, 'Further Correspondence Respecting the Proposed Release of Civilians Interned in the British and German Empires' [in continuation of Misc. No 25 (1916), CD 8296], Misc. No 35 (1916) CD 8352, November 1916, p. 2.
22  Page to Grey, 20 October 1916, ibid., p. 6.
23  J.C. Bird, *Control of Enemy Alien Civilians in Great Britain, 1914–18* (1986), p. 182.
24  Cabinet Paper CAB 37/155/36, 23 September 1916.
25  Bird, *Control of Enemy Alien Civilians*, p. 189.
26  Ibid., p. 183.
27  Jay Winter & Blaine Baggett, *1914–18 The Great War and the Shaping of the Twentieth Century* (1996), pp. 60–1.

## 2 Applying the Conventions

1  Richard B. Speed III, *Prisoners, Diplomats, and the Great War: A Study in the Diplomacy of Captivity* (1990), pp. 16, 97.
2  Speed, *Prisoners, Diplomats, and the Great War*, p. 194.
3  *The Times*, 18 August 1914, p. 2.
4  Ronald F. Roxburgh, *The Prisoners of War Information Bureau in London: A Study* (1915), pp. 12–4.

5   'Correspondence between His Majesty's Government and the United States
    Ambassador respecting the Treatment of Prisoners of War and Interned Civilians
    in the United Kingdom and Germany respectively' [in continuation of Misc. No 5
    (1915) March 1915, CD 7815], Misc. No 7 (1915), CD 7817, p. 4.

6   Daniel J. McCarthy, *The Prisoner of War in Germany: The Care and Treatment of the
    Prisoner of War, with a History of the Development of the Principle of Neutral Inspection and
    Control* (n.d.), pp. 158–9.

7   Memorandum concerning Prisoners of War, CD 7817, p. 14.

8   Statement of principles issued by the IFO, 28 February 1915, CD 7817, pp. 79–81.

9   'Correspondence between His Majesty's Government and the United States
    Ambassador respecting the Treatment of German Prisoners of War and Interned
    Civilians in the United Kingdom', Misc. No 5 (1915), CD 7815, pp. 2–3; and
    CD 7817, pp. 54–5.

10  CD 7815, p. 2.

11  Speed, *Prisoners, Diplomats, and the Great War*, p. 100.

12  CD 7815, p. 2.

13  CD 7817, p. 80.

14  'Regulations respecting the Maintenance of Prisoners of War', 24 April 1915, in
    'Correspondence with the United States Ambassador respecting the Treatment of
    British Prisoners of War and Interned Civilians in Germany' [in continuation of Misc.
    No 11 (1915), CD 7861], Misc. No 14 (1915) HMSO CD 7959, June 1915, pp. 23–6.

15  Grey to Page, 24 September 1914, 'Correspondence between His Majesty'
    Government and the United States Ambassador respecting the Treatment of Interned
    Civilians in the United Kingdom and Germany respectively' [in continuation of Misc.
    No 5 (1915), CD 7815], Misc. No 7 (1915) HMSO CD 7817, pp. 4–5.

16  The Treatment of Prisoners of War in England and Germany During the First Eight
    Months of the War, Based on Parliamentary Paper Misc. No 7 (1915), CD 7817 (1915),
    p. 13.

17  CD 7817, pp. 74–5.

18  Page to Grey, 26 November 1914; and Grey to Page, 21 December 1914,
    'Correspondence between His Majesty's Government and the United States
    Ambassador Respecting the release of Interned Civilians and the Exchange of
    Diplomats and Consular officers and of certain Classes of naval and military officers,
    Prisoners of War, in the United Kingdom and Germany Respectively', Misc. No 8
    (1915) HMSO CD 7857, April 1915, pp. 59–60.

19  Ibid., pp. 61–3.

20  'Convention for the Amelioration of the Condition of the Wounded and Sick in
    Armies in the Field, Geneva, 27 July 1929', Article 11.

21  Treaty of Versailles, Article 224.

## 3   Germany: Problems & Inspections

1   James W Gerard, *My Four Years in Germany* (1917), p. 157.

2   Gerard to Page, 2 October 1914, 'Correspondence between His Majesty's Government
    and the United States Ambassador respecting the Treatment of Prisoners of War and
    Interned Civilians in the United Kingdom and Germany respectively' [in continuation
    of Misc. No 5 (1915), CD 7815], Misc. No 7 (1915) HMSO CD 7817, p. 8.

3   Gerard, *My Four Years*, p. 164.

4   Grey to Page, 14 January 1915, CD 7817, pp. 41–2.

5   Gerard, *My Four Years*, pp. 164, 195.
6   Grey to Page, 19 March 1915, CD 7817, p. 82.
7   Gerard to Page, 11 March 1915, CD 7817, pp. 76–8.
8   Richard B. Speed III, *Prisoners, Diplomats, and the Great War: A Study in the Diplomacy of Captivity* (1990), p. 194.
9   Report by American Consul-General at Berlin, CD 7817, p. 11.
10  Jackson to Grey, 31 March 1915, Reports by United States Officials on the Treatment of British Prisoners of War and Interned Civilians at Certain Places of Detention in Germany [in continuation of Misc. No 7 (1915): CD 7817], Misc. No 11 (1915), HMSO CD 7861, May 1915, p. 2.
11  *The British Prisoner of War – Being the Monthly Journal of the Central Prisoners of War Committee of the Red Cross and Order of St John*, Vol. 1, No 8, August 1918, pp. 87–8.
12  Grey to Page, 19 April 1915, CD 7861, p. 7.
13  CD 7817, pp. 34–5.
14  Report by German military authorities, 19 July 1915, Foreign Office file FO 383/43, National Archives, Kew.
15  Letter from British Red Cross Society, 16 October 1914, FO 372/541.
16  CD 7817, pp. 12–4.
17  Report dated 15 May 1915, 'Correspondence with the United States Ambassador respecting the Treatment of British Prisoners of War and Interned Civilians in Germany' [in continuation of Misc. No 11 (1915): CD 7861], Misc. No 14 (1915), CD 7959, June 1915, p. 54.
18  CD 7817, pp. 30–3.
19  Report by German military authorities, FO 383/43.
20  CD 7817, p. 29.
21  Ibid.
22  Ibid., p. 40.
23  Report by German military authorities, FO 383/43.
24  Grey to Page, 26 December 1914, CD 7817, p. 29.
25  Damm to Gerard, 31 December 1914, CD 7817, pp. 42–3.
26  Jackson to Grey, CD 7861, p. 2.
27  Gerard to Page, 4 May 1915, CD 7959, pp. 30–3.
28  Gerard, *My Four Years*, p. 166.
29  Ibid., p. 162.
30  Gerard to Page, 4 May 1915, CD 7959, p. 32.
31  Daniel J. McCarthy, *The Prisoner of War in Germany: The Care and Treatment of the Prisoner of War, with a History of the Development of the Principle Neutral Inspection and Control* (n.d.), pp. 38, 170.
32  Jackson to Grey, CD 7861, p. 2.
33  Gerard, *My Four Years*, p. 186.
34  CD 7959, p. 32.
35  McCarthy, *The Prisoner of War in Germany*, pp. 36–9.
36  See for example report by Russell, 28 October 1915, 'Further Correspondence with the United States Ambassador respecting the Treatment of British Prisoners of War and Interned Civilians in Germany' [in continuation of Misc. No 19 (1915) CD 8108], Misc. No 16 (1916), HMSO CD 8235, May 1916, pp. 3–4.
37  'Convention relative to the Treatment of Prisoners of War, Geneva, 27 July 1929', Article 9.

38  Gerard, *My Four Years*, p. 160.
39  See Page to Grey, 17 March 1915; and Grey to Page, 20 March 1915, CD 7817, pp. 75, 84.
40  McCarthy, *The Prisoner of War in Germany*, pp. 32–3; and Speed, *Prisoners, Diplomats, and the Great War*, p. 28.
41  Ibid., p. 15.
42  Geneva Convention 1929, Article 86.

## 4 The British Experience

1  War Office report to Foreign Office, Foreign Office file, FO 369/800, National Archives, Kew.
2  Petition dated 3 November 1914, ibid.
3  Note by Sir W. Langley, 7 November 1914, FO 369/714.
4  Report dated 21 November 1914, Cabinet Paper CAB 37/123/37, 20 January 1915, National Archives, Kew.
5  Internal minute to Grey, 19 November 1914, FO 369/800.
6  Minute from Acland to Grey, ibid.
7  Letter from General Sir Alfred Turner to Lieutenant-General Bellfield, dated 17 December 1914, ibid.
8  FO minutes dated 24 November 1914 and 2 December 1914, FO 369/714.
9  Telegram dated 27 November from Grant Duff, HM Ambassador, Berne, ibid.
10  'Correspondence between His Majesty's Government and the United States Ambassador respecting the Treatment of Prisoners of War and Interned Civilians in the United Kingdom and Germany respectively' [in continuation of Misc. No 5 (1915): CD 7815], Misc. No 7 (1915), HMSO CD 7817, pp. 36–7.
11  The five prisoners killed were Christian Bickel, aged 25, a waiter; Ludwig Bauer, aged 31, a 'checker' from Brixton; Bernhard Warning, aged 25, a locksmith; Richard Hermann Mathias, aged 21, a sailor; and Richard Fuhs, aged 20, a waiter. See letter from US Embassy, Berlin, 19 January 1915, FO 383/35.
12  'Disturbance at the Aliens Detention Camp at Douglas on Thursday, November 19th 1914', Inquiry by the Coroner of Inquests in the Isle of Man and a jury, on Friday 20 November and Friday 27 November 1914, Official Report of the Proceedings.
13  The remit of the Destitute Aliens Committee, through which the Home Office operated, was to arrange for the repatriation, accommodation or relief of destitute aliens. It was later renamed the Civilian Internment Camps Committee. See J.C. Bird, *Control of Enemy Alien Civilians in Great Britain, 1914–18* (1986), pp. 131–2.
14  Home Office file, ref. HO 45/10946 File 266042/38, National Archives, Kew.
15  Robert Fyson, 'The Douglas Camp Shootings of 1914', *Proceedings of the Isle of Man Natural History and Antiquarian Society*, Vol. XI No 1 (2000).
16  War Office report to Foreign Office, FO 369/800.
17  Richard B. Speed III, *Prisoners, Diplomats and the Great War: A Study in the Diplomacy of Captivity* (1990), p. 99.
18  Report included with Page to Grey, 27 July 1915, FO 383/33.
19  Robert Jackson, *The Prisoners 1914–18* (1989), p. 136.
20  House of Commons: Parliamentary Debates (Hansard), 11 February 1915, Col. 746.
21  Hansard, 15 February 1915, Col. 982.
22  Speed, *Prisoners, Diplomats, and the Great War*, p. 103.
23  Hansard, 25 February 1915, Col. 381.

24  Hansard, 8 March 1915, Cols 1137–40.
25  Hansard, 15 March 1915, Cols 1877–94.
26  Speed, *Prisoners, Diplomats, and the Great War*, p. 105.
27  Ibid., p. 104.
28  FO minute dated 9 August 1915, FO 383/34.
29  Hansard, 9 September 1914, Cols 551–2.
30  Hansard, 16 November 1914, Col. 215.
31  Hansard, 24 February 1915, Cols 248–51.
32  Hansard, 24 February 1915, Cols 248-51, 258.
33  Hansard, 9 February 1915, Cols 448–88.
34  Letter from Sir Arthur Conan Doyle to the War Office, 14 January 1915, FO 383/32.
35  FO 369/800.
36  Report on visits to Handforth and Queensferry camps on 19 and 20 December 1914, ibid.

## 5  Wittenberg, Gardelegen & Typhus

1  Correspondence between Grant Duff (19 July 1916) and Grey (11 August 1916) in 'Correspondence with His Majesty's Minister at Berne respecting the question of Reprisals against Prisoners of War', Misc. No 29 (1916), CD 8323, September 1916.
 2  'Report by the Government Committee on the Treatment by the Enemy of British Prisoners of War regarding the Conditions obtaining at Wittenberg Camp during the Typhus Epidemic 1915', Misc. No 10 (1916), CD 8224, April 1916; and 'Report on the Typhus Epidemic at Gardelegen by the Government Committee on the Treatment by the Enemy of British Prisoners of War during the Spring and Summer of 1915', CD 8351, October 1916.
 3  James W. Gerard, *My Four Years in Germany* (1917), p. 172.
 4  Daniel J. McCarthy, *The Prisoner of War in Germany: The Care and Treatment of the Prisoner of War, with a History of the Development of the Principle of Neutral Inspection and Control* (n.d.), pp. 39–40.
 5  'Report on the Transport of British Prisoners of War to Germany, August–September 1914', Misc. No 3 (1918), CD 8984, February 1918, pp. 17–9.
 6  McCarthy, *The Prisoner of War in Germany*, p. 74.
 7  Report by Jackson, 16 March 1916, 'Further Correspondence with the United States Ambassador respecting the Treatment of British Prisoners of War and Interned Civilians in Germany' [in continuation of Misc. No 19 (1915) CD 8108], Misc. No 16 (1916), CD 8235, May 1916, p. 88.
 8  Gerard, *My Four Years*, p. 172.
 9  Report by Osborne, 2 November 1915, CD 8235, p. 6.
10  Report by Ohnesorg & Dresel, 10 March 1916, CD 8235, p. 85.
11  War Office file, WO 32/5608, National Archives, Kew.

## 6  From Capture to the Camps

1  'Correspondence between His Majesty's Government and the United States Ambassador respecting the Treatment of Prisoners of War and Interned Civilians in the United Kingdom and Germany respectively' [in continuation of Misc. No 5 (1915), CD 7815], Misc. No 7 (1915), CD 7817, p. 33.
 2  Cabinet Paper, CAB 37/128/17, National Archives, Kew.

3   Wolfgang Vormann, *Infanterie-Regiment Fürst Leopold von Anhalt-Desau (I. Magdeburg,)
    Nr 26, III* (n.d.), p. 536, cited in Christopher Duffy, *Through German Eyes: The British
    and the Somme 1916* (2006), p. 35. See pp. 34–40 for a general assessment of the
    treatment of prisoners on capture.

4   'Report on The Treatment by the Germans of Prisoners of War taken during the
    Spring Offensives of 1918' [in continuation of Misc. No 7 (1918), CD 8988), Misc.
    No 19 (1918), HMSO, CD 9106, October 1918, p. 8.

5   August Gallinger, *The Countercharge: The Matter of War Criminals from the German Side*
    (1922), pp.20, 22.

6   Ibid., pp. 24–5.

7   Ibid., pp. 25–7.

8   Ibid., pp. 26–7.

9   Duffy, *Through German Eyes*, p. 40.

10  Carl P. Dennet, *Prisoners of the Great War: Authoritative Statement of the Conditions in the
    Prison Camps of Germany* (1919), pp. 49, 77.

11  Ernst Gruson, *Das Königlich Preussiche 4. Thü. Infanterie-Regiment Nr 82 im Weltkriege*
    (1930), p. 245, cited in Duffy, *Through German Eyes*, p. 35.

12  Daniel J. McCarthy, *The Prisoner of War in Germany: The Care and Treatment of the
    Prisoner of War, with a History of the Development of the Principle of Neutral Inspection and
    Control* (n.d.), p. 39.

13  Dennet, *Prisoners of the Great War*, p. 39.

14  'Report on the Transport of British Prisoners of War to Germany, August–December
    1914', Misc. No 3 (1918) CD 8984, HMSO, February 1918, pp. 2–4.

15  CD 8984, pp. 32–3.

16  Ibid., p. 5.

17  Ibid., pp.8–10.

18  Ibid.

19  House of Commons: Parliamentary Debates (Hansard), 16 September 1914, Cols 867–8.

20  James W. Gerard, *My Four Years in Germany* (1917), pp. 166–7

21  CD 8984, pp. 19–20.

22  Ibid., p. 4.

23  David Vandeleur, letter to author, 13 August 1999. The letter includes that Major
    Vandeleur's son, Lt-Col Joe Vandeleur DSO, subsequently had a distinguished
    career in the Second World War, commanding the Irish Guards Battle Group in 30
    Corps at Arnhem, and his cousin, Giles Vandeleur, was his second-in-command and
    commanded the Armoured Battalion; Michael Caine took his part in the film *A
    Bridge Too Far*.

24  CD 7817, pp. 30–1.

25  Foreign Office file FO 383/43, National Archives, Kew.

26  CD 8984, p. 2.

27  Gallinger, *The Countercharge*, p. 34.

28  Ibid., p. 57.

29  *The British Prisoner of War – Being the Monthly Journal of the Central Prisoners of War
    Committee of the Red Cross and Order of St John*, Vol. 1 No 7 (July 1918), p. 83.

30  CD 9106, p. 3.

31  Manual of Military Law, War Office 1914, HMSO (1914), p. 248.

32  Foreign Office telegram to Rumbold, Minister at Berne, 9 April 1917, on War Office
    file, WO 32/5098, National Archives, Kew.

33  CD 9106, various reports.
34  'Convention relative to the Treatment of Prisoners of War, Geneva, 27 July 1929', Article 2.

## 7 Reprisals

1   House of Commons: Parliamentary Debates (Hansard), 10 March 1915, Cols 1518–31.
2   Foreign Office file, FO 383/32, National Archives, Kew, draft reply to German protest sent from Admiralty to Foreign Office dated 29 March 1915.
3   *The Times*, 20 March 1915, p. 8.
4   FO 383/32, manuscript note by Sir Edward Grey on telegram from German Foreign Office, received via Page on 20 March 1915.
5   FO 383/32, telegram from German Foreign Office dated 17 March 1915, received via US Ambassador Page on 20 March.
6   FO 383/32, manuscript note by Rumbold on Admiralty proposed reply to German protest.
7   *The Times*, 7 April 1915, p. 9.
8   *The Times*, 14 April 1915, p. 8.
9   Cabinet Paper, CAB 24/63, 12 September 1918, National Archives, Kew.
10  James W. Gerard, *My Four Years in Germany* (1917), p. 168.
11  *The Times*, 26 April 1915, p. 9.
12  FO 383/32, manuscript note from Rumbold to Primrose, 14 April 1915.
13  Report by Asquith to the king, dated 27 April, of the Cabinet meeting held on 26 April 1915, CAB 37/127/40.
14  Hansard, 27 April 1915, Col. 572.
15  On 4 December 1914, four German cruisers had bombarded Scarborough, Whitby and Hartlepool, killing forty civilians and wounding several hundred.
16  *The Times*, 28 April 1915, p. 9.
17  *The Times*, 29 April 1915, p. 5.
18  Gerard, *My Four Years*, pp. 169–70.
19  *The Times*, 13 May 1915, p. 5.
20  *The Times*, 20 May 1915, p. 7.
21  *The Times*, 2 June 1915, p. 3.
22  CAB 37/129/9, 5 June 1915.
23  Hansard, 9 June 1915, Cols 267–8.
24  *The Times*, 10 June 1915, p. 8.
25  Hansard, 30 June 1915, Col. 1787.
26  Gerard, *My Four Years*, pp. 170–1.
27  *The Times*, 10 June 1915, p. 8.
28  *Cologne Gazette*, quoted in *The Times*, 12 June 1915, p. 5.
29  FO 383/184, memoranda dated 24 February and 1 March 1916.
30  Richard B. Speed III, *Prisoners, Diplomats, and the Great War: A Study in the Diplomacy of Captivity* (1990), pp. 101–2.
31  FO 383/184, memorandum handed by Lord Newton to Lord Kitchener on 29 February 1916.
32  FO 383/184, Sir Arthur Nicholson to Grey, 1 March 1916, and manuscript note by Grey.
33  CAB 371/144/7, 3 March 1916.
34  FO 383/184, Kitchener to Crewe, 7 March 1916.

35 Grey to Sir G. Spring-Rice, 27 April 1916, 'Correspondence Respecting the Employment of British and German Prisoners of War in Poland and France Respectively', Misc. No 19 (1916), CD 8260 June 1916, pp. 2–3.
36 FO 383/185, WO memorandum, 17 October 1916.
37 FO 383/184, telegram from Page to Grey, 15 May 1916.
38 FO 383/185, telegram from Page to Grey, 30 June 1916.
39 FO 383/185, manuscript note by Rumbold, 24 July 1916.
40 FO 383/185, telegram from US Embassy, 5 October 1916.
41 FO 383/185, report by War Office, 20 October 1916.
42 Gerard, *My Four Years*, p. 175.
43 CAB 24/63.
44 *The Times*, 15 June 1916, p. 10.
45 Gerard, *My Four Years*, p. 168.
46 FO 383/185, telegram from Ambassador Spring-Rice, Washington, 25 July 1916.
47 FO 383/185, telegram from Ambassador Spring-Rice, Washington, 6 August 1916.
48 Note Verbale from the German IFO dated 24 January 1917, 'Report on the Treatment by the Enemy of British Prisoners of War behind the Firing Lines in France and Belgium With Two Appendices', Misc. No 7 (1918) HMSO CD 8988, April 1918, p. 12.
49 Report of Cabinet discussion on 30 March 1917, on War Office file, WO 32/5381, National Archives, Kew.
50 Note of Conference on 12 & 13 March 1917, on WO 32/5098, National Archives, Kew.
51 Reply from HMG dated 8 February 1917, CD 8988, p. 13.
52 War Office file, WO 32/5098, National Archives, Kew.
53 Daniel J. McCarthy, *The Prisoner of War in Germany: The Care and Treatment of the Prisoner of War, with a History of the Development of the Principle of Neutral Inspection and Control* (n.d.), p. 147.
54 Gerard, *My Four Years*, p. 176.
55 James W. Gerard, *Face to Face with Kaiserism* (1918), illustrations.
56 CAB 37/151/1, 5 July 1916.
57 Hansard (Commons), 5 February 1918, Col. 2061.
58 CAB 24/63
59 CAB 24/14, 30 May 1917
60 CAB 23/41, 30 July 1917.
61 CAB 24/63.
62 On 28 March 1915, Captain Charles Fryatt turned the steamer *Brussels* into an attacking German submarine in an attempt to ram it. The submarine fled, with Captain Fryatt receiving much publicity and being awarded a gold watch by the Admiralty. A few months later, the German navy intercepted the *Brussels* on one of its regular crossings from Harwich to the Hook of Holland, capturing Captain Fryatt and his crew and interning them at Ruhleben. The German authorities then court-martialled Captain Fryatt at Bruges on 27 July 1916 for piracy in relation to the original act, and despite Gerard's request to see him and arrange legal representation, executed him later the same day. Martin Gilbert, *First World War* (1994), pp. 141, 274; and Gerard, *My Four Years*, pp. 192–3.
63 CAB 23/8, 11 October 1918.
64 Hansard, 29 October 1918, Cols 1296–390.

65 'An Agreement between the British and German Governments concerning Combatant and Civilian Prisoners of War', Misc. No 12 (1917), CD 8590, July 1917.

66 'Convention relative to the Treatment of Prisoners of War, Geneva, 27 July 1929', Article 2.

# 8 Parcels, Assistance & Relief

1 Daniel J. McCarthy, *The Prisoner of War in Germany: The Care and Treatment of the Prisoner of War, with a History of the Development of the Principle of Neutral Inspection and Control* (n.d.), p. 187.

2 *The British Prisoner of War – Being the Monthly Journal of the Central Prisoners of War Committee of the Red Cross and Order of St John*, Vol. 1 No 12, December 1918, p. 137.

3 House of Commons: Parliamentary Debates (Hansard), 20 April 1915, Cols 248–9.

4 Letter from B.W. Young, Secretary, PWHC, to Sir Horace Rumbold, dated 30 June 1915, Foreign Office file FO 383/43, National Archives, Kew.

5 'Report of the Joint Committee appointed by The Chairman of Committees of the House of Lords and the House of Commons to enquire into The Organisation and Methods of the Central Prisoners of War Committee', Presented to the House of Commons by Command of Her Majesty, HMSO CD 8615, 1917.

6 FO 383/43, letter from B.W. Young, 30 June 1915.

7 CD 8615.

8 Ibid.

9 *The British Prisoner of War*, Vol. 1 No 1, January 1918, p. 1; and No 8, August 1918, p. 94.

10 Ibid., No 8, August 1918, p. 94.

11 Ibid., No 6, June 1918, pp. 63–6.

12 Ibid., No 3, March 1918, p. 36.

13 CD 8615.

14 *The British Prisoner of War*, Vol. 1, No 5, May 1918, pp. 51–3.

15 Ibid., No 1, January 1918, p. 11.

16 Ibid., No 2, February 1918, p. 20.

17 Ibid., No 3, March 1918, p. 26.

18 Ibid., No 9, September 1918, pp. 105–6.

19 Carl P. Dennett, *Prisoners of the Great War: Authoritative Statement of Conditions in the Prison Camps of Germany* (1919), pp. 45–6.

20 Danby Christopher, *Some Reminiscences of a Prisoner of War in Germany* (1918), p. 25.

21 *The British Prisoner of War*, Vol. 1 No 3, March 1918, p. 30.

22 'Correspondence with the United States Ambassador respecting the Treatment of British Prisoners of War and Interned Civilians in Germany' [in continuation of Misc. No 11 (1915)], Misc. No 14 (1915), CD 7959, p. 24.

23 *The British Prisoner of War*, Vol. 1 No 3, March 1918, pp. 33–4.

24 Martin Gilbert, *The First World War* (1994), p. 256.

25 Lyn Macdonald, *To The Last Man: Spring 1918* (1999), p xxiii.

26 McCarthy, *The Prisoner of War in Germany*, p. 188.

27 House of Lords: Parliamentary Debates (Hansard), 31 May 1916, Cols 249–68.

28 Robert Jackson, *The Prisoners 1914–18* (1989), p. 141.

29 Gerard to Page, 7 August 1915, FO 383/43.

30 CD 8615.

31 *The British Prisoners of War*, Vol. 1 No 10, October 1918, pp. 115–6.

32  Boylston A. Beal, report dated 7 March 1916, 'Reports of Visits of Inspection made by Officials of the United States Embassy to Various Internment Camps in the United Kingdom', Misc. No 30 (1916), CD 8324, p. 3.

33  *The British Prisoner of War*, Vol. 1 No 6, June 1918, p. 72; and No 7, July 1918, p. 73.

34  Ibid., No 8, August 1918, p. 86.

35  Ibid., No 7, July 1918, pp. 79–80.

36  Ibid., No 9, September 1918, pp. 101–2.

37  CD 8615.

## 9  Daily Life in Germany

1   Mrs Pope-Hennessey, 'Map of the Main Prison Camps in Germany and Austria' (New and Revised Edition with Gazetteer, n.d.).

2   Martin Gilbert, *First World War* (1994), p. 212.

3   James W. Gerard, *My Four Years in Germany* (1917), p. 192.

4   Pope-Hennessey, 'Map of the Main Prison Camps in Germany and Austria'.

5   Gerard, *My Four Years*, pp. 403–6.

6   Daniel J. McCarthy, *The Prisoner of War in Germany: The Care and Treatment of the Prisoner of War, with a History of the Development of the Principle of Neutral Inspection and Control* (n.d.), p. 44.

7   Ibid., p. 53.

8   Ibid., pp. 62–3.

9   Ibid., p. 60.

10  Ibid., p. 64.

11  'Correspondence Respecting the Use of Police Dogs in Prisoners' Camps in Germany', Misc. No 9 (1917), HMSO CD 8480, May 1917.

12  'Corrrespondence with the German Government repecting the Death by Burning of J P Genower, Able Seaman, when Prisoner of War at Brandenburg Camp', Misc. No 6 (1918), CD 8987, March 1918.

13  Carl P. Dennet, *Prisoners of the Great War: Authoritative Statement of Conditions in the Prison Camps of Germany* (1919), pp. 78–84.

14  McCarthy, *The Prisoner of War in Germany*, p. 90, and Gilbert, *First World War* (1994), p. 128.

15  Cabinet Paper CAB 37/151/35, circulated 18 July 1916, National Archives, Kew.

16  Gilbert, *First World War*, p. 114.

17  *To Make Men Traitors: Germany's Attempts to Seduce Her Prisoners-of-War* (1918) (author not indicated), p. 10.

18  McCarthy, *The Prisoner of War in Germany*, pp. 84–5.

19  *To Make Men Traitors: Germany's Attempts to Seduce Her Prisoners-of-War*, p. 10.

20  Ibid., pp. 24–6.

21  Ibid., p. 23.

22  *The British Prisoner of War – Being the Monthly Journal of the Central Prisoners of War Committee of the Red Cross and Order of St John*, Vol. 1 No 8, August 1918, p. 86.

23  *The British Prisoner of War*, Vol. 1 No 12, December 1918, p. 136.

24  Ibid., pp. 143–5.

25  Ibid., No 11, November 1918, p. 125.

26  McCarthy, *The Prisoner of War in Germany*, p. 128.

27  *The British Prisoner of War*, Vol. 1 No 4, April 1918.

28   Report by Dresel, 24 March 1916, 'Further Correspondence with the United States
     Ambassador respecting the treatment of British Prisoners of War and Interned
     Civilians in Germany' [in continuation of Misc. No 16 (1916) CD 8235], Misc.
     No 26 (1916) HMSO CD 8297, August 1916, pp. 4–5.
29   *The British Prisoner of War*, Vol. 1 No 12, December 1918, p. 147.
30   Ibid., No 10, October 1918, p. 116.
31   Ibid., No 3, March 1918, p. 26.
32   Dennet, *Prisoners of the Great War*, p. 76.
33   Report by Jackson, 18 November 1915, 'Further Correspondence with the United
     States Ambassador respecting the Treatment of British Prisoners of War and Interned
     Civilians in Germany' [in continuation of Misc. No 19 (1915) CD 8108], Misc. No 16
     (1916), CD 8235, May 1916, pp. 20–1.
34   Report by Osbourne, CD 8235, pp. 62–3.
35   McCarthy, *The Prisoner of War in Germany*, p. 95.
36   Richard B. Speed III, *Prisoners, Diplomats, and the Great War: A Study in the Diplomacy
     of Captivity* (1990), p. 77.
37   McCarthy, *The Prisoner of War in Germany*, pp. 96–8.
38   Dennet, *Prisoners of the Great War*, p. 6.
39   'Report on the Employment in Coal and Salt Mines of the British Prisoners of War
     in Germany', Misc. No 23 (1918) HMSO CD 9150, November 1918, p. 2.
40   McCarthy, *The Prisoner of War in Germany*, p. 118.
41   Ibid., pp. 113–4.
42   Ibid., p. 115.
43   Ibid., p. 124.
44   Speed, *Prisoners, Diplomats, and the Great War*, pp. 148–9.
45   'Correspondence between His Majesty's Government and the United States
     Ambassador respecting the Treatment of Prisoners of War and Interned Civilians
     in the United Kingdom and Germany respectively' [in continuation of Misc. No 5
     (1915)], Misc. No 7 (1915), HMSO CD 7817, p. 63.
46   CD 7817, p. 81.
47   'Report by DR A E Taylor on the Conditions of Diet and Nutrition in the
     Internment Camp at Ruhleben received through the United States Ambassador',
     Misc. No 18 (1916), HMSO CD 8259, June 1916.
48   'Further Correspondence Respecting the Conditions of Diet and Nutrition in the
     Internment Camp at Ruhleben' [in continuation of Misc. No 18 (1916), Cd 8259],
     Misc. No 21 (1916), HMSO CD 8262.
49   Gerard, *My Four Years*, p. 184.
50   McCarthy, *The Prisoner of War in Germany*, p. 142.
51   Gerard, *My Four Years*, pp. 177–8.
52   Ibid., pp. 178–9.
53   McCarthy, *The Prisoner of War in Germany*, p. 141.
54   Gerard, *My Four Years*, p. 180.
55   *The British Prisoner of War*, Vol. 1 No 6, June 1918, pp. 67–9.
56   Gerard, *My Four Years*, p. 181.
57   McCarthy, *The Prisoner of War in Germany*, p. 136.
58   Speed, *Prisoners, Diplomats, and the Great War*, p. 151.
59   Jackson, *The Prisoners*, p. 55.

## 10  Daily Life in the UK

1   J.C. Bird, *Control of Enemy Aliens in Great Britain, 1914–18* (1986), p. 132.
2   Report dated 18 May 1916, 'Reports of Visits of Inspection made by Officials of the United States Embassy to Various Internment Camps in the United Kingdom', Misc. No 30 (1916), HMSO CD 8324, September 1916, pp. 19–23.
3   Richard B. Speed III, *Prisoners, Diplomats, and the Great War: A Study in the Diplomacy of Captivity* (1990), p. 147.
4   Foreign Office file FO 383/33.
5   Letter dated 9 November 1915, FO 383/1.
6   Letter from Page, 9 November 1915, complaints from internees, 12 November, FO 383/1.
7   Petition to US Embassy, 29 November 1915, FO 383/1.
8   Report by Lieutenant-Governor, IOM, 29 November 1915, FO 383/1.
9   Report dated 18 May 1916, CD 8324, p.20.
10  Bird, *Control of Enemy Alien Civilians*, pp. 159–60.
11  Report dated 18 May 1916, CD 8324, pp. 17–9.
12  Bird, *Control of Enemy Alien Civilians*, pp. 165–6.
13  Report dated 20 June 1916, CD 8324, pp. 31–2.
14  Report dated 13 March 1916, CD 8324, pp. 4–5.
15  Report dated 2 June 1916, CD 8324, pp. 23–5.
16  House of Commons: Parliamentary Debates (Hansard), 24 April 1915, Cols 385–90.
17  Ibid, 8 March 1916, Col. 1526.
18  House of Lords: Parliamentary Debates (Hansard), 22 March 1916, Cols 442–7.
19  Cabinet Paper CAB 24/2, 23 September 1916, National Archives, Kew.
20  Cabinet Paper CAB 37/162/7, 10 January 1917.
21  Robert Jackson, *The Prisoners 1914–18* (1989), p. 140.
22  Speed, *Prisoners, Diplomats, and the Great War*, p. 102.
23  Report dated 7 March 1916, CD 8324, p. 4.
24  CD 8324.
25  *Handforth Camp Prisoners of War Newspaper*, held at Imperial War Museum.
26  Hansard, House of Commons, 24 April 1915, Cols 385–90.
27  Hansard, House of Commons, 27 April 1915, Col. 587.
28  FO 383/122.
29  August Gallinger, *The Countercharge: The Matter of War Criminals from the German Side* (1922), pp. 102, 107, 109.
30  Ibid., pp. 102–3.
31  *The British Prisoner of War – Being the Monthly Journal of the Central Prisoners of War Committee of the Red Cross and Order of St John*, Vol. 1 No 12, December 1918, p. 134.

## 11  Exchanges, Internments & Agreements

1   Grey to Page, 10 December 1914, 'Correspondence between His Majesty's Government and the United States Ambassador Respecting the Release of Interned Civilians and the Exchange of Diplomats and Consular Officers and of Certain Classes of Naval and Military Officers, Prisoners of War; in the United Kingdom and Germany Respectively', Misc. No 8 (1915), HMSO, CD 7857, April 1915, pp. 45–6.
2   HM Ambassador, Rome, to Grey, 19 December 1914, CD 7857, p. 46.
3   CD 7857, p. 55.

4   Daniel J. McCarthy, *The Prisoner of War in Germany: The Care and Treatment of the Prisoner of War, with a History of the Development of the Principle of Neutral Inspection and Control* (n.d.), p. 165.

5   Cabinet Paper CAB 37/155/36, 23 September 1916, National Archives, Kew.

6   *The Times,* 31 May 1916, p. 9.

7   Richard B. Speed III, *Prisoners, Diplomats, and the Great War: A Study in the Diplomacy of Captivity* (1990), p. 36.

8   Speed, *Prisoners, Diplomats, and the Great War,* pp. 35, 199.

9   Ibid., p. 36.

10  Robert Jackson, *The Prisoners 1914–18* (1989), p. 75.

11  War Office file, WO 32/5380, National Archives, Kew.

12  Note dated 19 April 1917, on WO 32/5380.

13  *The British Prisoner of War – Being the Monthly Journal of the Central Prisoners of War Committee of the Red Cross and Order of St John,* Vol. 1 No 4, April 1918, pp. 39–42.

14  McCarthy, *The Prisoner of War in Germany,* pp. 92–4.

15  CAB 37/139/50, 30 December 1915.

16  CAB 37/149/20, 9 June 1916.

17  CAB 37/151/21, 11 July 1916, and report of discussion by Asquith.

18  WO 32/5380.

19  House of Commons: Parliamentary Debates (Hansard), 28 June 1917, Col. 508.

20  'An Agreement between the British and German Governments concerning Combatant and Civilian Prisoners of War', Misc. No 12 (1917), CD 8590, July 1917.

21  J.C. Bird, *Control of Enemy Alien Civilians in Great Britain, 1914–18* (1986), pp. 157–8.

22  Carl P. Dennet, *Prisoners of the Great War: Authoritative Statement of Conditions in the Prison Camps of Germany* (1919), p. 3.

23  Hansard, 27 July 1917, Col. 1598.

24  *The British Prisoner of War,* Vol. 1 No 2, February 1918, p. 14.

25  Ibid., No 3, March 1918, p. 26.

26  Ibid., No 6, June 1918, p. 62.

27  *The Times,* 8 June 1918, p. 7.

28  *New York Times,* 7 June 1918.

29  Bird, *Control of Enemy Alien Civilians,* pp. 193–4.

30  'An Agreement between the British and German Governments concerning Combatant Prisoners of War and Civilians', Misc. No 20 (1918), CD 9147, October 1918.

31  'Report on the Treatment by the Enemy of British Officers, Prisoners of War in Camps under the 10th (Hanover) Army Corps, up to March 1918', Misc. No 28 (1918).

32  Hansard, 29 October 1918, Cols 1354–5; and CAB 24/66, 14 October 1918.

33  CAB 23/41, 30 July 1918.

34  CAB 24/66.

35  CAB 23/8, 11 October 1918.

36  Speed, *Prisoners, Diplomats, and the Great War,* p. 55.

## 12 The Armistice & Repatriation

1   Cabinet Paper, CAB 23/8, 11 October 1918, National Archives, Kew.

2   House of Commons: Parliamentary Debates (Hansard), 29 October 1918, Col. 1353.

3   Hansard, 11 November 1918, Cols 2454–9.

4 Stanley Weintraub, *A Stillness Heard Around the World: The End of the Great War: November 1918* (1985), p. 155.

5 Ibid., pp. 333–54.

6 Ibid., pp. 346–7.

7 *The Times History of the War, Vol XXI* (1920), pp. 219–20.

8 Richard B. Speed III, *Prisoners, Diplomats, and the Great War: A Study in the Diplomacy of Captivity* (1990), p. 176.

9 *The British Prisoner of War – Being the Monthly Journal of the Central Prisoners of War Committee of the Red Cross and Order of St John*, Vol. 1 No 12, December 1918, pp. 150–1.

10 Speed, *Prisoners, Diplomats, and the Great War*, p. 176.

11 *The British Prisoner of War*, Vol. 1 No 12, December 1918, p. 151.

12 Ibid., pp. 131, 151.

13 Ibid., pp. 134, 150.

14 Ibid., pp. 134, 151.

15 Weintraub, *A Stillness Heard Around the World*, p. 354.

16 *The British Prisoner of War*, Vol. 1 No 12, December 1918, pp. 134–5.

17 Ibid., No 5, May 1918, p. 50; No 8, August 1918, p. 91; No 9, September 1918, p. 107; No 10, October 1918, p. 109; No 11, November 1918, p. 129; and No 12, December 1918, pp. 134–5.

18 Ibid., No 12, December 1918, p. 135.

19 Carl P. Dennet, *Prisoners of the Great War: Authoritative Statement of Conditions in the Prison Camps of Germany* (1919), p. 217.

20 Speed, *Prisoners, Diplomats, and the Great War*, pp. 131–2.

21 *The Treaty of Versailles and After: Annotations to the Text of the Treaty*, US Department of State, Publication 2724 (1947), pp. 365–6.

22 Speed, *Prisoners, Diplomats, and the Great War*, p. 179.

23 Ibid.

## 13 Leipzig: The Aftermath

1 Note by Primrose on memorandum from Admiralty to FO, dated 29 March 1915, Foreign Office file FO 383/32, National Archives, Kew.

2 House of Commons; Parliamentary Debates (Hansard), 27 **April** 1919, Col. 174.

3 Cabinet Paper, CAB 23/8, 11 October 1918, National Archives, Kew.

4 'German War Trials – Report of the Proceedings before the Supreme Court in Leipzig with Appendices', Cmd 1450 (1921).

5 Ibid., p. 5.

6 Ibid., p. 8.

7 Ibid., p. 26.

8 Ibid., p. 29.

9 Ibid., pp. 34–5.

10 Ibid., pp. 29–30.

11 Ibid., p. 35.

12 Ibid., p. 41.

13 Ibid., p. 36.

14 Claud Mullins, *The Leipzig Trials* (1921), pp. 173–89.

15 Ibid., pp. 151–68.

16   Ibid., pp. 169–73.
17   *The Times*, 27 May 1921, p. 11.
18   Hansard, 30 May 1921, Cols 571–2.
19   *The Times*, 2 June 1921, p. 9.
20   *The Times*, 9 July 1921, p. 9.
21   *The Times*, 1 June 1921, p. 9.
22   Ibid.
23   *The Times*, 28 May 1921, p. 9.
24   Hansard, 23 June 1921, Cols 1538–40.
25   Mullins, *The Leipzig Trials*, p. 198.
26   Ibid., p. 208.
27   *The Treaty of Versailles and After: Annotations of the Text of the Treaty*, p. 379.
28   Record by Sir E. Crowe of a conversation with the German Ambassador, 3 February
     1922, *Documents on British Foreign Policy 1919–1939*, First Series Vol. 20, p. 375.

# BIBLIOGRAPHY

## Primary Sources

### Archives

*Cabinet Papers, The National Archives, Kew:*
CAB 23/8, CAB 23/41, CAB 24/2, CAB 24/14, CAB 24/63, CAB 24/66, CAB
37/122/182, CAB 37/122/185, CAB 37/123/10, CAB 37/123/37, CAB 37/125/2,
CAB 37/125/18, CAB 37/127/35, CAB 37/127/40, CAB 37/128/17, CAB 37/128/22,
CAB 37/129/9, CAB 37/129/21, CAB 37/130/6, CAB 37/139/50, CAB 37/142/19,
CAB 37/143/18, CAB 37/143/19, CAB 37/144/7, CAB 37/144/39, CAB 37/147/9,
CAB 37/148/3, CAB 37/149/20, CAB 37/150/3, CAB 37/151/1 (plus report of
meeting), CAB 37/151/21 (plus report of meeting), CAB 37/151/35, CAB 37/152/29,
CAB 37/154/17, CAB 37/155/36, CAB 37/157/10, CAB 37/159/44, CAB 37/162/7,
CAB 41/36/10, CAB 41/36/25.

*Foreign Office files, The National Archives, Kew:*
FO 369/714, FO 369/800, FO 371/2561, FO 372/541, FO 383/1, FO 383/18, FO 383/32,
FO 383/33, FO 383/34, FO 383/35, FO 383/43, FO 383/46, FO 383/52, FO 383/59, FO
383/122, FO 383/124, FO 383/158, FO 383/179, FO 383/184, FO 383/185, FO 383/474.

*Home Office files, The National Archives, Kew:*
HO 45/10946 File 266042/38.

*War Office files, The National Archives, Kew:*
WO 32/4868, WO 32/5098, WO 32/5188, WO 32/5371, WO 32/5373, WO 32/5380,
WO 32/5381, WO 32/5608.

## Conventions, Agreements & Treaty

'Convention for the Amelioration of the Condition of the Wounded in Armies in the
Field. Geneva, 22 August 1864', International Committee of the Red Cross.
[Accessed at http://icrc.org on 12 August 2008]

'Additional Articles relating to the Condition of the Wounded in War, Geneva, 20
October 1868' (Not brought into force), International Committee of the Red Cross.
[Accessed at http://icrc.org on 16 August 2008]

'Convention (III) for the Adaptation to Maritime Warfare of the Principles of the Geneva
Convention of 22 August 1864. The Hague, 29 July 1899', International Committee of
the Red Cross. [Accessed at http://icrc.org on 16 August 2008]

'Convention for the Amelioration of the Conditions of the Wounded and Sick in
Armies of the Field. Geneva, 6 July 1906', International Committee of the Red Cross.
[Accessed at http://icrc.org on 12 August 2008]

'Convention for the Amelioration of the Condition of the Wounded and Sick in Armies
in the Field, Geneva, 27 July 1929', International Committee of the Red Cross.
[Accessed at http://icrc.org on 27 June 2008]

'Convention (II) with Respect to the Laws and Customs of War on Land and its annex:
Regulations concerning the Laws and Customs of War on Land. The Hague, 29 July
1899', International Committee of the Red Cross. [Accessed at http://icrc.org on 12
August 2008]

'Convention (IV) respecting the Laws and Customs of War on Land and its annex:
Regulations concerning the Laws and Customs of War on Land. The Hague, 18
October 1907', International Committee of the Red Cross.
[Accessed at http://icrc.org on 7 August 2008]

'Convention relative to the Treatment of Prisoners of War, Geneva, 27 July 1929',
International Committee of the Red Cross. [Accessed at http://icrc.org on 27 June 2008]

'An Agreement between the British and German Governments concerning Combatant
and Civilian Prisoners of War', Misc. No 12 (1917), HMSO CD 8590, July 1917.

'An Agreement between the British and Ottoman Governments respecting Prisoners of
War and Civilians', Misc. No 10 (1918), HMSO CD 9024, April 1918.

'An Agreement between the British and German Governments concerning Combatant
Prisoners of War and Civilians', Misc. No 20 (1918), HMSO CD 9147, October 1918.

'Treaty of Peace between the Allied and Associated Powers and Germany, Signed at
Versailles, June 28th, 1919', HMSO CD 153.

## Government & Parliamentary Publications

'Correspondence between His Majesty's Government and the United States Ambassador
respecting the Treatment of German Prisoners of War and Interned Civilians in the
United Kingdom', Misc. No 5 (1915), HMSO, March 1915, CD 7815.

'Correspondence between His Majesty's Government and the United States Ambassador
respecting the Treatment of Prisoners of War and Interned Civilians in the United
Kingdom and Germany respectively' [in continuation of Misc. No 5 (1915), CD 7815],
Misc No 7 (1915), HMSO, Cd 7817.

'Correspondence between His Majesty's Government and the United States Ambassador
Respecting the Release of Interned Civilians and the Exchange of Diplomats and Consular
Officers and of Certain Classes of Naval and Military Officers, Prisoners of War; in the United
Kingdom and Germany Respectively', Misc. No 8 (1915), HMSO CD 7857, April 1915.

# Bibliography

'Reports by United States Officials on the Treatment of British Prisoners of War and
Interned Civilians at Certain Places of Detention in Germany' [in continuation of
Misc. No 7 (1915), CD 7817], Misc. No 11 (1915), HMSO CD 7861, May 1915.

'Correspondence with the United States Ambassador respecting the Treatment of British
Prisoners of War and Interned Civilians in Germany' [in continuation of Misc. No 11
(1915), CD 7861], Misc. No 14 (1915), CD 7959, June 1915.

'Correspondence with the United States Ambassador respecting the safety of Alien
Enemies repatriated from India on the SS *Golconda*', Misc. No 4 (1916), HMSO CD
8163, January 1916.

'Further Correspondence with the United States Ambassador respecting the safety of
Alien Enemies repatriated from India on the SS *Golconda*' [in continuation of Misc.
No 4 (1916), CD 8163], Misc. No 8 (1916), HMSO CD 8178, March 1916.

'Report by the Government Committee on the Treatment by the Enemy of British
Prisoners of War regarding the Conditions obtaining at Wittenberg Camp during the
Typhus Epidemic of 1915', Misc. No 10 (1916), HMSO CD 8224, April 1916.

'Further Correspondence with the United States Ambassador respecting the Treatment of
British Prisoners of War and Interned Civilians in Germany' [in continuation of Misc.
No 19 (1915), CD 8108], Misc. No 16 (1916), HMSO Cd 8235, May 1916.

'Correspondence with the United States Ambassador respecting the transfer to
Switzerland of British and German Wounded and Sick Combatant Prisoners of War',
Misc. No 17 (1916), HMSO CD 8236, May 1916.

'Report by Dr A F Taylor on the Conditions of Diet and Nutrition in the Internment
Camp at Ruhleben received through the United States Ambassador', Misc. No 18
(1916), HMSO CD 8259, June 1916.

'Correspondence Respecting the Employment of British and German Prisoners of War in
Poland and France Respectively', Misc. No 19 (1916), HMSO CD 8260, June 1916.

'Further Correspondence Respecting the Conditions of Diet and Nutrition in the
Internment Camp at Ruhleben' [in continuation of Misc. No 18 (1916), CD 8259],
Misc. No 21 (1916), HMSO CD 8262.

'Further Correspondence Respecting the Conditions of Diet and Nutrition in the
Internment Camp at Ruhleben and the proposed Release of Interned Civilians'
[in continuation of Misc. No 21 (1916), CD 8262], Misc. No 25 (1916), HMSO CD
8296, July 1916.

'Further Correspondence with the United States Ambassador respecting the Treatment of
British Prisoners of War and Interned Civilians in Germany' [in continuation of Misc.
No 16 (1916), CD 8235], Misc. No 26 (1916), HMSO CD 8297, August 1916.

'Correspondence with His Majesty's Minister at Berne respecting the question
of Reprisals against Prisoners of War', Misc. No 29 (1916), HMSO CD 8323,
September 1916.

'Reports of Visits of Inspection made by Officials of the United States Embassy to Various
Internment Camps in the United Kingdom', Misc. No 30 (1916), HMSO CD 8324,
September 1916,

'Report on the Typhus Epidemic at Gardelegen by the Government Committee on the
Treatment by the Enemy of British Prisoners of War during the Spring and Summer
of 1915', HMSO CD 8351, October 1916.

'Further Correspondence Respecting the Proposed Release of Civilians Interned in the
British and German Empires' [in continuation of Misc. No 25 (1916), CD 8296], Misc.
No 35 (1916), HMSO CD 8352, November 1916.

'Further Correspondence Respecting the Proposed Release of Civilians Interned in the British and German Empires' [in continuation of Misc. No 35 (1916), CD 8352], Misc. No 1 (1917), HMSO CD 8437, January 1917.

'Further Correspondence with the United States Ambassador respecting the Treatment of British Prisoners of War and Interned Civilians in Germany' [in continuation of Misc. No 26 (1916), CD 8297], Misc. No 7 (1917), HMSO Cd 8477, March 1917.

'Correspondence Respecting the Use of Police Dogs in Prisoners' Camps in Germany', Misc. No 9 (1917), HMSO, CD 8480, May 1917.

'Report of the Joint Committee appointed by The Chairman of Committees of the House of Lords and the House of Commons To enquire into The Organisation and Methods of the Central Prisoners of War Committee', HMSO, CD 8615, 1917.

'Reports on the Treatment by the Germans of British Prisoners and Natives in German East Africa', Misc. No 13 (1917), HMSO CD 8689, September 1917.

'Report on the Transport of British Prisoners of War to Germany, August–December 1914', Misc. No 3 (1918), HMSO CD 8984, February 1918.

'Correspondence with the German Government respecting the Death by Burning of J P Genower, Able Seaman, when Prisoner of War at Brandenburg Camp', Misc. No 6 (1918), HMSO CD 8987, March 1918.

'Report on The Treatment by the Enemy of British Prisoners of War behind the Firing Lines in France and Belgium, With Two Appendices', Misc. No 7 (1918), HMSO CD 8988, April 1918.

'Report on The Treatment by the Germans of Prisoners of War taken during the Spring Offensives of 1918' [in continuation of Misc. No 7 (1918), CD 8988], Misc. No 19 (1918), HMSO CD 9106, October 1918.

'Report on the Employment in Coal and Salt Mines of the British Prisoners of War in Germany', Misc. No 23 (1918), HMSO CD 9150, November 1918.

'Report on the Treatment of British Prisoners of War in Turkey', Misc. No 24 (1918), HMSO CD 9208, November 1918.

'Further Report on the Treatment by the Germans of Prisoners of War taken during the Spring Offensives of 1918' [in continuation of Misc. No 19 (1918), CD 9106], Misc. No 27 (1918), HMSO [no date, no number shown].

'Report on the Treatment by the Enemy of British Officers, Prisoners of War in Camps under the 10th (Hanover) Army Corps, up to March 1918', Misc. No 28 (1918), HMSO [no date, no number shown].

'German War Trials – Report of the Proceedings before the Supreme Court in Leipzig with Appendices', Cmnd 1450 (1921).

## Publications of the Government Committee on the Treatment of British POWs

'The Treatment of Prisoners of War in England and Germany During the First Eight Months of the War', based on Parliamentary Paper Misc. No 7 (1915), CD 7817. Published under authority of HMSO, Crown Copyright [n.d.].

*The Horrors of Wittenberg: Official Report to the British Government by the Government Committee on the Treatment by the Enemy of British Prisoners of War, Chairman Sir Robert Younger, 6 April 1916* (London: C. Arthur Pearson Ltd, 2nd Edn).

*British Civilian Prisoners in German East Africa: A Report by The Government Committee on the Treatment by the Enemy of British Prisoners of War, London 1918* (London: Messrs Alabaster, Passmore & Sons Ltd).

## Other Official Publications
Documents on British Foreign Policy 1919–1939.
House of Commons and House of Lords: Parliamentary Debates (Hansard).
Manual of Military Law, War Office 1914.
'Disturbance at the Aliens Detention Camp at Douglas on Thursday, November
  19th 1914', Inquiry by the Coroner of Inquests in the Isle of Man and a Jury, Friday
  20 November and 27 November 1914, Official Report of the Proceedings (Douglas:
  Brown & Sons Ltd) [Copy held on HO 45/10946 File 266042/38, The National
  Archives, Kew].

## Memoirs
Danby, Christopher, *Some Reminiscences of a Prisoner of War in Germany* (Eyre and
  Spottiswoode, March 1918).
Dennet, Carl P., *Prisoners of the Great War: Authoritative Statement of Conditions in the Prison
  Camps of Germany* (Cambridge MA: Riverside Press Cambridge, 1919).
Gerard, James W., *My Four Years in Germany* (New York: George H. Doran Co., 1917).
————, *Face to Face with Kaiserism* (London: Hodder & Stoughton, 1918).
McCarthy, Daniel J., *The Prisoner of War in Germany: The Care and Treatment of the Prisoner
  of War, with a History of the Development of the Principle of Neutral Inspection and Control*
  (London: Skeffington & Son Ltd, n.d.).

## Other Primary Sources
*The Handforth Camp Prisoner of War Newspaper*, held at the Imperial War Museum.
*The Times.*
Mrs Pope-Hennessey, 'Map of the Main Prison Camps in Germany and Austria' (London:
  Nisbet & Co. Ltd, n.d.).
*List of Places of Internment*, Prisoners of War Information Bureau, London.
Gerard, James W., *Speech to the Ladies Aid Society of St Mary's Hospital, New York,
  25 November 1917*, at http://www.firstworldwar.com/audio/loyalty.htm [Accessed
  9 February 2009].

## Secondary Sources

Bailey, Gordon Wallace, *Dry Run for the Hangman: The Versailles-Leipzig Fiasco, 1919–21:
  Feeble Foreshadow of Nuremburg* (Michigan: unpublished dissertation, 1988).
Bird, J.C., *Control of Enemy Alien Civilians in Great Britain, 1914–18* (New York & London:
  Garland Publishing Inc., 1986).
Duffy, Christopher, *Through German Eyes: The British and The Somme 1916* (London:
  Weidenfeld & Nicholson, 2006),
Fyson, Robert, *The Douglas Camp Shootings of 1914, Proceedings of the Isle of Man Natural
  History and Antiquarian Society Vol XI No 1* (Kendal: Titus Wilson & Son, 2000).
Gallinger, August, *The Countercharge. The Matter of War Criminals from the German Side*
  (Munich: Süddeutsche Monatshefte, 1922).
Gilbert, Martin, *First World War* (London: Weidenfeld & Nicolson, 1994).
Holland, Thomas Erskine, *The Laws of War on Land* (Oxford: Clarendon Press, 1908).
Jackson, Robert, *The Prisoners 1914–18* (Routledge, 1989).

Kampmark, Binoy, *James W. Gerard, His Image of Imperial Germany, 1913–1918*, at http://www.unc.edu/depts/diplomat/archives_roll/2003_01-03/kempmark_gerard/kam [Accessed 8 July 2008].

Macdonald, Lyn, *To the Last Man: Spring 1918* (London: Penguin, 1999).

Moynihan, Michael (ed.), *Black Bread and Barbed Wire: Prisoners in the First World War* (London: Leo Cooper, 1978).

Mullins, Claud, *The Leipzig Trials* (London: H. F. & G. Witherby, 1921).

Myerson, M.H., *Germany's War Crimes and Punishment: The Problem of Individual and Collective Criminality* (Toronto: Macmillan, 1944).

Palmer, Alan, *The Kaiser: Warlord of the Second Reich* (London: Orion Books Ltd, 1997).

Picton, Harold, *Das Besseres Deutschland im Krieg* (Süddeutsche Monatshefte, c.1921).

Roxburgh, Ronald F., *The Prisoners of War Information Bureau in London: A Study* (London: Longmans, Green & Co., 1915).

Seymour, Charles (ed.), *The Intimate Papers of Colonel House* (London: Ernest Benn, 1926).

Sharp, Alan, *The Versailles Settlement: Peacemaking in Paris, 1919* (Basingstoke & London: Macmillan Education Ltd, 1991).

Speed, Richard B. III, *Prisoners, Diplomats, and the Great War: A Study in the Diplomacy of Captivity* (Connecticut: Greenwood Press, 1990).

Stephens, Waldo, *Revisions of the Treaty of Versailles* (New York: Columbia University Press, 1939).

Stibbe, Matthew, *British civilian internees in Germany: The Ruhleben Camp, 1914–1918* (Manchester: Manchester University Press, 2008).

*The British Prisoner of War – Being the Monthly Journal of the Central Prisoners of War Committee of the Red Cross and Order of St John, Volume 1, Numbers 1 to 12, January to December 1918* (London).

*The Times History of the War* (London: The Times, 1920).

*The Treaty of Versailles and After: Annotations of the Text of the Treaty*, US Department of State, Publication 2724 (Washington: US Government Printing Office, 1947).

*To Make Men Traitors: Germany's Attempts to Seduce Her Prisoners-of-War* (London, New York & Toronto: Hodder & Stoughton, 1918).

Tuchman, Barbara, *The Proud Tower: A Portrait of the World before the War 1890–1914* (London & Basingstoke: Macmillan Press Ltd, 1980).

Van Emden, Richard, *Prisoners of the Kaiser: The Last POWs of the Great War* (Barnsley: Pen & Sword, 2000).

Vandeleur, David, letter to author, 13 August 1999.

Weintraub, Stanley, *A Stillness Heard Round the World – The End of the Great War: November 1918* (London, Sydney & Wellington: Allen & Unwin, 1986).

Winter, Jay & Baggett, Blaine, *1914–18: The Great War and the Shaping of the Twentieth Century* (BBC Books, 1996).

Winter, J.M., *The Experience of World War 1* (Oxford: Papermac, Equinox (Oxford) Ltd, 1988).

# ACKNOWLEDGEMENTS

I am grateful to the staff of the Imperial War Museum Reading Room for their help in identifying much of the material used in this study. I am also grateful to the museum for allowing me access to their picture library and for arranging the showing of relevant film footage from their archive.

# INDEX

Treves (Trier) Camp 132–3
Trinke, Sergeant Heinrich
  Leipzig Trials 190–1
Trotha, Admiral von
  Leipzig Trials 195

Valenciennes 67, 81
Vandeleur
  Major C.B. 43–5, 82–6
  The Hon. Mrs 109
  Mrs L.B. 109
  Miss Vera 109
Vanselow, Captain 72
Versailles, Treaty of 37, 181
Vidal, Captain, RAMC 67–8, 71

Villingen Camp 135
Vischer, Dr A.L. 163

Wahn Camp 124
walks on parole
  Germany 132–3, 141
  UK 151
Wilson, US President Woodrow 11, 101
Wittenberg Camp 48, 65–75, 126
Woking Camp 154

Younger, Sir Robert 12, 162

Zossen (Crescent) Camp 129
Zossen (Wuhnsdorf) Camp 124, 129